The Changing
Catholic College

norc

NATIONAL OPINION RESEARCH CENTER
MONOGRAPHS IN SOCIAL RESEARCH

The Changing Catholic College

By

ANDREW M. GREELEY

With the assistance of

WILLIAM VAN CLEVE
GRACE ANN CARROLL

ALDINE PUBLISHING COMPANY
Chicago

*The research reported herein was supported by
a grant from the Carnegie Corporation.*

*First published 1967 by
ALDINE Publishing Company
320 West Adams Street
Chicago, Illinois 60606*

*Library of Congress Catalog Card Number 67-27393
Designed by Greer Allen
Printed in the United States of America*

Preface

Almost all of America's private colleges and universities (and some public ones as well) started out as denominational schools. Harvard was founded as a seminary to turn out Calvinist divines, and Chicago was an offshoot of a midwestern Baptist educational society. For most of the schools originally closely associated with the major Protestant denominations, connections with their sponsoring churches have gradually attenuated over the last century so that only vestiges of such ties are left: Dwight Eisenhower had to declare himself an Episcopalian to become the president of Columbia University, but that great institution's ties to Episcopalianism are less than nominal.

The fundamentalist Protestant denominations and the Roman Catholics are the only churches that still maintain colleges and universities closely tied financially and in spirit to their denominations. Catholic higher education is the largest of these denominational systems, producing a significant proportion of America's college graduates, trained professionals, and Ph.D's.

There can be little doubt that a few decades ago Catholic colleges and universities as a group were not on a par with the rest of academia. Knapp's studies of the undergraduate origins of scientists and scholars showed that as late as the thirties these schools were contributing very little to the training of our scientific and scholarly elites. But changes have taken place since those days, as Father Greeley's earlier study indicates, and to judge from the ferment in the Catholic press, still further changes are taking place at the moment.

Whether the movement in Catholic higher educational circles toward setting standards of quality as high as those of the best of secular schools will succeed or not, only the future can tell. Whether this movement will result in the same secularization as occurred to Protestant colleges of the nineteenth century also must be left to the future. What we can study at the moment is how colleges and universities manage to change. This is the purpose of Father Greeley's study.

The methodology employed by Father Greeley is of considerable interest, since it represents an attempt to employ essentially qualitative procedures with a built-in quantitative check. In designing the study, we felt that not enough was known about the factors leading to organizational change to specify rigorous data collection procedures. Yet it was possible to determine through our previous studies of American colleges and universities those schools which show evidence of change in recent times. We chose a sample of schools varying in the degree to which such changes were evident, without revealing to the investigators which were which. Father Greeley and his field team visited each of the schools, interviewing significant segments of each. The analysis of his data had to accomplish two tasks in order to be considered a successful research endeavor. First of all, the researchers had to correctly characterize each school in terms of its recent growth toward excellence. Second, they had to identify those elements in the organization of each school which were critical in fostering and supporting such changes. If the researchers were unable to correctly characterize each school, then the plausibility of their analysis of causal factors would have been considerably undermined. The fact that they were able to do so (to a surprisingly successful degree) raises the credibility of their causal analysis although it does not, of course, guarantee its accuracy. It does indicate that the researchers were sensitive and skillful observers.

Father Greeley's main findings concerning the importance of vigorous and imaginative administrators in fostering growth toward excellence are findings with which most sociologists and most faculty will be uncomfortable. As sociologists, we tend to underplay the role of individuals and as faculty we tend to regard academic administrators either as traitors to scholarship or as natural-born enemies of the scholarly enterprise.

The policy implications of these findings are also unsettling. To improve a school we should install a vigorous administration, but to identify men who will become vigorous administrators is not an easy task. In short, although Father Greeley has told us much about the working of academia, his findings do not lead to pat formulae that can be applied as indicated. The governance of universities and colleges is still an art rather than an engineering skill.

It would be easy to mistake Father Greeley's monograph as a study of Catholic education rather than as a study of educational institutions that are Catholic. The same processes at work in the Catholic colleges and universities are at work in the secular schools. Hence this work is a contribution to the sociology of education generally. As such it will come to take its place high in the list of studies that have aided in the understanding of the complex enterprise of higher education in America.

PETER H. ROSSI
Director
National Opinion Research Center
March, 1967

Acknowledgments

The director of NORC Study No. 476 wishes to acknowledge first of all the generous patience and dogged cooperation of his two colleagues in the survey; that two people could survive the rigors of so much jet plane travel and especially countless Friday afternoons circling in snowstorms over O'Hare International Airport and remain friends is a tribute to their patience, or their virtue, or possibly the intervention of some higher authority.

Speaking of higher authority, we must also acknowledge the ingenious assistance of NORC's Director, Peter H. Rossi, whose insights at critical times were of great help. We must further thank James Beckwith for handling the data processing involved in the study and for replying with such comprehensibility to the incomprehensible memos that turned up on his desk at odd hours on weekends. We further are grateful to Norman Bradburn and Donald Treiman of the NORC staff who did the regression analysis which was essential to the design of the study and whose helpfulness will lead us to forgive the superior "I've got a secret" attitude with which they viewed our efforts. There aren't very many words that are adequate to express the debt of the survey team to our staff secretary, Mrs. Virginia Quinn, whose genius at handling reservations prevented us from freezing or starving to death more than once, and whose organization of our travels prevented the study from going into complete chaos. It is a wonder that she found any time to type the vast reams of memos that flowed into the office through the course of the survey. Bonnie McKeon labored over the manuscript with editorial care that in a book not dealing with religiously affiliated schools we might call devout.

We must also thank the group of ten Catholic educators who carefully read a preliminary draft of the report and offered many helpful and penetrating comments. We will not mention these educators by name because in most instances they were on the staffs of schools we had visited. Further, we must express our gratitude to our sociological colleagues who read and commented on the manuscript: David Riesman, Joseph Katz, William D'Antonio, and Robert Hassenger. Comments were also received from certain members of the NORC staff: Robert McNamara, James Vanecko, Robert Crain, and Joe L. Spaeth. Needless to say, none of those mentioned in this paragraph can be held responsible for the content of the report.

Finally, our deepest gratitude of all goes to the administrators, faculty, and students of the Catholic and non-Catholic colleges we visited during the study for their patient, enthusiastic, and generous cooperation with our work.

The entire study was made possible by a grant from the Carnegie Corporation.

A.M.G.

Contents

List
of
Tables

1

Introduction

One of the most fascinating aspects of human behavior is the phenomenon of institutional change. The constant growth and decline of institutions that men create is so much a part of the human condition that we are inclined to take it for granted even though theoretical explanations of change as well as empirical measures of its pace are still anything but satisfactory. However, if human institutions can both grow and decline, the former kind of change seems to be, at least in American society, the more important and the more difficult to understand. Various refinements of the "iron law of oligarchy" can explain how means become ends and how once vital institutions lose their vigor and force and begin to ossify. As the late Gustav Weigel once remarked, "All things human, given enough time, go badly."

But the phenomenon of growth is not so easy to deal with, especially in a dynamic society like the United States. The persistent technological expansion of American society makes it possible for an institution to grow without another institution having to decline to make room. The spirit of expansionism, which is so much a part of American culture, seems to demand that every day in every way every institution must get better and better, since the need for institutions to decline seems to be eliminated, or at least reduced, by the constantly expanding gross national product.

Thus it is not particularly surprising that there has always been considerable interest in American social science in the qualitative improvement of social institutions. Nor, given the massive commitment of American society to education, and more recently to higher education, is it at all surprising that there is considerable interest in educational institutions and in the qualitative growth of higher educational institutions. Not only does every American college want to become excellent, it wants to become more excel-

1

lent; and it would be a very rare college president who would admit that his school is not moving rapidly forward in the pursuit of this mythical and mystical excellence. One can hardly imagine an American college president remarking that his school was not improving and that he really did not want it to improve because he was firmly persuaded that there was no need to improve. Nowhere in American society is the faith in the possibility of limitless quantitative and qualitative expansion so obvious as it is in higher education.

But granted that everyone wants to be excellent and that everyone feels he is proceeding toward excellence, it is not immediately clear what are considered to be the criteria of excellence. Presumably the best measure of whether a school is getting better is the product; if the graduate from a college today were better educated than his predecessor five or ten years ago, it could be safely assumed that the school had indeed improved. But what constitutes a well-educated young person, and what measures can be devised to measure this quality of being well educated? The educated person has a capacity for critical thought, a familiarity with the best in the Western intellectual and cultural tradition, and an awareness of the possibilities of his own personal development through the enriching experience of participating in that tradition.

While there may be little controversy that these are the goals of the higher educational experience, it is considerably more difficult to agree on what indicators can be used to measure how successfully a college or university is pursuing these goals. For most practical purposes, there seems to be reluctant agreement that a school can be said to be improving if it is acquiring a better faculty and better students; if the faculty has more advanced degrees, better training, and is more productive in scholarly publications; and if the students score higher on standardized measures, such as the college entrance board test. It is also fairly widely assumed that an extremely useful measure of the quality of the faculty and the student body is the proportion of graduates who go on for further academic training (and especially the proportion who do so with impressive fellowships). Implicit in this assumption is the notion that those young people who become more intellectually aware during their college experience will wish to continue their intellectual training at the graduate level and that, therefore, attending graduate school is some measure of the college's success in creating intellectual awareness. Even if it be argued that young people are more and more likely to come to college with graduate school plans, it can still be said that the high productivity of graduate students is an indication that the excellence of the school is such as to attract large numbers of young people who think that institution can facilitate their entrance into graduate school.

Obviously, graduate school attendance is something less than a completely satisfactory measure of academic excellence. At best it is only a useful shorthand measure that can be rather quickly computed and that does seem to correlate both with improvement in faculty and with improvement in student intelligence. Nonetheless, while sociologists universally, if reluctantly, use the productivity of graduate students and eventually of Ph.D.'s as a rough measure of the excellence of the school, graduate school registration is still hardly the same thing as a sophisticated understanding of the best in the Western intellectual tradition, coupled with an ability to critically evaluate the world in which one lives and works. But even if one can register in graduate school and obtain the Ph.D. without either the ability to think critically or a taste for the best in Western culture, all other things being equal, the proportion of students going to graduate school is a fairly useful measure of academic excellence, and a relative improvement in the proportion going to graduate school can safely be used as a shorthand indicator of academic growth.

But if the growth of academic improvement in higher educational institutions is a matter of considerable interest both theoretically and practically, the question of growth among the more than three hundred colleges affiliated with the Roman Catholic Church has some unique and intriguing aspects:

1. While many American colleges began with some sort of religious affiliation, the Catholic schools have demonstrated an ability to preserve the close link between religion and higher education that many other institutions have long since lost.

2. The sheer number of Catholic schools—more than three hundred institutions enrolling more than 400,000 students—make them an impres-

sive and important part of American higher education. Even though one might prefer to rule them out of the pale of the American higher educational enterprise, they are simply too many in number and too coherent in organization to be ignored.

3. Not only are these institutions religously affiliated, but they are affiliated with a large and important religous minority group within American society. Changes occurring in the higher educational institutions of this minority group can be expected to be important not only for the group but also for the group's relationship with the rest of society.

4. There is vast evidence available that American Catholic immigrant groups are entering into the later stages of the acculturation process and are becoming in many ways indistinguishable from other American population groups. Thus, the changes in Catholic higher education may be symbolic of the acculturation of the immigrant ethnic groups into American society.

5. Finally, under the impetus of the reforms of Pope John and the Second Vatican Council, the Catholic Church has begun a major process of restructuring. At the precise time that the American Church is becoming more thoroughly American, the universal Church is attempting to become more thoroughly contemporary. These two transitions not only are bound to have an impact on developments in Catholic higher education but are also likely to impart a special and rather interesting flavor to what is going on in Catholic colleges. Hence, the intriguing question about the change in Catholic higher education is not merely how Catholic colleges improve, but how they improve while simultaneously remaining the same. How do they shift many of their emphases and goals and at the same time maintain whatever goals are thought to be essential in order that they may continue to be Catholic?

What is going on, then, in Catholic colleges is not merely self-improvement but, as the immigrant and the pre-Vatican ghettos are left behind, self-transformation. Many other religiously affiliated schools have gone through similar processes, in most instances losing many of their religious dimensions in the self-transformation. But self-transformation of higher educational institutions has rarely, if ever, occurred on so large a scale or so abruptly, or with the same vigorous intention to preserve a uniquely religious character in the process.

Given the change in the Catholic population, it is not at all surprising that Catholic colleges would change; on the contrary, such change is almost inevitable, and evidence reported in previous National Opinion Research Center studies indicating that the graduates of Catholic colleges were as likely to go on to graduate training in the arts and sciences as graduates of other colleges ought not to come as a shock. The more important question is why some Catholic colleges have changed more rapidly than others and why some apparently do not change at all. Given these favorable environmental conditions and the pressure from the changing population for academic growth, why do some schools put aside the old and more parochial norms that guided their early years and choose new norms very similar to those of other American colleges and universities, while other Catholic schools continue in the tradition of the past, acquiescing only minimally to the goals and values of the larger American educational enterprise? Why do some schools continue to defend the faith, while other institutions seem more interested in improving their faculties? Why do some continue the traditional familistic and paternalistic approach to academic organization while others become much more professional and collegial in their styles of administrative behavior?

A school can be viewed as a system of relationships, both internal and external, among faculty, students, administrators, alumni, parents, contributors, other schools, ecclesiastical authorities, and the civic community. Somewhere in this pattern of relationships there must be found an explanation of why one school changes and another does not. Financial resouces play a crucial role in the qualitative improvement of almost any American institution, educational or other, but only in rare instances is money unsolicited, so the mere availability of financial resources is not in itself a sufficient explanation of growth. One must ask, rather, what the higher educational institution does about the resources that are available, how they are collected, and then how they are spent. The social class of students is a relevant factor, since well-to-do students are an indication of parental resources that the school can tap and also a promise of future well-to-do alumni who can safely be expected to support their alma mater. On the other hand, money must be collected and it must be spent, and the mere presence on campus of well-to-do young people is not in itself a guarantee that the money will be either collected or spent wisely.

Furthermore, the physical location of the school could play an important part in its academic improvement. If the school, for example, must compete with a large number of similar institutions in the same area, it may not be able to amass the resources that will make for a favorable balance among the various relationships that are part of its social system. Again, a school that is located far from a center of Catholic population may not have an adequate base of Catholics either to fill its desks or to provide the finances necessary to keep it going, much less to create the margin necessary for improvement. Finally, given the rather close relationship between a Catholic school and the ecclesiastical authority of the Church, it is quite possible that a favorable ecclesiastical setting will be highly conducive to academic improvement. If Church authorities in particular areas are resistant to change and development, then it might be rather difficult for a college to improve, while if the ecclesiastical atmosphere is progressive and dynamic, then there may even be pressure for academic improvement.

Sheer size could be either an asset or a liability for a Catholic college or university. If the school is too small, then it may simply not have enough students or enough finances to sustain the overhead necessary to make academic growth feasible. If, on the other hand, it is too big, it is quite possible that its resources will be spread out in too many diversified projects for there to be the sort of focus required for qualitative improvement. Given the relatively authoritarian stance of the Catholic Church in the centuries after the Council of Trent, it could well be that an absolute prerequisite for academic growth is a decline of paternalism in the Catholic college and an increase of academic freedom and faculty participation. Thus, measures of freedom and faculty participation might be very useful indicators of whether the school has broken out of its old ecclesiastical ghetto and begun the pursuit of excellence, however this concept is defined.

Since most Catholic colleges and universities are owned and administered by various religious orders of the Roman Catholic Church, it may well be that the traditions and spirit of the religious community play a crucial role in the school's improvement, with some of the more progressive orders presiding over schools that are rapidly improving, while others, more careful and conservative in their traditions, being more reluctant to break with the methods and the goals of the past.

However, even the most cursory reading of the history of colleges and universities makes it quite clear that the administrative leadership of the school is crucial in its attempts to improve. While the William Rainey Harpers of the world are few and far between, it is not hard to find a name or series of names that can be linked to the dramatic growth of almost any great school. Without necessarily subscribing to the great man theory of history, it could still be affirmed that the leadership of a college or university president often means the difference between stagnation and growth. Some of the "multiversities" are so big and complex that it may well be that no one man can have a major influence on their development. But none of the Catholic schools are terribly large or complicated as American universities go, so an explanation of why one Catholic school grows more rapidly than another must take into account the personalities and the abilities of the presidents of the two institutions.

Money, social class, location, size of population base, ecclesiastical setting, decline of paternalism, increase of academic freedom and size, and attitudes of the religious order that owns and administers the school—all these, or combinations of these, might be the explanation of why one Catholic school improves academically and another does not. But there is a special dimension to the problem of qualitative improvement in Catholic colleges that may provide us with a hint of the most likely explanation for improvement. Anyone who has had even a brief experience with Catholic colleges knows that there is a complicated problem in the relationship between the religious order that owns the school and the educators who administer it. Indeed, the structure of the relationship between the educational institution and the religious community is perhaps the most critical aspect of the school's organization and operation. In most instances, the trustees who are the legal owners of the school are appointed by the religious superior of the community, generally the person called the provincial.[1] The trustees are either identical with the provincial council (that is to say, the advisory body that surrounds the provincial), or are administrators of the school wearing a slightly different hat. The administrative officers of the school themselves are appointed either directly by the provincial or indirectly by the provincial through the general of the religious community in Rome and then are constituted officers from the point of view of civil law by the routine action of the legal trustees.

The relationship among these various sources of authority and power is quite complex and delicate. The legal trustees themselves are generally without any real power. If they are the same people as those who administer the school, then when they meet as trustees they in effect sit in judgment on their own efforts and evaluate their own work. On the other hand, if the trustees are the provincial consultors, they act, in most instances, as agents of the provincial. In either case, the administrative officers of the school are not at all responsible to their legal trustees but rather to their religious superior, who may or may not know anything about the administration of a higher educational institution.

The religious community can traditionally be expected to emphasize obedience, discipline, loyalty, order, and respect for familiar, diffuse, particularistic, and ascriptive values. The higher educational institution, insofar as it trys to imitate typical American institutions, will be more likely to emphasize initiative, imagination, creativity and specific achievement, and universal values. A man can have all the talents necessary to be an extraordinarily effective college administrator and yet the provincial, as a representative of the religious community, may think that he cannot safely be trusted with power and responsibility. Similarly, from the point of view of the provincial, the person who would be an ideal religious superior might be a very poor academic administrator. In addition, the provincial and the religious community are very likely to have many other works under their direction in addition to higher education. High schools, parishes, missions, retreat houses—all of these are the responsibility of the

---

[1]The province is a subdivision of the entire religious order. Thus, for example, the American Jesuits are divided into eleven provinces.

provincial, and he must view the total needs of the religious order as being superior to the needs of any one specific kind of institution, even if it happens to be a university that aspires to greatness.

As a result, the administrators of Catholic colleges are all too frequently chosen by people who do not understand the needs and problems of higher education and who must be concerned about other needs that sometimes seem more pressing than those of a college or university. In addition, community pressures and the multiple responsibilities of his office may often force a religious superior to view with great concern the innovations that a college administrator might attempt. He may be warned that community traditions are being violated or that the school is being given away to the laity or that grave financial risks are being taken that may bankrupt the religious order. Even if the provincial does not take these pressures seriously, the very fact that the members of the order are in a position to bring these pressures to bear may severely inhibit the freedom of university administrators, especially when the financial officer of the school is more the agent of the provincial or the religious superior than he is of the college president. Under such circumstances, it might be that a Catholic college president would be most effective in accelerating the growth of his school if he were able to structure the relationship between the school and the religious community in such fashion as to guarantee the maximum freedom and independence of the school compatible with its being owned by a religious community. In the preliminary thinking that went into the survey reported in this volume, it was therefore hypothesized that, given a reasonably favorable geographic environment and a reasonably favorable financial situation, the key to the academic improvement of a Catholic college would be the competence of the top-level administrator—a competence manifested both by his understanding of what an American higher educational institution ought to be and how it is created, and by his ability to create a situation in which he could minimize interference and maximize support of the religious community. Political skills are necessary for all administrators of large corporate bodies, but Catholic college administrators may need not only the intellectual and political skills that any college president might be expected to have, but also the special skill of obtaining the freedom necessary to exercise their more strictly academic and administrative competencies.

Since the legal nature of the relationships between college and religious order has been changed in only a very few Catholic schools, we assumed that the ability of the president to obtain such freedom and to use it to restyle the school's operation from the familial to the professional and from the paternalistic to the collegial would be based on informal working agreements (and often implicit ones at that) that he had managed to arrange with or extort from his superiors. It therefore seemed that the basic question was whether the religious orders that still staff the principal administrative positions in Catholic colleges and universities can produce the kind of academic administrator and bring into Catholic higher education the academic and administrative norms operative in most American colleges and universities without so affecting the relationship between the order and the university as to endanger the continuity of the administration.

There are two elements in our hypothesis: The first is that the school that will improve academically more rapidly is the one that has an administrative leadership that accepts the basic American higher educational values and styles. The second is that, since these styles are at variance with what has traditionally been considered the proper spirit of a Roman Catholic religious order, the leadership of an academically improving Catholic school must, by one means or another, create acceptance within the religious order for the innovations it proposes.

We therefore began to expect that if a rank ordering of Catholic higher educational institutions could be based on a sophisticated perception of the amount of enlightenment and independence observed at the administrative leadership level, such a rank ordering ought to be highly predictive of academic improvement in Catholic higher education. If there were a positive rank-order correlation between academic improvement and the competence and independence of the school's administrative leadership, it would follow that the secret of even greater improvement in Catholic higher education would be the appointment of academically qualified administrators who would have the maximum amount of freedom to transform Catholic colleges and universities into schools that were typically American in every way that was compatible with their remaining in some essential sense Roman Catholic institutions.

In attempting to reduce this theorizing to an operational study, we decided that a useful and interesting way to proceed with the problem of the rank ordering of schools on this measure would be to have a team of sensitive researchers visit a number of Catholic institutions and observe the patterns in relationships existing among faculty, students, and administrators. We were encouraged in this study design by the highly successful efforts of Robert Crain and his team of colleagues in their study of the politics of school desegregation, and, as Crain states in the introduction to the preliminary report:

If there is any part of our research we are pleased with it is the method of data collection. Our fears that a week of interviewing in each city would not be enough time proved to be unfounded. We had no difficulty learning a detailed study of a decision. There may be some well kept secrets which we did not uncover but we think that in almost every city we have a story complete enough for analysis. In addition, we found, as other researchers have noted, that a clear impression of a particular tone or style of the city is apparent, although sometimes we were not successful in identifying all the factors which go into making up a city's style of action.

The plan that evolved, then, was that the three researchers would visit a number of Catholic institutions on which NORC already had considerable information from its previous studies and would attempt to rank them according to the enlightenment and independence of the institution as viewed through the eyes of the students, faculty, and administrators. The particular schools to be investigated were selected by Norman Bradburn and Donald Treiman of the NORC staff, who had determined by an objective measurement which Catholic schools could be considered academically improving schools and which could not. Bradburn and Treiman prepared a regression of school quality in 1956 on school quality in 1964 for all the schools that were in the 1961 and 1964 NORC samples (by a method described in the Appendix). Nineteen Catholic schools and six non-Catholic schools were then selected from the regression line for the survey team to visit. (The non-Catholic schools were included largely for comparative purposes to determine to what extent the problems of Catholic higher education were similar to the problems experienced in most American colleges.)

The nineteen Catholic schools were selected from various points on the regression line so that some of the schools were rapid improvement institutions, others moderate improvement institutions, and still others slow improvement institutions. The research team was then assigned to go out into the field and separate the educational sheep from the educational goats. It is important to stress that the interviewing team not only did not know where any of the schools were on the regression line of academic growth but also were unaware of what specific variables were used by Messrs. Treiman and Bradburn in preparing the regression line.

The nineteen schools were divided into two groups: the five small women's colleges and the fourteen larger colleges and universities, of which all but two were at least in some fashion coeducational. Each of the three researchers prepared a ranking of the school from the viewpoint of his own particular specialty. The interviewer who worked principally with administrators achieved a correlation of .79 for the coeducational schools and .8 for the women's colleges. The interviewer who worked principally with faculty members achieved a rank order correlation of .83 for the coeducational schools and .8 for the women's colleges. The interviewer who worked with students achieved a .96 rank order for the coeducational schools and a 1.0 rank order for the five women's schools.

We now turn to a more direct description of the procedure used in the survey itself. In the fall of 1965, letters were sent to the presidents of nineteen Catholic and six non-Catholic schools describing very briefly the purpose of the study, assuring the presidents of the complete confidentiality of the interviews and asking permission to visit the school some time in the course of the year. On the schools approached, one non-Catholic school asked to be excused from the study (for reasons that had to do with an internal reorganization), and one Catholic school (a very well-known and very prominent women's college) did not deign to answer the initial letter or two follow-up letters. Both these schools were replaced by two similar schools from the regression analysis. Worth noting, in passing, is the willingness (in some instances, eagerness) of Catholic college presidents to permit such a survey— an interesting indication of the new openness on the Catholic campus.

After a letter of acceptance was received from the college president, a second letter was dispatched indicating when the survey team hoped to visit the school and asking that a coordinator be appointed to schedule interviews for the team when they arrived. In addition, all available descriptive literature about the school was solicited. The coordinator was then informed of the plans of the interviewing team. The researcher concerned with administration indicated his interests in academic officers, registrars, directors of admission, directors of development, librarians, and other key figures in the college or university administration. The faculty interviewer noted that he would like to speak with "some of the old and some of the young; some of the new and some of the not so new; some of the more favorable and some of the more critical." In addition, he asked that he be permitted to interview the chairman of the faculty senate, if there were such an organization, and the president of the AAUP chapter, if there were one on the campus. Finally, the student interviewer expressed a desire to speak with the student officers and leaders and the newspaper editors of the college and asked for permission to drift around campus gathering interviews with students.

Of the nineteen institutions visited for the specific analysis with which this report is concerned, three were west of the Mississippi, two were south of the Mason-Dixon line, and the others were in the northeast and middlewestern sections of the country. Five were women's schools and two were all-male schools, while the others were coeducational. In addition to the five women's schools, four other schools were liberal colleges and the others were universities, though only some of the universities had authentic arts and science graduate programs leading to the Ph.D. Nine of the schools were administered by the Society of Jesus, five were administered by religious orders of women, one was a diocesan college, and four others were administered by various religious orders. (It is worth noting that the most rapidly improving and the least rapidly improving schools were Jesuit institutions.) Approximately 20 per cent of the students in Catholic colleges and universities are enrolled in these nineteen schools. The oldest school in the sample is 140 years old; the newest was spawned immediately after World War II. The largest school has in excess of eight thousand students, the smallest has less than eight hundred. While the complete confidentiality promised to the college presidents before the study began makes it impossible for us to present a list of the schools that were visited, it is our conviction that they are quite typical of American Catholic higher education, at least for the specific purposes of this study.

In addition to the nineteen schools described in the present analysis, eleven other institutions were visited either because they happened to be readily at hand when we were inspecting another college or because there was something in particular about the school that made it worth visiting. Some of the phenomena observed at these eleven schools were taken into account in the observations made in subsequent chapters.

The visits to the schools lasted anywhere from two to five days, depending on the size and complexity of the institution. The administration interviewer would usually talk to about ten people. The faculty interviewer would speak with from twelve to fifteen. And the student interviewer, who often was able to speak to several students at the same time, would work with perhaps as many as twenty respondents. Thus, in the course of the year's grand tour of American Catholic higher education, more than fifteen hundred interviews were completed.

Elaborate interview schedules were not used, but rather each of the researchers decided on five or six general questions with which key subjects could be introduced. The direction the interview would take depended in most instances on the direction that the respondent wanted to give it. Indeed, many of the respondents noted that the conversation seemed almost too relaxed and casual to be a real sociological interview. (Apparently, the image of contemporary sociology is such that unless something is marked on a printed questionnaire, it is not taken to be serious.)

In many interviews, particularly with faculty members, and especially with faculty members in the social sciences, it was necessary to ask only one question—What are the problems here at your university?—and to listen and take rapid notes, sometimes for several hours. Virtually all the respondents were eager to talk, and questions from the interviewer were not particularly necessary.

As a matter of fact, near the survey's end, the senior researcher gave a paper at the annual meeting of the Jesuit Educational Association in which he had some very forceful words to say about the problems of Jesuit higher education; he deemed it safe to do this since there was only one Jesuit school left in the sample. There was some risk (though by this time it was clear to us that the risk was minimal) that such a talk would provoke a hostile reaction at the remaining Jesuit institution. The reaction was, in fact, just the opposite. The various faculty respondents (thoughtfully equipped by someone in the university with a copy of the JEA paper) came to the interview with detailed outlines of what they wanted to say and pursued their critical comments on the given school with a great deal more vigor and care than we had encountered at many other institutions. In addition, one department in this university was quite upset that it was not represented among those being interviewed and insisted that a member of the department be permitted to talk to the researcher.

It is very important to note that the cooperation of the faculty and the administration was almost universally excellent. At only one school was there suspicion, distrust, and aggressive opposition, and even here the suspicion was masked under a display of overwhelming, if rigidly controlling friendliness. But even at this school the first faculty member interviewed was one who had just been discharged from her position by the school administration. Indeed, it seemed to us that in most instances the school administrations were eager to display every possible bit of their dirty linen for the survey team to inspect. The faculty interviewer routinely checked with the AAUP chairman or with a contact he had on the campus to determine whether the interviews arranged for him by the coordinator of the visit were in fact such as to give him a representative view of the problems the faculty faced. In every single instance the "reality check" indicated that the administration had indeed "played it straight."

Of course, no mathematical proof can be adduced to establish that in given instances the survey team was not deceived. However, to those who might contend that we were consistently deceived across the entire system we can only point with modesty to the very high rank-order correlations between our evaluation of the schools' academic improvement and the objective evaluation made by the computer. Deceptions, whatever they may have been, did not prevent us from sizing up the schools' relative positions along this dimension.

The researchers took notes during the interviews and then dictated memos describing each interview. At no time were tape recorders used during the interview sessions, because it was felt that the use of tape recorders might be construed as a violation of the privacy of the respondent and also because the tape recorder might inhibit the frankness of the respondent's answers. (At the one college where we were clearly not welcome, bitter accusations were made that we had somehow or other concealed tape recorders with which to "bug" the conversation.)

It must be borne in mind that the methods we used were tailored to fit the specific goals of the study rather than the goals of the study being altered to fit what is taken to be "standard methodology." Thus, we were not interested in a random sample of the faculty or the student body of the school; we were interested rather in the sort of analysis of the school and its problems that could be obtained from the more sophisticated, reflective, and penetrating members of the school community. We were not so much interested in what a representative sample of a faculty of a school might think as we were in understanding how the school operated, how its areas of decisions were defined, how the decisions were made, and what processes were used in carrying out the decisions. In such a situation, a perceptive informant is of far more use than a random sample. Further, we were not concerned with whether a given number of faculty members would respond "yes," "no," or "don't know" to a question that had been printed on a previously prepared questionnaire. We were much more interested in the tone, the color, and the style of the school as it could be conveyed not in a simple precoded answer but in all the nuances that a personal encounter in a relaxed, casual conversation might reveal.

The research team feels very strongly that the style and methods of its survey do not constitute second-class sociology simply because they cannot be reduced to statistical tables or to regression analyses. We contend that for the specific goals of this particular study the methods and the style were the most appropriate. We therefore make no apologies for our procedures.

In conclusion, it is safe to say that, in varying degrees, the three researchers felt at the beginning of the study and still feel that (1) there are many things wrong with Catholic higher education; (2) considerable improvement has taken place in recent years and will continue to take place; and (3) there is a vast diversity and pluralism within Catholic higher education, with some schools being very promising and exciting and others being very dull and discouraging.

But the purpose of this project is not to recommend either the continuation or the discontinuation of Catholic higher education. Our feeling is that the three hundred or more Catholic colleges and universities are here to stay. We are concerned rather with the factors that make for academic improvement in Catholic colleges and with the precise question of why one college improves and another does not. We had hypothesized that the crucial variable is the independence and intelligence of the top administrative leadership, particularly the president. We further determined that one way to test such a hypothesis was to compare rank ordering of schools on this variable, compiled after visiting a large number of Catholic colleges and universities, with a rank ordering of the schools based on some objective measures of academic improvement. We found that the correlations between the research team's evaluation of the schools rate of improvement and that provided by more objective measures was very high indeed, and we feel quite safe in suggesting that in the absence of intelligent and independent leadership, a Catholic college or university would do little more than stagnate.

There are three qualifying comments that are necessary before we turn to the next chapter:

1. Any study of higher educational institutions is bound to be a critical study. Since the goal of research in higher education is usually, at least in some remote fashion, the improvement of higher education, the researcher will concentrate on describing the problems and difficulties in the school he is studying. If there were no problems, there would be little need for research. But American Catholic education is in a rather special situation. Critics both inside and outside the Church have, for some time, been demanding a complete elimination of a religiously-affiliated Catholic school system. Under these circumstances any report on Catholic education that makes any critical comments at all is considered by the opponents of Catholic education to be more ammunition for their attack and by the defendents of Catholic education as a further weakening of their already threatened position. It is almost impossible for a serious researcher to avoid having his material claimed by one side or the other in support of their position, even though the terms of the dispute may appear to the outside observer to be quite unrealistic.

2. A second problem is that, because of the controversy arising about Catholic schools, sociological reports on the subject run the risk of being quoted out of context to support one or the other side of this great debate. To disown such distortions does not prevent them from occurring, as NORC has learned in its previous research on Catholic education. Nonetheless the authors wish to strongly warn that journalists who quote this report out of context do so against the authors' wishes and at their own risk.

3. The researchers were somewhat surprised (although perhaps they should not have been) to discover that those who read the preliminary draft of this report were particularly eager to identify the colleges described in Chapters 3, 4, and 5 and especially eager to learn whether the colleges under discussion were in fact their own schools. On some occasions, readers wrote to observe that in a given passage we were obviously talking about their school but

we had misunderstood the situation being described. However, in practically every instance, we were not talking about the alma mater of the reader who thought we had misunderstood a situation at his institution. It is a case, one supposes, of, "If the shoe appears to fit, then we must put it on." There is no way to stop readers from guessing the names of the schools that are being described, but we warn in advance that their guesses are far more likely to be unsuccessful than successful.

In several points in the course of the report we insist that nothing we encountered in our research on Catholic higher education in any notable way indicated that it is inferior to the general run of American higher education. One can make this assertion a limited number of times without boring one's readers. Nevertheless, a few of the committee of Catholic educators who read the first draft of this report expressed the fear that the report would be interpreted as indicating the inferiority of Catholic higher education. Despite the fact that the criticisms are intended, rather obviously we thought, to lead to the improvement of Catholic colleges and universities rather than to their elimination, these educators still felt that their enemies would use the material in this report as more evidence that the Catholic Church should get out of higher education.

It is safe to conclude from the present document that the quality of many Catholic colleges and universities is none too impressive. But it is important to emphasize that the quality of most of American higher education is none too impressive, and that Catholic schools are no better and no worse than the vast majority of other American higher educational institutions. We simply do not think that this report can in any sense be interpreted as an attack on Catholic higher education. Those who do interpret it in such fashion do so not only against the intentions of the authors but also, in the authors' judgment, against the obvious sense of the substance of the report.

The following plan will be followed in the presentation of this report. In the next chapter we will briefly summarize available information on the past history of Catholic higher education and the sociological literature dealing with the current situation on the Catholic campus. In three succeeding chapters, we will give generalized descriptions of three rapid improvement, three medium improvement, and three low improvement schools. Then, in Chapter 6, we will attempt to summarize, through rather simple statistical analysis, the evidence that it is indeed quality of administrative leadership and not any other variable that predicts academic improvement in a Catholic college or university. In Chapters 7, 8, and 9, we will comment in considerably greater detail about the administrations, faculties, and student bodies at Catholic colleges and universities with our recommendations as to the sorts of improvements that would be desirable in these institutions. Finally, we will conclude with some very general remarks about the future outlook for Catholic higher education in the United States.

2

Social and Historical Background

While is it anything but adequate, the literature on Catholic higher education is becoming more and more extensive. It is not our intention in this volume to attempt a review of the literature, since such review would merely duplicate the excellent review already done by Hassenger (1967). Nevertheless, certain sociological and historical data ought to be summarized in a preliminary chapter to the present report. Since the report assumes the existence of a change in Catholic higher education it is of some importance to document the fact that such change has apparently occurred. Second, for those whose interests do not go beyond the scope of the present volume it is important that there be presented a summary of the historical, social, and demographic background of the Catholic colleges and universities. Third, since this report is oriented to policy planning, it is appropriate for the readers to know what sociological and historical presuppositions the researchers had in mind when they began their analysis.[1]

The present chapter will have two sections. First of all, we will discuss as adequately as possible, given the rather minimal information available to us, certain historical trends in the development of Catholic colleges and universities. Secondly, we will summarize existing sociological information about the current graduates of Catholic colleges, information drawn to some considerable extent either from previous NORC reports or from NORC data not yet published in any formal report.

[1]Catholic grammar schools are generally affiliated with parishes and owned directly by the diocese of which the parish is a part. The Catholic high schools are sometimes diocesan-owned and sometimes owned by the religious orders which in the Roman Catholic Church are in many ways independent of the bishop. The overwhelming majority of Catholic universities, however, are owned by the religious orders, with only twelve of the more than three hundred institutions

22

The Changing Catholic College

TRENDS IN THE HISTORY OF CATHOLIC HIGHER EDUCATION

In his extremely important essay on the history of Catholic higher education, Philip Gleason comments, "It is hardly an exaggeration to say that Catholic higher education is entering its identity crisis in a state of virtual amnesia, with no meaningful grip on the history that has played so crucial a role in forging its present identity. It is supremely ironic that the Catholic academic community which is more and more disposed to accept the developmental review of reality, has only the sketchiest notion of the pattern of its own development. What is even more unfortunate and, from the developmental viewpoint simply bewildering, is the disposition sometimes manifested to treat the earlier efforts of Catholic educators with condescension or scorn because they are not what we are doing or trying to do today" (Hassenger, 1967).

It would be no exaggeration, in fact, to say that American Catholicism almost lacks a history of its own and that the history of Catholic higher education is in even worse condition. There are a handful of first-rate scholars specializing in serious research on the historical development of American Catholicism, but given the magnitude and the complexity of the field, their work has only begun to furnish us with understanding of the meaning of the American Catholic phenomenon. In the area of Catholic higher education there exists one comprehensive book, that by Edward J. Power (1958). Only the history of The Catholic University of America, done by Ellis and his students (Ahern, Barry, and Hogan), the history of St. John's Abbey and University by Colman Barry (1956), and a few other works provide high quality historical background for individual institutions. The Power book,

---

being "diocesan" colleges. The precise relationship in canon law between the diocese and any college administered by a religious order within the bounds of the diocese are obscure, though in practice the college is generally run independently of the diocese and there is frequently some awkwardness in the relationship between the diocese and the college. There is little in the way of coordination and cooperation among Catholic higher educational institutions. There are some loose consortia, and the colleges belonging to a given religious community may have some sort of coordinating agency such as the Jesuit Educational Association. Further, there is a higher education division of the National Catholic Educational Association with a very small staff in Washington. However, none of these agencies has anything more than advisory power.

while extremely useful, has relatively little to say about the progress of Catholic higher education in the last forty years, a time
that would be of particular interest to those interested in the
changes of the past half-decade or two. But if Gleason is right
when he says, "the whole story of [Catholic higher education] may
be understood in terms of the social evolution of the Catholic
population and the institutional and ideological adjustments the
colleges have made in order to adapt to the American scene without compromising their Catholicity," then we are hindered not
only by lack of a social history of Catholic higher education, but
also by lack of a comprehensive social history of the American
Catholic population. Under such circumstances, the bewildered
sociologist trying to deal with the contemporary phenomenon of
Catholic higher education is forced to rely on impressions, guesses,
and sweeping generalizations which, there is every reason to believe, the careful historians of the future will find somewhat more
than just faintly amusing.

Nonetheless, we would think that some understanding of the
historical development of Catholic higher education can be had
if these three statements are kept in mind:

1. At the present time American Catholics are as likely to
graduate from college as are other Americans.

2. Half the adult Catholic population are either immigrants or
the children of immigrants.

3. In Gleason's words, "The development of Catholic higher
education has in fact followed the same general pattern as that of
non-Catholic colleges and universities, but with a chronological
lag."

The Catholic population is an immigrant population only now
entering the mainstream of the social and economic life of the
country and, hence, only now are its colleges and universities
turning aside from the posture of an immigrant religious group
and taking on the posture of a typically American educational
institution. It would be a mistake, however, to argue that there
is some sort of historical inevitability in the process, that simply
the passage of time and the development of an adequate social
and economic base will lead to a system of Catholic higher education in which the range of schools from top to bottom will be not

unlike the range of American higher education. It could very well be that there are some structural or ideological inhibitions built into the American Catholic social system which will prevent the social forces making for evolution of Catholic higher education from carrying the Catholic colleges along the path other schools have blazed but with ever-decreasing chronological lag. It is the purpose of this study to uncover possible obstacles to such development.

A Look at Origins

It is reasonably well known that the first Catholic university founded in this country was Georgetown in Washington, D.C., in the year 1789. After Georgetown, eighty-two more colleges were founded before the beginning of the Civil War. Of these eighty-two, only twenty-eight have survived until the present time. In the decade before the Civil War, forty-one colleges were formed, of which only fourteen have survived. (This fantastic rate of college foundation has continued unabated. Between 1904 and 1910, for example, twenty-four colleges were formed, of which none has survived. At least for some of the years of the past decade it has been estimated that three Catholic colleges were founded each year, though in our present more enlightened age with financial help available from the Great Society program as well as the increased demand for college admission, the mortality rate among colleges is not nearly what it used to be.) For the most part, it would seem that these colleges were founded by missionary bishops in the American dioceses that were multiplying even more rapidly than were institutions of higher education. The bishop, perhaps for reasons not altogether clear to himself, felt that it was one of his prime responsibilities in organizing a new diocese to establish a higher educational institution, a tradition that dates back to Archbishop Carroll's founding of Georgetown. However, only in rare instances was the bishop able to staff the college himself and so one of the various religious orders was asked to take over first of all the staffing, and eventually the administration of the school. Since the Jesuits were the most famous of Catholic educators, they were the ones a bishop most frequently would seek for his college. Some of the foundations were at best tenuous and others, which did manage to survive, did so in many instances by the sheerest chance, especially since a good number of bishops, once they had called in a religious order to staff the college, left its success or failure, both financial and academic, entirely in the hands of the religious community.

It is fashionable to say that the colleges were founded to provide a place for the training of clerics, and surely it is true that much of what they did was in effect preseminary training, though the institutions were also founded to preserve the faith of those few Catholic lay people who sought a higher education. But it would be a mistake to feel that these two rather simple motivations were the only factors at work. It is to be suspected that a good number of bishops and college administrators in the early days of American Catholicism felt instinctively that an institution of higher education was something that was needed. If we casually read some of the letters of early American bishops, we can see that the idea of having a college of their own was something that was very dear to the hearts of most of them, and a respect for learning as an element in Catholic life appealed to the missionary bishops.

The schools were, for the most part, colleges in the European rather than in the English or contemporary American sense. They combined what we would now consider to be high school and college in one institution, three years of "academic" course work being roughly equivalent to preparatory school, and three years of "humanities" being roughly equivalent to what we would consider college. However, given the poor state of primary education of the Catholic population, most of the early colleges were much more high schools than colleges in our sense. The curriculum was traditional, stressing the classics, rhetoric, and philosophy. Since the training received at these early Catholic colleges was a somewhat edited version of the famous Jesuit *ratio studiorum,* the philosophy of education, insofar as there was one behind such schools, tended to be static and conservative. It was assumed that the Catholic Church had an organic "integrity of vision" about the meaning of the world and of life, and it was the purpose of the college to pass on this vision of meaning to the student in order that he might have an integrated personality in an organic world view. The goal of Catholic higher education was then considered to be "the development of the whole man" (a cliché repeated consistently in Catholic college catalogues even today). The schools were not so much concerned with the pushing back of the frontier of truth as with passing on a given tradition of truth in which little in the way of addition or alteration was necessary.

It would be a mistake to assume that this static philosophy of education ended with the end of the nineteenth century, or even that it is totally absent today. In Gleason's words, "To an age whose education was secular, scientific, and technical in spirit, particularized in vision, flexible in approach, vocational in aim, and democratic in social orientation, the Jesuits thus opposed a system that was religious, literary, and humanistic in spirit, synthetic in vision, rigid in approach, liberal in aim, and elitist in social orientation. There was no place in it for interchangeable parts, electivism, or vocationalism. These were simply the educational heresies that sprang from the radical defect, the loss of a unified view of reality. To tell a student that he could 'elect' anything was to admit that one was no longer sure what was worth knowing, or the order in which it should be learned; to award a degree to those who elected this, that, and the other thing until the whole collection added up to 128 'credits' was utter academic and intellectual irresponsibility."

"In a famous address to 'the assembled Faculties of the largest Catholic University in the world,' Father Bull argued that Catholicism was a culture, a way of life, a view of reality; that the characteristic mark of this view of reality was its totality of vision, the way it ordered all knowledge and values into a comprehensive organic unity; and that it was the function of the Catholic college to impart to students this Catholic culture, this synthetic vision. A few years later, Father Bull argued in another essay that the function of the Catholic graduate school was precisely the same as that of the Catholic college, only on a higher level; he specifically denied that research was the function of the graduate school. In fact, he asserted, to accept the primacy of research would be to attempt 'the impossible task of being Catholic in creed and anti-Catholic in culture.' Research, as an '*attitude,*' Bull declared, was concerned not with truth, but with the *'pursuit of truth'*; its tendency was vocational and particularistic, 'its spontaneous bent [was] toward the apotheosis of the principle of disintegration,' and its ultimate consequence was dehumanization. Between the Catholic view and the research view there were only antinomies— organic unity vs. disintegration; the 'sense of tradition and wisdom achieved vs. "progress"; . . . principles vs. fact; . . . contemplation vs. "research."' Education at the graduate level, as elsewhere, was for Bull, 'the enrichment of human personality, by deeper and deeper penetration into the velvety manifold of reality, as *Catholics possess it*'" (Hassenger, 1967).

This view of the purpose of higher education is certainly held by relatively few Catholic educators today (though it is not by any means absent from their official statements of purpose), nor was it a universal position even thirty to forty years ago, but it represents a deeply-felt system of goals that profoundly influenced Catholic higher education in its formative years and remains, at least in its residual effects, part of the Catholic higher educational picture.

With the exception of the few lay-founded colleges that did not survive very long, the typical college administrator was a member of a religious order, and his qualifications to serve as a president or a dean were primarily his seminary training. The faculty members were chosen from the religious community, though even at the very beginning a few lay auxiliaries were to be found, men whose role as second-class citizens was all too clear. The students were not entirely future seminarians, though this made little or no difference in their life, since the rigidly structured and closely supervised academic life of the future layman was precious little different from that of the future cleric.

Thus, at the beginning of the twentieth century Catholic colleges were small, in constant financial difficulty, academically inferior, static in educational philosophy, traditional in curriculum and pedagogy, rigid in discipline and student life, clerical in faculty and administration, and isolated almost completely from the mainstream of American higher education. On the other hand, it is worth noting that many of the faults then, as now, were to be found in most other American colleges and universities.

Into the Twentieth Century

In the time between 1900 and the end of World War II four major developments contributed to the forward academic movement of Catholic colleges as well as their movement toward a closer relationship with other American colleges. (1) Under pressure of the college division of the Catholic Educational Association, the six-year college curriculum was revised into a four-year preparatory school curriculum and a four-year college program with gradual divorce of the preparatory school from the college— a divorce which was not completed in many of the Jesuit institutions until the early 1920's. (2) At the same time, pressures from the CEA and from powerful educational theorists within the Catholic colleges forced the schools to move toward a greater standardization of program and curriculum requirements with the gradual adoption of the credit system. (3) Such a process was accelerated by the increasing need to meet the requirements of the accrediting agencies, although many Catholic schools were reluctant to adopt the "secularist" standards of these agencies, which were felt by Catholic accrediting agencies of the old school to be at variance with the integrated and organic nature of Catholic education. For example, St. John's University in Minnesota moved toward accreditation only in the years after World War II. (4) In the midst of the process of accreditation, standardization, and curriculum reform, many of the Catholic schools also became universities, not so much by moving into doctoral programs (only The Catholic University of America was truly a doctoral school), but rather by acquiring various professional schools, such as engineering, law, commerce, medicine, music, and journalism. The favorite way of converting a college into a university was not so much to found a new school as to purchase or pick up by default one of the many small and faltering professional schools that could be found in the major metropolitan areas—a method popular with non-Catholic urban schools as well.[2] This "instant

[2]For the fascinating story of how Marquette University managed to collect virtually every professional school in Milwaukee that was not "nailed down," see Hamilton (1953). The book is also interesting for its accounts of the almost incredible financial problems and manipulations of Marquette in its early days, as well as for its rather bold introduction of the principle of coeducation.

transformation" from a small liberal arts college into a multi-purpose university was justified on the very persuasive grounds that the school's role in a large city was to serve the many needs of the urban population. Such schools also provided professional training for many Catholics in the metropolis who otherwise might not have obtained it or might have obtained it under what would be deemed dangerous, non-Catholic auspices. Whether one thinks this transformation into an "instant university" was greatly courageous or foolhardy depends on one's point of view. In any event, the move was made and, with the exception of the medical schools, it did not seem to have been a financially unprofitable move. Whether the concentration on professional schools inhibited the development of a more academic atmosphere in the Catholic colleges remains to be seen, although in the present study we were readily persuaded that at least the Catholic medical schools represent a tremendous drain on the resources, time, and personnel of Catholic universities.

What would have happened in the development of Catholic education in the years after World War I if the catastrophe of the Great Depression had not struck the United States is unclear. However, between 1928 and 1940 the only possible role that occurred to most Catholic administrators was survival. It should be kept in mind that many of the men in the senior administrative positions in the Catholic universities at the present time, and the major superiors of the orders that oversee the universities, went through their formative years during the Great Depression and have yet to be persuaded in their heart of hearts that it could not happen again.

The Post-war Decades
To the many college administrators who had managed to survive World War II only with the help of various officer training programs, the years immediately after were an incredible experience, half dream and half nightmare. Where previously there had been not enough students and too many faculty, there was now an overwhelming number of students and not nearly enough faculty. While there may have been some who argued that the schools should have limited their enrolment and continued to be what

they were—small liberal arts colleges—this counsel to prudence
was ignored and the Catholic colleges expanded at a fantastic
rate in the late 1940's. The expansion jolted to a temporary stop
during the Korean conflict (a stop that acutely embarrassed some
of the smaller schools that had overexpanded) and then proceeded
at even more frantic rates of growth until the present time. Thus,
in 1916 there were 32,000 students enrolled in Catholic colleges,
many of them in the pre-college preparatory programs. By 1930
there were 102,000, and by 1940 the numbers had inched up to
162,000. At the present time, the enrolment is around 400,000,
more than twice what it was a quarter of a century ago, and nobody projects anything but a continued exponential increase. Not
only were the enrolments in the schools themselves going up, but
the number of schools were expanding as well, so that at the present time there are over three hundred Catholic institutions of
higher education, the exact number depending on how many of
the seminaries and the small "sister formation" colleges one
wishes to count as institutions of higher learning.[3] This expansion
has largely been uncontrolled because, despite the impression that
many non-Catholics have, American Catholicism is a loosely organized institution with precious little in the way of centralized
control and direction. Any bishop can permit the foundation of a
college within his diocese and any religious superior can, either
at the invitation of the bishop or on his own initiative, propose
that a new college be formed. In the Chicago standard statistical
metropolitan area alone, for example, there are, if one counts the
seminaries and sister formation schools, more than twenty-five
Catholic schools claiming to offer higher education. In addition,
we shall note later in the report, despite a good deal of happy talk,
any institutional collaboration that does exist besides the theoretical is very minimal indeed.[4]

[3]For the problems of the so-called sister formation colleges and the general
multiplication of institutions of higher learning, see the forthcoming report by
Charles Ford of St. Louis University.

[4]Many of the other religious orders are extremely critical of the Jesuits for their
refusal to engage in inter-institutional cooperation. They contend that the Jesuits
presiding over twenty-eight institutions of higher learning and playing a controlling role in American Catholic higher education are academic imperialists who
simply do not even want to recognize the existence of other colleges. While such

Along with this pell-mell expansion there has been a tendency towards laicization and professionalization on the Catholic campuses out of sheer necessity. Laymen in large numbers had to be hired to service the needs of the post-World War II students who inundated the Catholic campuses. It gradually and painfully became clear that the old familial patterns of relationships that existed among faculties when most of its members were clerics were no longer appropriate. Even though the change has been slow and not nearly as enthusiastic as would be to the liking of the lay faculty members or the liberal Catholic critics, the gradual replacement of familial norms with professional norms is continuing and is accelerating with each passing year. This tendency is one of the major focuses of concern of the present report.

Third, Catholic universities since the end of World War II have moved toward the establishment of authentic arts and sciences graduate schools. While only The Catholic University of America can claim admission in the strict sense to the fraternity of true universities (granting 1 per cent of the Ph.D.'s in the country) there are several other Catholic institutions that are seriously planning to become major graduate institutions, and still others that are flirting with the idea without counting the costs of the problems. We will return to this phenomenon later in the report. In our judgment, at the present time there are at least four, and possibly five, metropolitan areas where it would be technically, academically, and economically feasible for there to be major Catholic graduate centers, but more will be said of that in a later chapter. Gleason's comments are once again singularly appropriate: "No one would deny that there is still room for much more improvement, but it is equally important to recognize, in evaluating the present situation, that graduate work on the doctoral level is hardly older than yesterday in the Catholic universities."

Finally, in the more recent years since the end of the war, there has been a considerable amount of talk, and not an inconsiderable amount of activity, directed toward the entry of Catholic academia into the mainstream of American higher education. John Tracy Ellis' famous essay in 1955 about the failures of Catholic

charges would be demonstrably false if leveled against certain Jesuit administrators, there seems little reason to doubt that it is true in a fair number of instances.

intellectualism in this country both symbolized and accelerated the pace of this development. The "quest for excellence" in the Catholic colleges, while in many instances misdirected and in other instances abortive, is nonetheless sincere (at least more or less so) and powerful. Whether this quest has any chance for success is one of the concerns of the present volume. Or, to put the matter more specifically, the present report is concerned with the circumstances under which and the types of structure within which one can reasonably expect the quest for excellence to be successful.

Gleason notes that the "adjustment was an ongoing process of accommodation, responding to this pressure or that need as it became noticeable to the point of demanding action. Catholic educators have always been struggling to keep up with the situation; they have never been able to get on top of their problems or to dispose matters according to some ideal scheme. The same is largely true of all American educators, of course, but there are some special complexities involved with Catholic institutions. All colleges and universities had to adjust themselves to changing needs in American society, but Catholic educators had the additional problem of adapting their adjustments to the general pattern followed by non-Catholic institutions."

Gleason's statement is as true now as it was in any time in the history of Catholic higher education, but there is some reason to think that at the present time the final stages of the dialectical process may be near. The fact that American Catholics are assimilating very rapidly into the mainstream of American economics, polity, and society may give some reason to expect that the same assimilation is taking place in Catholic higher academia; if given perhaps another generation the differences, other than the purely religious, between Catholic colleges and non-Catholic colleges may well be minimal. Surely some of the sociological data reported in the second half of this chapter confirms this suspicion. If one believes, as the present researchers are inclined to believe, that economic and social forces can provide adequate explanations for the problems of Catholic higher education with only occasional reference needed to ideological variables, then one would assume that economic and cultural parity would also soon lead to educational parity. But it is by no means clear that there are not structural and cultural problems within American Catholicism in general, and its educational enterprises in particular, that will impede, if not prevent completely, the further development of Catholic higher education.

SOCIOLOGICAL DATA CONCERNING CATHOLIC HIGHER EDUCATION[5]

Demography and Social Class
Socially and demographically the typical graduate of the Catholic college or university is not very different from the typical American college graduate, though he is rather more different from his coreligionist who attended a non-Catholic college (Greeley, 1963, Chaps. 2 and 5). A Catholic college graduate is as likely to be a girl (43 per cent) and to come from a family where both parents went to college as is a typical American college graduate (about two-fifths of the graduates' parents also attended college). Furthermore, the graduate of a Catholic college is just as likely as is the Protestant graduate to come from a family whose income was over $7,500 a year and whose father was a professional man or a manager. On the other hand, a Catholic who attended a non-Catholic college is much less likely to be a girl (only 31 per cent) and to come from a smaller city and from a distinctly lower socioeconomic background (only one-fifth of the fathers of the Catholics who went to non-Catholic colleges had themselves gone to college). Furthermore, almost a third of the Catholics who went to non-Catholic colleges were either married or planning marriage before the fall after graduation (a proportion about the same for Protestants who graduated from college), but only a fifth of the graduates of Catholic colleges were either married or contemplating immediate marriage.

Three years after college graduation the Catholic college graduate was still much less likely to be married than either the Catholic or non-Catholic who had not attended a Catholic college. But if he or she were married, he or she was more likely to have children

[5]Tables that already exist in a previous publication (Greeley, 1963) will not be duplicated here.

than the non-Catholic and more likely to have two or three children than the non-Catholic graduate. However, as far as having children was concerned, the Catholic graduates of non-Catholic colleges were not notably different from their coreligionists (Table 2.1).

The graduates of Catholic colleges were also considerably more likely to be from the area north of the Mason-Dixon line and east of the Mississippi River, with 89 per cent coming from this area while only 68 per cent of the Catholics who went to non-Catholic colleges were from this area (Table 2.2). Indeed, it is well worth noting that better than a third of the graduates of Catholic colleges came from the five states of the old Northwest Territory: Illinois, Indiana, Michigan, Ohio, and Wisconsin.[6] One of the

[6]There may possibly be some sampling variation at work in this distribution since none of the Catholic colleges which fell into the NORC sample on which the table is based came from the West Coast.

Table 2.1 Marriage and Religion for College Graduates (Per Cent)

Marital Status	Catholic Graduates of Catholic Colleges	Catholic Graduates of Non-Catholic Colleges	Non-Catholic Graduates
Single	40	32	28
Married, with children	80	78	65
Married, more than one child	42	37	28
Married, more than two children	14	15	8

Table 2.2 Region and Catholic College Attendance (for Catholics) (Per Cent)

Region	Catholic College	Non-Catholic College
Northeast	22	6
Middle Atlantic	32	37
East North Central	35	25
West North Central	6	6
South	4	8
West	1	15
Other	1	3
Total	100	100

most important facts about the graduates of Catholic colleges is that almost two-fifths of them were of Irish ancestry, while approximately one-fifth the proportion of the Catholic graduates of non-Catholic colleges were Irish (Table 2.3). In comparison with the Irish, all of them were slightly underrepresented among graduates of Catholic colleges. Other NORC data indicate that the 37 per cent Irish in the 1961 graduating population represents a substantial decline from the proportion in past graduation classes; among Catholic adults who went to college, almost half had Irish ancestral background. It is no secret, of course, that the Irish, because of their early arrival, knowledge of the language, and political skills, have been the dominant ethnic group within the American Church. It is also no secret that the Irish have traditionally been extremely loyal to Catholic institutions. Hence, both because of organizational control and organizational loyalty it is not unexpected that Catholic higher education is so heavily an Irish phenomenon.

In summary, then, the graduates of Catholic colleges are not different from typical American college graduates in socioeconomic background, though they are different in their tendency to marry either during college or shortly after college graduation. They are rather different from their confreres who did not go to Catholic colleges in the size of the cities from which they come,

Table 2.3 Ethnicity and Catholic College Attendance (for Catholics) (Per Cent)

Father's Ethnicity	Catholic College	Non-Catholic College
English	10	13
Irish	37	18
German	23	25
Italian	11	17
French	5	4
Polish	6	7
Other East Europeans	3	4
Spanish	1	3
Others	4	9
Total	100	100

in the regions of the country in which they grew up, in their socio-economic background, and in their ethnicity.

Politics

It has been lamented frequently by liberals, both Catholic and non-Catholic, that American Catholics, even though they may belong to the Democratic party, are not in fact "liberal" Democrats. It has been further lamented that the Catholic colleges have turned the Democratic children of the immigrant working class into conservative Republicans. It is also quite fashionable among some Catholic liberals to tell rather terrifying stories of the "Birchite" conservatism to be found among their students in Catholic colleges and universities. Unfortunately for these lamentations, the data in Table 2.4 provide no support for their continuation. Thus, about 29 per cent of Catholics who went to college (no matter what kind of college they went to) still would describe themselves as liberal Democrats, and only 14 per cent would describe themselves as conservative Republicans. If anything, college education seems to make it more likely for a young person to be a liberal Democrat than his parents were. The

Table 2.4 Politics and Religion for College Graduates and Their Parents (Per Cent)

Politics	Catholic Graduates of Catholic Colleges		Catholic Graduates of Non-Catholic Colleges		Non-Catholic Graduates	
	Respondent	Parents	Respondent	Parents	Respondent	Parents
Conservative Republican	14	17	14	18	21	18
Liberal Republican	13	13	16	12	22	17
Conservative Democrat	15	19	14	10	10	12
Liberal Democrat	29	25	29	25	20	17
Conservative independent	14	14	9	4	11	14
Liberal independent	13	9	15	4	13	13
Other	2	3	2	2	2	3
Total	100	100	100	100	100	100
N	(1,969)		(2,664)		(2,579)	

graduate of a Catholic college is more likely to describe himself
as a Democrat, and as likely to describe himself as a liberal than
the non-Catholic who went to college. Attending a Catholic college does not make someone from a conservative family liberal;
neither does it make someone from a Democratic family Republican. It can only be said that the tendency of young people to
inherit political affiliation and orientations of their parents seems
remarkably unaffected by the kind of college they attend.

Religion
However, graduates of Catholic colleges are much more likely
to remain in the Church and to attend church weekly than are
Catholics who do not attend Catholic colleges. Of those who said
their religion was Catholic, 97 per cent of those who had been to
Catholic colleges and only 80 per cent of those who attended non-
Catholic colleges would still describe themselves as Catholic three
years after their graduation. Almost half of the defection from
the Catholic Church, among those who went to non-Catholic colleges, apparently occurred before college education began (Table
2.5). And four-fifths of the Catholics who did not attend Catholic
colleges would describe themselves as Catholics three years after
college graduation. Thus, it would not seem that Catholic higher
education has been necessary to keep young people in the Church.
On the other hand, there does seem to be some relationship between a Catholic college education and church attendance, with
better than nine-tenths of those who attended Catholic college
reporting church attendance as opposed to only two-thirds of

Table 2.5 Religious Defection among Catholic Graduates (among
Those Who Were "Raised Catholics") (Per Cent)

"Raised Catholics"	Attended Catholic College	Attended Non-Catholic College
Catholics at beginning of college	98	92
Catholics now	97	80
Married to Catholics	86	67
Married to Catholics (spouse "raised Catholic")	81	57
Weekly church attendance	92	67

those who did not attend Catholic colleges. Furthermore, those in Catholic colleges were 19 percentage points more likely to have married a fellow Catholic than those who had attended non-Catholic colleges.[7] Whether the strong relationship between church attendance and Catholic college education can be attributed to the college itself or to the previous influence of the families from which the student was predisposed to go to Catholic college is not known. We will defer this question to a later section in which we discuss the religious impact of Catholic colleges.

Career Choices

The career choices of the Catholic college graduate are not so very different from the career choices of other Americans who went to college (Greeley, 1963). Catholics are somewhat overrepresented in large business and somewhat underrepresented in primary and secondary education, but there are no differences between the graduates of Catholic colleges and other Americans in their choice of scientific and academic careers or, within the sciences, in their choice of the so-called hard sciences, such as mathematics, physics, and chemistry. Neither are Catholic graduates any less likely to enroll the year after their graduation in full-time graduate work or to plan an eventual doctorate or a career in college teaching or research. Within the broad categories there are some differences: Catholic college graduates are less likely to choose biological sciences and a little bit more likely to choose the humanities; within the social sciences, Catholics are especially interested in political science, perhaps because they also seem predisposed to government service. But the overall picture from the June, 1961, data is that whatever influence the "religious factor" or religious education may have had in years gone by, there is precious little difference between Catholics and Protestants or between Catholic school Catholics and non-Catholic school Catholics in their career aspirations, their graduate plans, or their occupational values.

[7]Eighty-one per cent of the spouses of the Catholic college graduates were raised Catholics as opposed to 57 per cent of the spouses of Catholics who did not go to Catholic colleges. In both instances, there is evidence of a fair amount of "marriage conversions" of people marrying Catholics who had graduated from college.

It is carefully noted in *Religion and Career* (Greeley, 1963) that the mere plans to go to graduate school do not an intellectual make, nor does the possession of the Ph.D. a distinguished scholar make. But it is also remarked that the absence of Catholics in the ranks of academia, carefully documented by previous research, seems to be rapidly coming to an end. It would seem, therefore, that some sort of dramatic change went on in American Catholicism in general, and within American Catholic higher education in particular, in the years between the end of World War II and the inauguration of John Kennedy.

The findings reported in *Religion and Career* were not accepted by all scholars concerned with the question of the influence of the religious factor on career choice and occupational values. Some writers questioned the validity of the NORC sample and other suggested that, even though Catholics might have great aspirations for graduate school training and academic careers, such aspirations would weaken through the years as the anti-intellectualism of their religion began to take its toll.

Fortunately, there exist in the NORC studies of college graduates two very rare phenomena in contemporary social science—a panel study and a replication. The June, 1961, graduates were followed for the first three years of their post-college experiences so that it could be determined whether in fact the Catholic graduates were likely to defect from their career aspirations. Furthermore, working with a completely independent sample of the June, 1964, graduates, Michael Schiltz at NORC could find nothing that did not confirm the conclusions of *Religion and Career*. While the interested reader is referred to the Schiltz work, at least one table from it should be noted in passing. It is obvious from Table 2.6 that with controls for sex and socioeconomic status, kind of high school attended, and academic performance in college, the graduate of Catholic colleges is no less likely than other Americans (and somewhat more likely than other Catholics) to aspire to a higher degree or to plan a career in the academic life.

The fact that the 1964 study replicated the findings of the 1961 study, with a completely different sample, virtually eliminates the possibility that the 1961 findings could be explained away as the result of sampling variation. However, a more serious criticism is the argument that with the passage of time those who had been tabbed as future Catholic scholars would drift away from graduate school. In June of 1964, there was no sign of the massive defection of 1961 graduates from academic plans (Table 2.7). While the differences between Jews and Gentiles persisted into the third year of graduate study, there was no discernible difference between American Protestants and the graduates of Catholic colleges in the proportion still in graduate school, the proportion attending graduate school full time, the proportion with M.A.'s, the proportion expecting a Ph.D., the proportion expecting to finish their doctoral studies by 1967, the proportion having chosen a Ph.D. topic, the proportion studying in the arts and sciences, and the proportion expecting academic careers. The mass exodus from academia that certain writers anticipated clearly had not occurred by June of 1964. Furthermore, it should be emphasized that the data in Table 2.6 have built-in controls for sex, socioeconomic status, race, size of hometown, and region in which the respondent was raised. (The differences that exist between Catholics from Catholic colleges and Catholics from other colleges, with the latter scoring somewhat less high on matters of academic commitment, are not so readily explained. Controls for ethnicity, generation, and more specific SES controls do not eliminate the differences.)

Table 2.6 Degree and Career Plans of 1964 Graduates by Religion and School Background (Upper SES, Upper API Males Only) (Per Cent)

Degree and Career Plans	Non-Catholic Graduates	Catholic Graduates Who Attended:			
		Catholic High School and Catholic College	Catholic High School but Non-Catholic College	Non-Catholic High School but Catholic College	Non-Catholic High School and Non-Catholic College
Those aspiring to "higher degree"*	57	55	52	53	48
Those planning academic careers	15	13	8	9	11
N	(3,619)	(255)	(198)	(78)	(217)

*Ph.D. or professional degree.

Academic Performance

But it might be contended that while Catholics are going to graduate school and planning academic careers they are still not intellectual enough or Protestant enough to get into the top-quality graduate schools or at least to do well in these schools. Actually, however, one-sixth of the arts and sciences graduate students in each of the Christian analytic groups are in one of the top twelve schools; and there is nothing in Table 2.8 to indicate that the graduates of Catholic colleges are underperforming in the context of the great secular universities. They are just as likely to continue in the schools as American Protestants, a little more likely to have an A grade-point average, just as likely to be expecting the Ph.D. and to have it finished in the middle 1960's, and just as likely to have their thesis topic approved. Neither is there any sign that they have in the secular graduate school atmosphere

Table 2.7 Graduate School Status, by Religion, of June, 1961, College Graduates (Only White Males from Upper Half SES Backgrounds Who Grew Up in New England or Middle Atlantic Cities with a Population of Over 500,000)* (Per Cent)

Graduate School Status	Protestants	Catholics from Catholic Colleges	Catholics from Non-Catholic Colleges	Jews
Those still in graduate school (spring, 1964)	45	46	44	60
Those with M.A.	12	15	11	24
Those expecting Ph.D.	21	20	15	26
Those expecting academic careers	20	19	15	43
Those in arts and sciences graduate programs	20	22	18	30
Those in graduate school who attend full time	58	57	38	55
Those expecting Ph.D.—when it is expected:				
by 1965	38	28	26	26
by 1967	78	79	62	89
Ph.D. topics chosen	65	70	55	68
N	(163)	(510)	(316)	(121)

*Subsample includes all respondents whose original religion was Catholic and one of every six whose original religion was not Catholic.

been tempted to defect from their faith (though this surely cannot be said of the Catholics in secular graduate schools who did not have Catholic undergraduate training).

Not only did the Catholics who graduated from Catholic colleges and universities in June, 1961, show as much interest in graduate school, the arts and sciences, and academic careers as did non-Catholic fellow Americans, there was no evidence three years later that in their graduate school performance or attitudes there was the slightest deviation from their original intention. It should be emphasized (though one grows weary of re-emphasizing it) that graduate school performance is not the same necessarily as academic eminence. The Catholic scientists and scholars do not as yet fill the pages of *Who's Who*. But at least on the basis of their graduate school performance, there is no evidence to say that the June, 1961, graduates will not some day have their fair share of names listed in that august publication.

Table 2.8 Graduate School Status, by Religion, of Arts and Sciences Students from the June, 1961, Class Who in the Spring of 1962 Were Attending Top Twelve Graduate Schools (Whites Only)* (Per Cent)

Graduate School and Religious Status	Protestants	Catholics from Catholic Colleges	Catholics from Non-Catholic Colleges	Jews
Those still in graduate school (spring, 1964)	95	100	100	88
Those with A grade point average	10	16	17	14
Those planning Ph.D.	97	98	66	100
Those expecting Ph.D.—when it is expected:				
by 1965	59	56	33	24
by 1966	79	96	47	86
Those having thesis topic approved	50	59	22	19
Those still in religion in which they were raised	55	85	52	71
Those still in religion to which they belonged at college graduation	81	98	54	79
N	(40)	(54)	(27)	(21)

*Subsample includes all respondents whose original religion was Catholic and one of every six whose original religion was not Catholic.

As they look back on their academic experience what will the graduates of Catholic colleges think of the education they received? At least on the average, they are no more likely to be critical than any other American graduate (Warkov and Greeley, 1966). However, the one important group of Catholic graduates, the high-performing males who plan to go to graduate school and expect academic careers (especially if their undergraduate college was Jesuit), tended to be much more critical of the education they received than were members of a comparable group who did not attend Catholic colleges.

Thus, while the average graduate of a Catholic college was reasonably satisfied with his education, the young person from whom presumably the Catholic colleges are going to have to recruit their faculty members in years to come was something less than enchanted with the academic experience he had received. Since we are not able to find any objective measure of school quality that would correlate with this criticism (as indeed it was of the very best Catholic colleges that the criticism took place), we are led to deduce that it is very likely that this criticism among the future academicians was part of the self-critical inferiority complex phenomenon currently so very powerful in the American Church, and that indeed it might be a reaction in the bright future academicians created by the dissatisfactions of the younger lay members of the faculties of those universities with whom there was some evidence these students had closely identified.

The overwhelming evidence reported thus far in this section is that the graduates of Catholic colleges, while they may be somewhat different in their religious commitment from either other Catholics or other Americans, do not differ very much on any other measure of behavior available to us, and that the "religious factor" is not an important predictor of career plans, occuptional values, or academic performance. Nor does it seem (Table 2.9) to be much of a predictor of a young person's expectations, three years after college graduation, of what his life is going to be. The graduate of a Catholic college, for example, is just as likely to feel that he is going to write a book, to become important in his field, to publish a magazine article, to make an important contribution to science or technology, to have literary works published,

Table 2.9 College Students' Expectations of Their Future, by Religion and Type of School Attended (Per Cent)

Future Expectations—Want Very Much To:	Catholic Graduates of Catholic Colleges	Catholic Graduates of Non-Catholic Colleges	Non-Catholic Graduates
Write a book	22	21	23
Make an innovation in my field	26	24	25
Have a great deal of authority	28	25	22
Become well known in my field	41	41	30
Publish in a magazine or professional journal	29	29	33
Be a leader in a community organization	36	29	22
Make a theoretical contribution to science	7	6	7
Become well known nationally	7	6	7
Become an authority on a special subject in my field	40	39	41
Be influential in public affairs	21	15	18
Make a contribution to technology	8	12	10
Be elected to public office	11	17	6
Have poems, novels, or short stories published	11	8	9
Produce original paintings, sculpture, etc.	6	7	7
Have a musical composition played or published	1	2	2
Become famous or eminent	8	4	6
Make a significant contribution to literature or the arts	5	5	7
Make at least $20,000 a year	50	48	41
Develop a very successful business of my own	18	18	18
Be elected to a high office in a professional organization	11	8	9
Be a good parent	40	42	43
Have plenty of time for leisure activities	51	52	54
Do something which I consider useful	34	35	35
Have a big family	46	31	16
Be helpful to others	32	30	29
Have a close family relationship	26	24	24
Have good, close friends	21	20	21
Have enough money to live well	60	57	58
Be active in community organizations	56	53	53
Attend concerts, plays, and other artistic or cultural events	41	40	39
Have a nice, well-furnished home	62	58	61
Help my children develop as I think they should	44	43	45
Have freedom from pressures to conform in my personal life	28	26	25
Live in a good neighborhood for my children to grow up in	49	42	45
Do something important	39	38	38
Be able to travel	50	49	51

to produce original works of art or music, to become famous or eminent, to be financially and occupationally successful. And he is just as eager to hope to be a good parent, to have time for leisure activities, to enjoy close friendships, to make enough money to enjoy the good life, to have a nice home, to be close to his children, to have freedom in his personal life, to do something important with his life, and to be able to travel. About the only difference between the Catholic college graduate and the other respondents is that he is more likely to expect (and more likely to want very much) a big family.

Social and Religious Consequences of Catholic Higher Education

In the previous section we pointed out that the graduate of a Catholic college was more likely to stay in his church and attend Mass every Sunday than Catholics who had not gone to Catholic college. At least some Catholic educators, as well as some critics of Catholic higher education, would demand far more than this from a higher educational system affiliated with the Church. Without attempting to enter into the difficult question of how much religious and ethical formation can be expected of a higher educational institution, we can refer to another body of NORC data which gives some idea of the social and religious consequences in adult life of having gone to a Catholic college.

In a previous NORC study (Greeley and Rossi, 1966, p. 167) significant and substantial differences were found between Catholics who had gone to Catholic colleges and Catholics who had gone to other colleges on their reception of the Sacraments, acceptance of the Church as teacher, in their ethical and doctrinal attitudes, and in their level of religious knowledge (Table 2.10). It is worth noting that the very substantial differences recorded in Table 2.10 are not appreciably affected when controls are introduced for sex, social class, or the religiousness of family background. Furthermore, as Table 2.11 establishes, Catholics who attended Catholic colleges scored significantly lower on indexes that measure anti-Semitism, anti-civil liberties, religious extremism, and "Manichaeanism." These differences also are not notably affected by an introduction of demographic and socio-economic controls.

It is of some interest to glance briefly at the responses to individual opinion items of which the indexes in the two previous tables were composed. Thus, we can observe in Table 2.12 that there are very strong negative correlations between attending Catholic colleges and opinion items that could be expected to measure racism, anti-Semitism, and authoritarianism. Indeed, on one of the anti-Semitism items, Catholics who attended Catholic colleges are apparently significantly less prejudiced than American Protestants who graduated from college.

Table 2.10   Religious Behavior of College Graduates, by Kind of College Attended (Per Cent)

Religious Behavior	Catholic College	Non-Catholic College
High on sacramental index	49	24
High on Church-as-teacher index	44	34
High on ethical orthodoxy index	44	33[a]
High on doctrinal orthodoxy	56	26[a]
High on religious knowledge index	65	26[a]
Children in Catholic schools	73	69
Mass more often than weekly	20	7[a]
N	(117)	(250)

[a]Significantly different from "Catholic."

Table 2.11   Social and Cultural Attitudes and Behavior of College Graduates, by Kind of College Attended (Per Cent)

Social and Cultural Attitudes	Catholic College	Non-Catholic College
High on community involvement index	43	41
High on racism index	19	20
High on anti-Semitism index	16	31[a]
High on anti-civil-liberties index	31	44[a]
High on "Manichaean" index	13	31[a]
High on religious-extremism index	18	29[a]
High on anti-Protestant index	39	42
N	(117)	(250)

[a]Significantly different from Catholic.

Opinion items and social behavior are by no means identical, but the very considerable differences presented in the last three tables would at least call into question the frequently-heard assumption that Catholic colleges have been quite ineffective in teaching the social doctrines of the Roman Church.

In addition to the NORC national sample data on which we have relied thus far in this section, there are a considerable number of other studies of the "impact" and the "atmosphere" of the Catholic campus. In Chapter 5 of his book (1967), Robert Hassenger reviews in great detail this literature. And, as Hassen-

Table 2.12 Comparisons of Opinions of Those Who Attended Catholic Colleges with Those Who Attended Other Colleges (Per Cent)

Questionnaire Item (Response in Parentheses)	Catholics Who Attended Catholic Colleges	Catholics Who Attended Other Colleges	Protestants
Two people who are in love do not do anything wrong when they marry, even though one of them is divorced (agree)	24	50[a]	87[b]
White people have a right to live in an all-white neighborhood, and Negroes should respect this right (disagree strongly)	40	30	31
I would strongly disapprove if a Negro family moved next door to me (disagree strongly)	36	24[a]	27
Jews have too much power in the United States (disagree strongly)	75	57[a]	54[a]
People who don't believe in God have as much right to freedom of speech as anyone else (agree)	74	63	–
The Catholic Church teaches that large families are more Christian than small families (agree)	12	27[a]	–
Protestant ministers should not be permitted to teach things publicly which are opposed to Catholic doctrine (disagree strongly)	67	44[a]	–
The Catholic Church teaches that a good Christian ought to think about the next life and not worry about fighting against poverty and injustice in this life (agree)	10	31[a]	–
Husband and wife may have sexual intercourse for pleasure alone (agree)	47	37	–
N	(117)	(250)	(159)

[a]Significantly different from those who went to Catholic colleges.
[b]Significantly different from both Catholic groups.

ger himself ruefully notes, much of it is of dubious value since it deals with small numbers of respondents or one school or a handful of nonrandomly selected schools. Furthermore, some of the sociopsychological instruments used in these studies are of dubious value and could very well have a "culture bias" against Catholic respondents. The reader interested in pursuing this literature is referred to the Hassenger volume. However, at least three different studies deserve mention at this point.

First of all, the Williamson and Cowan study of attitudes towards student freedom in American higher education (1966) is of very high quality both in its coverage and its analysis. Williamson and Cowan conclude that, at least on the average, Catholic colleges and universities score somewhat lower in their respect for freedom of student press and the right of student organizations to invite outside speakers to campus. They carefully note that the standard deviations from mean scores from Catholic schools tend to be quite high, which is to say that there is a vast variety of practice in the area of student academic freedom within the Catholic college and university system. Some of the schools apparently grant complete freedom of press and complete freedom of student organizations, while others seem to grant practically no freedom, with the vast majority of Catholic colleges somewhere in between, though on the average scoring lower than the private colleges and universities of the nation. Surely nothing that we encountered in our grand tour would lead us to question the Williamson and Cowan observation. Catholic college administrations, by and large, are afraid of "what might happen" if student organizations and student publications were given not absolute freedom (which is rare on the American campus), but freedom comparable to that enjoyed by their peers in non-Catholic colleges. While it is a mistake to consider that Catholic colleges are completely closed, there is vast room for improvement in the Catholic colleges in the area of student freedom.

A second research project well worth noting is the Environmental Assessment Technique of Alexander Astin of the National Merit Scholarship Corporation. Astin attempted to evaluate the environment of a college on the basis of scores of entering freshmen. Eight separate dimensions emerged—the estimated selectivity of the student body (based on the number of the national merit semi-finalists considering the school), size which, according to Astin, tends to correlate with "atmosphere," and six personal orientations: "realistic," "scientific," "social," "conventional," "enterprising," and "artistic." In the Hassenger book, Weiss reports on the scores of the Catholic colleges on these eight dimensions. Catholic colleges tend to be somewhat smaller than the average and very close to the mean on estimated selectivity, scientific orientation, social orientation, and artistic orientation. They are lower than the mean in the realistic orientation which is "characterized by a preference for the practical and concrete rather than the abstract . . . [and] reflects the proportion of baccalaureate degrees in such fields as agriculture, engineering, physical education, forestry, and industrial arts." Thus, there is precious little in the Astin data that would indicate that the Catholic colleges are very different from the typical American college.

The Astin data is particularly important because it is based on a population of over one thousand colleges and, hence, is not likely to be biased by the influence of one particular college or another that turns up in a nonrandom sample.

Finally, something should be said about the Pace College and University Environmental Scales. Weiss (in Hassenger, 1967) summarizes the data for twenty-seven Catholic institutions to which the CUES have been administered. Catholic schools tend to score about the mean on the "practicality" scale (which deals with "practical instrumental emphasis in college environment, particularly personal status and practical benefits"), higher than the mean on the "community" scale (which "is concerned with the extent to which the campus is friendly, cohesive group-oriented"), 17 percentage points below the mean for the "awareness" scale (which "reflects a concern and emphasis upon the personal, poetic, political meaning, upon understanding and identity, upon a sense of personal involvement with the world's problems"), high on the "propriety" scale (which "measures the degree to which the environment emphasizes politeness, consideration, caution, and thoughtfulness"), and lower on the "scholarship" scale (which "describes an academic environment, one in which there is stress on comparatively high academic achievement and serious interest in scholarship").

It would appear, therefore, that the twenty-seven Catholic campuses—and there is no reason to believe that these twenty-seven are necessarily representative—are more friendly and considerate than involved or serious.

While our own impressions from the grand tour would not necessarily contradict Pace's findings, we believe that some cautions are in order. To label a response to a series of items as "scholarship" or "awareness" is a useful shorthand device but the answers to a scale of questions do not present anything more than answers to a scale of questions; the exact interpretation of the Pace instruments seem to us to be still uncertain, especially when it is not clear what reference groups students would have in mind when answering the questions. Thus, one Catholic college we visited was a place of academic growth and considerable intellectual and scholarly concern, but it was located very close to one of America's great universities, and its students scored it quite low on Pace's scholarship scale, apparently because their referent was this great university. In addition, it must be kept in mind that the massive inferiority complex of American Catholic intellectuals permeates the atmosphere of a good number of Catholic institutions. Thus, while we feel that the Pace material must be used with considerable caution in arriving at any overall description of Catholic higher education, we nevertheless have the impression that there are certain things in the academic environment of the Catholic institutions that are not conducive to those dimensions that Pace has characterized as scholarship or awareness. We shall make use of the Pace scores of some of our schools in further analysis in this study. However, if one can with safety generalize from the Catholic schools to which the CUES have been administered to the whole Catholic higher educational system, the lack of scholarly or imaginative orientations in the schools' atmospheres has not affected the academic plans or the graduate school performances of people who have gone to these schools. It may well be that there is a reverse application of the conclusions of the Jacob report. Just as it is very difficult for a college to produce notable changes in student personality in one direction, so it may be difficult for it to produce changes in the other direction. Quite possibly, the ordinary undergraduate college can a potential academician neither make or unmake.

At least one commentator on the controversy over Catholic higher education has noted that while it must be conceded on the basis of NORC data that Catholics are indeed going to graduate school and performing well in these graduate schools, nonetheless, these phenomena merely depict the ambition of the American Catholic and not his scholarly or academic interests; this assertion is backed up by references to the Omnibus Personality Inventory scales which have been administered in several Catholic colleges, though hardly in such fashion as to persuade us either of their utility or their validity.

It might be replied to this assertion that at least the sociologist is more concerned with people's behavior than their responses to opinion items on questionnaires, and that the "ambition" of American Catholics is a new element being introduced into the discussion, since one would have believed from the Protestant ethic assumptions that this is precisely what American Catholics did not have. Finally, it is not at all certain that ambition need be an obstacle to scholarly productivity or even scientific eminence. The man with moderate scholarly abilities and orientations and considerable ambition is much more likely to be a productive scholar than the man with deep scholarly orientations and little ambition. We do not need the McClelland research to convince us that the "hungry" man is likely to be an achiever, though McClelland's data certainly confirm this (1961). In any event, it will take more than a single personality scale administered in a handful of colleges on the West Coast to persuade us that the tremendous Catholic influx into graduate school is the result merely of ambition. There is no reason to doubt that the notable change that has taken place in the career orientations of the American Catholic involves an element of ambition, but it does not follow therefore that ambition excludes scholarly productivity and that the graduates of Catholic colleges who are doing so commendably in their graduate school work are to be assumed, in some way or the other, to be anti-intellectual. As we noted before, only the future can tell what kind of scholarly distinction they will achieve. But the point of the NORC data, past and present, is that, for whatever motives, the graduates of Catholic colleges are now turning up in the graduate schools, particularly the top-quality graduate schools, in considerable quantities and are doing very well indeed in these schools, that this alone represents a major change, and that it is precisely this change that the present study is designed to investigate.

In summary then, the typical Catholic college graduate is somewhat more likely to be Irish, and somewhat more likely to come from a big city in the Northeast or Middle West, and is also considerably more likely to be religious than the Catholic who did not go to Catholic schools. But he is also inclined to be a liberal Democrat politically and is virtually no different from his non-Catholic fellow American who graduated from college at the same time in his career orientations, his academic plans, or his scholarly and professional values. And this similarity apparently applies despite the fact that there is less in the way of student academic freedom in Catholic colleges and despite the fact that there is some reason to believe that the atmosphere of the Catholic campus places less emphasis on scholarship and imagination.

It is possible, of course, and indeed probable, that the career plans and occupational values of the graduates of Catholic colleges are influenced more by the socioeconomic changes in the Catholic population than they are simply by the college experience. Catholics are going into graduate school and going into academic careers largely because the Catholic population has now reached a socioeconomic level where such plans are feasible for a considerable number of Catholic students. Indeed, the socioeconomic forces are probably so powerful as to sweep aside the inhibiting influence of the campus culture at Catholic colleges. The young people are going to be academicians even if their student papers are not free and even if the scholarly orientation is not as strong on the campus as it ought to be. Thus, it would be feasible to contend that the change of the academic plans of the Catholic population has nothing to do with the change in the colleges and indeed takes place despite this change. However, a more sophisticated view would be that if a population is undergoing sweeping socioeconomic changes then the institutions that service this population will themselves inevitably change, too. As American Catholics become full-fledged, if still junior, partners in the American experience, it is inconceivable that the Catholic colleges and universities would not undergo major changes in the direction of assimilating the norms of the larger American educational enterprise. Therefore, it seems reasonable to conclude that there is a mutual causality at work. The Catholic colleges are, to some extent, promoting the change within the Catholic population, and the change within the Catholic population in its turn is affecting the colleges. There is every reason to expect that the Catholic campus is changing because so many Catholic students are planning to go to a graduate school and, at the same time, it is also true that more students are planning to go to graduate school because the Catholic campus is changing.

CONCLUSIONS

The central theme of this chapter is that Catholic higher education reflects the development of the Catholic population. When Catholics were an immigrant group existing on the fringes of a larger society, Catholic higher education was a fringe enterprise, proceeding on its own values and towards its own goals. But as the openness of the ecumenical era and the socioeconomic parity of Catholics change the stance of the Catholic population and the Catholic ecclesiastical structure, it is not unreasonable to assume that Catholic higher education will undergo profound changes as it strives to reflect the acculturation of its constituency to the larger American society and perhaps to shape and direct this acculturation.

But it is of the nature of transitions that they are combinations of the old and the new; hence, it is to be expected that the present state of Catholic higher education will reflect both the isolation and fears of the past as well as hopes for excellence in the future. Further, since acculturation is not assimilation, it can be expected that as Catholic higher education strives to enter the mainstream of the American educational enterprise it will attempt to bring with it certain elements which are thought to be essential to its continuation as a distinctively Catholic endeavor. Some of these distinctively Catholic elements could conceivably represent a net gain for American higher education, but others could also constitute obstacles—perhaps insurmountable obstacles—to the pursuit of excellence, at least of excellence as American education defines it.

3

Rapid Improvement
Schools

In this, and the subsequent two chapters, we shall attempt to describe the characteristics of the Catholic colleges that seem to have improved academically, those that are improving somewhat, and those where the process of improvement seems to be relatively slow. The simplest and most interesting way to proceed would be to describe in great detail a number of the schools in each of the three categories, perhaps maintaining the useful social science fiction that if the name of the school is changed slightly, no one will recognize it. But it seems to us that at least in this particular report and given the delicacy of the matter, the promise of anonymity to the schools and to respondents, and the harm that might be done to some institutions if they could be identified, it is absolutely necessary that every precaution be taken that a school not be recognized, even by the interviewees of that school. The general social structural principles at work in the academic improvement of an institution of higher education can be substantiated in a fashion sufficiently generic to maintain the anonymity of the schools being discussed. While some concrete detail may be lost, we do not believe that the goals of the study will be impaired by maintaining the level of generality that will emerge in this and the two subsequent chapters.

BACKGROUND

The three institutions that we propose to describe in this fashion are all rather large universities (and large for a Catholic university would be more than five thousand students) with arts and sciences graduate programs as well as professional graduate schools. Two of the three are located in large metropolitan centers; one location is somewhat more rural. All three are in, or close to substantial concentrations of the Roman Catholic population. Ecclesiastically, the regions in which two of the schools are located could be described as very conservative, while the third school is in a far more liberal district. Two of the schools are located close to major non-Catholic universities, in addition to sharing their regions with several other Catholic colleges and universities. The third school has few competitors in its immediate area.

All three schools have national reputations, particularly from their long involvement in intercollegiate athletics (though one of the three is no longer heavily involved in such athletic programs). Only one of the three can be seriously said to have a national enrolment, though the other two do have some students from areas of the country beyond their immediate province and are engaged in vigorous recruiting on the national level. Two of the schools are operated by one religious community, and the third by another order. One has almost no coeds on its campus (though a small women's college is relatively close by); the other two do have coeds but, as yet, none are formally admitted to their arts and sciences college and must be content with other forms of citizenship. None of the three schools have laymen on their board of trustees, though in two of the three plans are afoot for such developments, and, in one instance, the spending of considerable amounts of donations made to the school is in the control of a separate group which does have a lay board of trustees.

All three schools are moving into substantial arts and sciences graduate programs and aspire to become great universities, not merely within the Catholic system but within the larger mainstream of American higher education. All three schools seem to have a strong sense of identity and direction. Faculty, administrators, and students, it appeared to us, all knew where the school was, where it was going, and seemed quite confident that it was eventually going to achieve its aims; in no instance did the optimism seem to be unrealistic. Indeed, we would judge that these three schools were not only among the most rapidly improving Catholic higher educational institutions in the country; they probably were also three of the very best by any absolute standards of academic quality that one could apply to Catholic colleges and universities.[1]

ADMINISTRATIONS

In two of the three institutions, the president had had a very long term of office, while at the third a new president had just been installed, replacing one whose tenure had been rather brief.[2] All three schools had extremely vigorous, determined, and informed leadership at the top level. Two of the three presidents had excellent academic credentials; one had been a president of a smaller college before being promoted to the larger university, and had been a successful dean before that. Only one of the three, however, had his doctorate from a non-Catholic institution. All three were substantially involved in local community activities beyond the school, and one of them had become a national figure of some importance. All three were imaginative, creative, and outgoing individuals who would be ill at ease in no social situation and could probably charm anyone from a cabinet member to a conservative and very wealthy widow.

One of our team, thoroughly skeptical of the most famous of these three charismatic presidents, attended a lecture that the president gave to a large group of freshmen, recounting his most recent lengthy tour to several different countries of the world.

[1] A fourth school that is not considered in the present description, although it does show academic improvement, was an arts and science college without any graduate programs. Thus, we do not think it can be said that the mere presence of graduate programs in itself guarantees academic improvement or even is a necessary precondition for it.

[2] Four of the nine institutions that we are describing in these chapters had new presidents the year of the study, a proportion that seems to be true of all Catholic colleges. Indeed, the opening phrase, "We're in the midst of a transition around here," was perhaps the most frequently heard comment as an introduction to a Catholic college. In some instances, the new president simply represented a continuation of a past tradition of presidential leadership, whereas in others, the change of office represented a drastic change of style in the school. We will indicate in these pages when discussing the school whether the change represented a transformation or continuation. In the academically improving school that has a new president, we were persuaded that the new administration represented merely a substantially more vigorous continuation of an already intelligent and perceptive presidential tradition.

Our colleague reported that it was an incredible performance. The president recorded his hectic journeyings, described the many different countries and the many important people he had visited, and yet succeeded in recounting the tale in such fashion that he did not seem at all to be bragging of his exploits but rather merely reflecting the glory that such trip brought to the university and the student body in the university. The ovation from the freshmen after the talk was thunderous, and our researcher, who had come prepared to scoff, had to admit that he, too, joined in it. Priest, president, friend of the student, Catholic, American, citizen of the world—all these titles seemed to rest rather lightly on the vigorous and muscular shoulders of the president. Our researcher reported that, in an age when phoney sincerity seems to abound, this man's dedication and enthusiasm was awesome.

One wonders if it takes such characteristics to make an ordinary Catholic college into a great university. They may not be absolutely necessary, but they certainly help.

There wasn't any doubt that the three men immensely enjoyed their jobs as college presidents and were not waiting for the day when they could give them up. We heard no complaints from them about the rigors of their jobs or about the lack of time for other things, nor did they seem at all reluctant to use the immense powers their jobs brought to them. With two of the three presidents we could only have brief interviews and had to evaluate their administration through the reports of others. But the third president entertained two of us for most of the morning in his vast, oak-paneled office and spelled out in great detail and with considerable Gaelic charm and wit his philosophy of Catholic education. (Half-way through the conversation, one researcher finally identified the president. He resembled for all the world Spency Tracy playing Frank Skeffington in "The Last Hurrah.") This priest radiated the same kind of confidence that his two presidential colleagues seemed to possess in superabundant quantities. He was under no illusions about the problems his school faced and, indeed, he pointed them out more clearly than most of the school's severest critics had, but we could not escape the impression that he thoroughly relished the problem and would have found the school quite dull and uninteresting if it did not offer him intellectual and political challenge. Even though he fully respected the immense inertial powers that the older members of the religious community could use to slow down his campaign of transformation of the school, he seemed totally secure and unthreatened in the face of this power and dismissed its importance by saying that the other day he had heard two men who had opposed most of his reforms in faculty relationships commenting apropos of a major scandal at another Catholic university, "It's a good thing for us that Pat took care of those problems long ago." With a Skeffingtonian wink, Pat noted, "I never thought I'd live to see the day when those two guys would be on my side."

Finally, all three knew exactly what a university was, and were pretty sure how they were going to lead their respective schools down the path of greatness. If the three of them had not been priests, and were not members of a religious community, but simply academicians in non-Catholic colleges, it would be a safe guess to say that all of them would be college presidents in any event (if they had not become major political figures in the Kennedy administration).

At one of the universities, the president and the executive vice-president (both rather recently appointed) constituted the most impressive team that we encountered anywhere in the grand tour. The executive vice-president reminded one of the researchers of a powerful diesel locomotive proceeding down an open track at full speed, spitting out ideas and plans much as locomotive wheels spit out sparks as they move along the track. This gentleman had on his desk a list of prominent lay people whom he was going to approach to accept vice-presidential positions at the university. While we would not dream of revealing the names of the people on the list, it suffices to say that Lyndon Johnson was about the only prominent person whose name we cannot recall being included.

Even though the faculties in these three schools could be critical of the mistakes of these three men and had a fair number of complaints about certain aspects of the school's development, all three presidents enjoyed the confidence of their respective faculties. Indeed, nowhere in the grand tour in either Catholic or non-Catholic schools did we encounter such confidence in presidential leadership. In the one school, where the president was brand new, even though the faculty had vigorous objections to some of the administrators who were holdovers from the previous administration, this did not seem to shake their confidence that the new man (whom they had known previously as a dean) was precisely the sort of president for whom they had long waited.

Two of the three men, however, had reputations for not being too good at delegating authority and responsibility, and the feeling seemed to persist in the school that this overcentralization of authority had in the past created certain bottlenecks in the implementation of presidential decisions. In one instance, it appeared that the president, while a very able and distinguished person himself, had not been able to surround himself with lesser administrators of the same caliber. As one man in his school observed, "If there's any boat-rocking to be observed, Tom rocks it himself; he doesn't want anybody to do it for him." The other two schools had extraordinarily competent second-level administrators who were able to remove substantial day-to-day burdens from the president's shoulders while, at the same time, guaranteeing continuity to the school's academic improvement should anything happen to the president.

In two of the three schools, there had been past regimes which, while not as dynamic as the present ones, had nonetheless notably prepared the way for the present rapid growth. Only in the third school were the innovations of the current president revolutionary instead of evolutionary. In all three instances, the president had very sympathetic religious superiors, though in only one of the three was there a long tradition of the religious order leaving to university administrators the administration of the university. None of the three presidents seemed at all insecure in the face of higher authority and, while they were political realists with little in the way of the martyr instinct about them, they also knew when it was necessary and imperative to resist pressure from higher ecclesiastical authorities. As a matter of fact, about two of the men there had grown up mighty legends of what happened when higher ecclesiastics mistakenly attempted to apply too much pressure to them. Legend has it that the secretary of the provincial of the religious order called one of the presidents to warn him against having students march in a civil rights protest. The president replied by bluntly advising the secretary to inform the provincial that if he had any message to deliver, he could deliver it personally. The legend continues that that was the last that was ever heard from the provincial's office about the civil rights demonstration.

We judged that there were three particular characteristics that were most essential to the success of the three presidents of the rapidly improving schools. First of all, they were men with masterful political skills. They had been able to stitch together a consensus among the religious superiors, the older members of the order, the younger members of the order, the lay faculty, the lower-level administrators, and the major financial contributors to the university. While in some instances the consensus was tenuous, and in all instances it represented an alliance of forces some of which could be considered natural enemies, and while the binding power of the consensus seemed to be little more than the personality of the president, it was still true that the consensus existed and that there were no particular signs of it collapsing.

Perhaps the secret of the three leaders could be best summarized by saying that they possessed "style" of the sort that made them natural political personalities. Humor, physical vigor, striking physical appearance, and great self-confidence were obvious parts of their personality. Each of them was the kind of person who would stand out in a group of his fellow human beings. Unfortunately for Catholic higher education, it was our impression that there are a substantial number of other people with the same personal resources who would not be trusted in presidential positions for fear that they would "rock the boat" too much.

Second, the president was a man who was able to "create an image" for the school. While this phrase is taken from the jargon of public relations, we would emphasize that it is not merely a public relations phenomenon. By word and by deed the president conveyed to his various publics a strong sense of what the school was doing and where it was going. Whatever the school's catalogues might have said about its theoretical goals, in practice faculty, students, administrators, and contributors knew that the school's objectives were what the president said they were. Their own personal warmth and energy initiated programs that were successful in the school's academic improvement, and their confidence and enthusiasm generated the expectation of even more success. Thus, if one asked the faculty member, "Why is this university moving?" the answer almost invariably would be the name of the president, so completely had he captured the imagination of his faculty.

Third, the three presidents seem to have a clear idea of what a great university is supposed to be. Their concept of the university was not substantially different from that found in any successful American university president. One of the men summed it up for us when he said, "How is this school different from any other American school? Well, I suppose we teach four or five themes here that you might not find at every school." We asked him if this meant four or five courses and he said, "Oh, no, it just meant four or five themes, like there is a God, there is a human soul, there is a life after death, that sort of thing." We then asked him if what his particular religious order was doing in its schools was any different from what was being done by another one of the top Catholic universities and he shrugged his shoulders and said that he couldn't think of any particular difference. In short, this man and his two colleagues did not have a notion that Catholic higher education differed from other American higher educational institutions, save that certain extra things were added at the Catholic school. The three presidents not only knew what an American university was, they also knew what steps were necessary to build such a school.

It may seem from the foregoing description that we had determined that the three presidents had almost by themselves been responsible for the academic growth of their schools. Such a statement would not be too strong. We would not hesitate to say that in the absence of these three men, or men similar to them, we very much doubt that these three schools would be any different from the average schools to be described in the next chapter. At one school, the lesser-level administrators seem generally to be of the same quality as the president and his immediate staff. In the second school, there were some fairly impressive lower-level administrators, though the competence of some (apparently on the way out) was not reassuring. In the third school, a few of the lower-level men seemed to be excellent, but we felt that the majority left something to be desired. In all three of them it appeared to us that the financial officers knew their place, though two of the three financial officers were quite obviously thorns in the presidential side.[3] In all three of the schools, the men in charge of development and fund raising were top flight professionals. Indeed, we would judge that one, and quite possibly two of them, could be numbered among the very best in the country. All three had vigorous recruiting campaigns for promising students and impressive professional admissions standards. Communication among the various elements of the administration seemed to be adequate (though not without some strain), but in all three, the lines of responsibility and authority were clear, and no one was in doubt as to who had what decision-making powers and roles, although in one school the presidential leadership style tended to be of a highly personal variety. Finally, in one of the schools library facilities were excellent; in the other two, they were adequate, but just barely, with new library construction apparently of top priority in the immediate future. In summary, the administrative leadership of the three academically improving schools was academically well informed, organizationally professional, and enthusiastically resourceful. The charismatic personalities of the three leaders added a dimension of confidence in the faculty and administration that went beyond simply rational explanation.

Above all else, these three presidents seemed to be quite independent in their administration of the school. Despite the rapid innovations they had introduced, they seemed to have maintained the full confidence of their religious superiors and a broad consensus among their colleagues and the religious community. The apparent secret of their ability to obtain independence from the religious order and to make the religious community not only tolerate the change but also, at least in two of the three cases, actually rejoice in it, was the ability of all three presidents to judge what were the critical areas in the relationship between the

[3]We will say more about the peculiar power of financial officers at Catholic colleges in a later chapter.

school and the religious order in which quick, incisive, and important progress could be made. One of the presidents summarized his strategy this way: "You take three steps forward, then one step sideways, then one step backwards and, while they're not looking, you run for ten yards." Of course, the very fact that religious superiors had appointed someone with these political and personal skills to the presidency, gave some indication that they were already themselves disposed toward change. As a superior general of one order wrote to a colleague who was protesting the changes at one of the three universities, "What concern of ours is it what these administrators do with their school?"

FACULTY

It would not be accurate to say that the faculty of any of the three schools was distinguished, but all three were surely better than adequate. A high proportion (approximately three-quarters of the arts and sciences faculties) had doctorates, and a Ph.D. seemed to be virtually required for a new professor coming on the faculty. While some of the older faculty members may have had their degrees from Catholic universities (occasionally at least the university in which they were teaching), most of the younger members had degrees from non-Catholic universities, and a substantial number of them from the very best of the universities. One of the three schools had a publishing faculty, in the sense that in virtually all its departments there were a good many publishing scholars. The other two schools had some research departments and at least a few research men in most of their departments. Even though the publish or perish pressures were not as rigorous at any of these schools as they are at many of the great non-Catholic institutions, the pressure still existed, and promotion was very difficult, if not impossible to obtain, without at least some evidence of research and publication. All three schools were vigorously involved in recruiting new faculty and seemed to have given their departmental chairmen adequate powers to pursue the recruiting. (We will see later that such a policy is not pursued in all Catholic schools, by any means.) Nor did this recruiting seem to be unsuccessful. While not all the new members coming on the faculty approached the highest professional promise, at least a handful did have this promise, and many others certainly seemed to be very competent young people. None of the schools had overcome the handicap of being part of a somewhat separate system, apart from the main body of American higher education, but if the schools continued to improve the quality of their faculty recruits this apartness would become a very minor thing in years to come.

Faculty salaries were excellent, particularly at the lower level, where assistant professors in all three schools were receiving salaries at the A scale in the AAUP ratings. Two of the schools' average scales were B. The other school's was C, though it was hoping to make a B rating at the end of the year. All three schools had expressed their intention to raise the salary level to the A scale, and one of the schools had announced its determination to do so in the near future. The fringe benefits at two of the schools were quite good, though at the third school they were surprisingly inadequate compared to the impressive salary level at the school. One of the three schools had not yet sufficiently improved to prevent the necessity of moonlighting among many of the senior faculty, but the administration hoped to remedy this situation in the very near future. For all the improvement in salary, there were still a fair number of men who were remaining on these faculties at some financial sacrifice and who would do better if they left the Catholic higher educational system. It seemed likely that some of them would leave unless the improvement in salary structure proceeded at an even faster rate than it had in the preceding half-decade.

Though there were some complaints and fears about academic freedom at the three schools, at least two of them showed no evidence at all of serious interference with the academic freedom of the members of the faculty. In the third school, there was still a bitter memory of a case in which a young professor had been refused promotion and tenure after a career of very vigorous criticism of the administration. However, as nearly as we could determine, the young professor had little claim to tenure since he had published nothing in his six years at the school. A number of other colleagues had been refused tenure at the same time for the same reason. We suppose, however, that the administration of the school was not particularly unhappy to see this young man go;

we can conclude that if the young faculty member intends to vigorously criticize an administration and expects to make a convincing case that his academic freedom has been abused when he is not promoted, he should establish some kind of scholarly record to stand along with his record of criticism.

Two of the schools had moderate amounts of faculty participation both in academic councils and in faculty committees and the participation, while consultative in the council, seemed to be reasonably effective in both council and committee. The third school had lagged rather surprisingly behind the other two in establishing faculty participation, though at the time of our visit, it was making up for this mistake by engaging in a highly public and quite democratic effort to compose a new faculty manual which would include a functioning and significant university senate. At all three schools faculty participation and citizenship still had a way to go before it would be adequate by the standards of most great American universities, and indeed some of the smaller and less impressive schools we visited had considerably more faculty participation; nonetheless, there seemed to be reasonable expectation on the part of the faculty members that continuous development in the direction of faculty participation was a certainty.

Though the lay faculty was certainly not willing to abdicate its prerogative of criticism, and while the criticisms were many and pointed, it remained true that in these three schools the lay faculty had confidence in the future of the school and in the competence of the administration. As a result, we would conclude that faculty morale at these three schools was extremely high despite the vigorous and articulate criticism that could be heard from faculty members. One social scientist who turned down a tenure appointment at a prominent Eastern university to assume a chairmanship at the Catholic school which he had served for several years noted, "This is the place where the action is. We make all kinds of mistakes; we have all sorts of problems. But Father Jim and Father Gus (an educational elder statesman who had brought his immense wisdom to the service of the administration of the school) have made this a moving institution. There's no point in going somewhere else where all the fun is over when this place has new thrills every week." And a younger colleague in the English department remarked, "I came here because I thought this might be a place where I could help a pretty good school get much better. Nothing that's happened in the year and a half I've been here has persuaded me that this was a wrong decision, and there's an awful lot of evidence that it was a right one."

However, in all the schools it seemed to us that the morale of the religious faculty was much less impressive. In two of the schools the conflict between the old guard and the new breed among the religious order was all too painfully obvious, while in the third school the new breed was much more concerned with its own identity and the relevance of its own role than it was with fighting the old guard who had long since lost the day. In all three schools even the younger and more liberal religious faculty members contended that there was better communication between the administration and the lay faculty than between the administration and the religious faculty. While the religious faculty at these schools was a rather small minority, the deterioration in their relationship with their own confreres who were administrators was, we judged, a more serious problem than the administrators themselves were willing to admit. One member at one of the schools remarked, "For all practical purposes, our religious order doesn't exist anymore. About the only difference it makes in our lives is the clothes we wear. Community life, at least for those of us who teach full time and live in the residence hall, stopped a good number of years ago. If we really want to have any kind of community, we have to put it together ourselves on a weekend a month."

In conclusion, the standards governing the administration-faculty relationships in the three rapidly improving schools were beginning to approximate the standards of typical American universities. While salaries were improving rapidly and faculty participation somewhat less rapidly, faculty criticism continued vigorously but had not, in our judgment, notably impeded faculty confidence in the administration on the general level of lay faculty morale. The religious faculty, however, presented a far more serious problem than the administration realized.

STUDENTS

There was evidence in the three schools of a rapid liberalizing of the regulation of student life, though in all three of them there were still restrictions of the sort that would not be found at most other American colleges. Thus, in two of the three schools it was required that students wear suit coats when attending class and in the other school student handbooks had somewhat more detailed regulations than many non-Catholic student handbooks would list. However, all three handbooks showed the effects of liberalizing tendencies and were simpler and less legalistic than the handbooks to be found at most other Catholic schools. At all three universities the student press was apparently completely free (though at one of them this freedom was a practical rather than theoretical one). None of the three schools had obligatory retreats and there was little evidence of any attempt at compulsory religious life. Nevertheless, at all three schools there were clerics serving as prefects in the residence halls and, in one of the three, a routine room check was made in freshman halls to make sure the students were in their beds at the proper time.

While intellectual concern was quite strong at these schools, the students were deficient in both social awareness and social commitment. The general apathy of the student body was often excused on the grounds that the majority of the students were the first ones in their family to attend college, but at all three schools more than two-fifths (in one case, more than half) of the students came from families where the father had attended college.

Furthermore, there was no evidence at any of the schools that with some minor exceptions there was much in the way of a vigorous religious or liturgical life on campus. The students were serious academically but there was little in their behavior and only a small amount in their education that could be called distinctively Catholic. Theology courses were better than the theology courses in most of the Catholic schools we went to but still were not anywhere near up to the standards that one would expect in the Catholic Church after the Vatican Council, and were surely not satisfying to the students. It seemed to us that the schools were in the process of putting aside most of the outmoded practices of student regulation and compulsory religious behavior which they had inherited from previous generations, but that they had yet to devise anything in student life that was distinctively Catholic, or even distinctively religious. Furthermore, the liberalization of the rules, while it was going on at a fairly rapid pace, was not proceeding rapidly enough to guarantee that there would not be serious problems of student unrest in the future. Although the students in all three schools had a deep admiration for the president, their feelings toward the religious order that administered the school were quite mixed, and in two institutions the students also had powerful feelings of inferiority about the school, since they took as a referent major secular universities that were close by. Their argument seemed to be that they were not getting as good an education at their alma mater as they would at the secular university and that this poor education was not being compensated for by anything in the way of an authentically Catholic religious experience. Although most of the students of all three schools were distinctly middle class both in their backgrounds and their goals, there was little behaviour that could even remotely be called "beat" to be observed. Nevertheless, the restlessness and the dissatisfaction was, we thought, considerably more serious than the administrators of the school apparently were aware of. Even though the young people were quite intelligent and performed impressively in graduate fellowship competition they seemed to us to be rather cynical about both their schools and their religion and not at all committed to sending their own children to the school that they themselves had attended.

Yet, it would be a mistake to think the picture was totally black in the student bodies at these three schools. In each of them, there were small groups of intellectually and socially concerned students who had left behind the certainties and the prejudices of their upper middle-class background and who had, at least in some instances, managed to blend curiosity and enthusiasm with a fairly sophisticated awareness of the social and humanistic implications of Catholic teaching. Our student interviewer had in early days dated a number (one would gather, a very large number) of young men from one of the schools, and she reports that she was amazed at the dramatic change in the student body in the space of two or three years. Conceding that the overwhelm-

ing majority of the students were still quite limited in their outlook, she maintained that the younger brothers of some of her
friends were very, very different from their predecessors. The
senior researcher was persuaded of the necessity of buying dinner
for a number of these young men in an excellent restaurant that
the university maintains on campus (though there is reason to suspect that the three young men could much more readily afford to
pay for the researcher's dinner). They described for our amuse-
ment how they had headed off a student riot a couple of weeks
previously in protest over what was alleged to be the failure of
the police in the local town to protect the students from some of
the local violent gangs. What was impressive about these three
young men was not merely that they had been smart enough to divert the riot (or that they had even been smart enough to have
a "Plan Two" available in case the riot had not been diverted),
but that their view of the situation that led to the protest was
informed, sophisticated, and sensitive. They were not merely concerned about the school but also about the social problems the
city faced. They had come a long, long way from the football pep
rallies of a few years ago.

It is not to be supposed that the student malaise at these three
institutions is any worse than that to be found at any other American college at the present time. Indeed, as far as overt action goes,
these schools have only moderate problems in their students. But
granting the rapid growth in other areas in these schools the level
of student enthusiasm was disappointingly low. While the schools
had improved considerably in liberalizing the minute regulations
of student life and had abandoned most compulsory religious
practices, their progress had not been such as to find any adequate
replacement for the old methods. Even if these schools do not
have more trouble with student restlessness in years to come,
they may very well find themselves forced to face the question
of whether there is anything at all in their religious atmosphere
that justifies their existence as distinctive institutions. We are
inclined to believe that this problem is not insoluble but we do
not find much evidence that there is any progress being made toward a solution.

CONCLUSIONS

These three institutions obviously had a considerable amount of things going for them: their size, their reputation, their national image, the tradition of contributions to the schools—all were surely *sine qua nons* for their present growth, but we cannot escape the conclusion that the key factor in the growth was the personality and ability of the top administrator. By a combination of political skill, public relations competence, and academic understanding, these three men had been able to gain the confidence of their faculty and the admiration of their administrative colleagues. They had professionalized the administration of the school and were rapidly accomplishing the professionalization of the faculty. Reinforcing faculty confidence with increased salaries and decreased teaching loads as well as greater faculty participation, they were making the schools increasingly attractive places for older academicians to stay and for younger academicians to begin their professional careers. Only in the area of religious faculty morale and student life would we have deemed the presidents to have been less than successful. In the former they had, in establishing better communications with the faculty, somehow forgotten about maintaining excellent communications with the religious faculty members, especially the younger ones. In the replacing of outmoded restrictions and compulsions of student life with more liberal attitudes they had not, it seemed to us, discovered a program of religious and social commitment that was relevant to contemporary young people. While both of these problems were soluble we found no ground for confidence that they were about to be solved.

Finally, there was the question of succession at the three schools. In only one could we fell certain that the religious community would surely appoint a successor of the same caliber, though in another instance, we thought it was at least very likely that such a successor would be appointed. One of the officials of the religious order remarked, "Each year when it comes to appointment time I have nightmares about what would happen to us if Jimmy's plane should crash in Transania or some other damned fool place like that." Since so much of the growth of these three schools in recent years was the result of the personality and the understanding of the incumbent president, it was quite possible that a change in office could decelerate, if not completely end the academic progress in two of the three universities. Thus, barring a major change in the way university presidents are recruited, the academic growth even in the best Catholic institutions at the present time must still be considered quite fragile.

4

Medium Improvement Schools

If one had visited two of our three top-level schools and all three of the middle-level schools fifteen years ago, there is considerable reason to suspect that one would not have discovered very much in the way of differences among the schools and one might even have made some erroneous predictions about which schools would be most likely to progress. All three of the middle-level schools are in substantial metropolitian regions of which two are quite conservative both politically and ecclesiastically. At the present time, the conservatism of two of these cities tends to permeate the academic institution to a very considerable extent, though one would suspect no more so than it did at one of the three rapidly improving schools not so many years ago. Two of the three universities are large, indeed sprawling institutions, while the other is a medium-sized liberal arts college with some professional and graduate additions. The two large schools both have substantial graduate programs in the arts and sciences and very extensive professional commitments (which commitments create considerable financial problems). The graduate arts and sciences commitments of these schools are increasing very rapidly as new Ph.D. programs proliferate. Enrolment at all three schools tends to be more local than national though one of them does have at least some students from distant regions. Two of the three schools are completely coeducational. All three have fairly impressive athletic reputations. The income and social class of the students coming to two of the schools is no different from that of two of the rapid improvement schools.

While the differences might not have been very great ten years ago, today one has an overwhelming impression that the three medium improvement schools have nowhere near the coherent sense of identity that the three rapid improvement schools have. Quite the contrary, in fact, two of the three schools seem to have little or no sense of identity or direction on almost any level of their activity. They are rather large city service institutions with only the most amorphous goals beyond continuation and expansion in every possible direction. The third school makes a pretense of being a liberal arts teaching institution, but its faculty is quite undistinguished and there do not seem to be any concrete policies to build up the level of teaching. We do not mean to say that there was no institutional planning at these schools, but simply that the planning did not seem to take place within a framework of clearly articulated goals.

ADMINISTRATION

In two institutions the presidents had very long tenures, while in the third, a new president had succeeded at the end of an administration that had been something less than a complete success. One of the administrators had training and experience in educational administration; the other two men, as far as could be determined, had no academic training or experience. All three presidents were personable, responsible men who were conscientiously trying to do the best they could in a job for which they had had meager preparation. The new president had inspired some hope and confidence in his faculty, but their judgments were quite guarded and reserved. The two other presidents were bitterly criticized by their faculty, by lesser administrators, and particularly by the members of their own religious community on the precise grounds that neither of these men knew what a university was or had any clearly thought-out goals for their own schools. At none of the three schools did the president have the confidence either of his own staff or of the faculty. The administrative philosophy of at least two of the three schools was summarized by one high-level administrator when he said, "The longer I'm in the business here, the more I am persuaded that the best way to run a university is the way you run a religious order. You tell somebody to do a job and he goes and does it without asking any questions why, or trying to negotiate with you why the job ought to be done." The man who made this remark was anything but a tyrant; he was a terribly harassed person, faced with responsibilities and burdens that were far too much for one man to have to put up with. As the university expanded more and more and became saddled with more and more problems, as the pressures of students and faculty and religious order and civic community built up, there was simply not time in his life for the kind of consultation and dialogue needed in the academic world. Thus, he found himself increasingly tempted to fall back on the superficially more efficient methods of the religious order.

The presidents described in this chapter are as different from the presidents described in the previous chapter as day is from night, although the possibility exists that in our descriptions we are accentuating differences that did not exist. But as we reread the interview protocols from the two classes of schools we are convinced that, if anything, we are underestimating the differences between the leadership styles of the rapid improvement and medium improvement schools. Just as consistently as the faculties at the top-level schools give credit to the president for the growth and movement that they claim is occurring in their institution, so the faculties of the middle-level schools are vigorous in their denunciation of what they argue is the poor leadership responsible for the stagnation of their schools. And just as the lower-level administrators not only greatly admire their presidential leader, but even bask in some of his reflected glory, so the administrators at the middle-level schools were anything but satisfied with the positions in which they found themselves.

Two of the presidents had reputations for being both aloof and indecisive, for centralizing all decision-making in their own hands, and for interminable procrastination. In addition, one president was accused of being a reactionary who governed with the help of a clique of close personal friends. In one of the schools, two of the medium-level administrators went to supper with the research team and, in the relaxed atmosphere of the meal, became quite blunt about the problems of their institution. It was perfectly clear to the two of them that their president (who was also their religious superior) made it impossible for them to do their jobs by what they would have considered to be even the most minimal professional standards. If they had been laymen working under such circumstances, they would almost certainly have quit, but their religious vows made it impossible for them either to leave or to engage in open revolt against the president. One could not help but feel compassion for these two men (a bitter conversation repeated in some other Catholic schools); they held some fairly clear notions about how a college or university ought to develop. They knew that their school was not developing along these lines. They were fully aware of the reasons why, and yet they could neither eliminate the reason nor withdraw from the situation. It seemed to us that religious superiors ought to be aware of what happens to human morale under such circumstances.

Not only was the morale of the lower-level administrators quite poor, but their competence was anything but impressive. At one school in particular the deanship positions were very poorly manned. All three schools pursued extremely conservative financial policies. The development offices were not reassuring (though they at least were not amateurish).[1] The financial officer of the school was an extremely important person in the ruling clique, and his approach in each instance seemed to betray a considerable fear of risk-taking. Concern about money and the problems of going bankrupt was very strong in each of these three schools, though we would judge that their financial condition was no worse than that of at least two of the rapid improvement schools where money seemed to be much less an important consideration. While all three presidents were somewhat involved in civic affairs in their communities, they were not at ease outside the Catholic ghetto or outside the sphere of rather conservative civic personages and would be quite ill at ease in the company of academicians and administrators of non-Catholic colleges.

At least two of the three men apparently obtained their jobs because they had reputations for being successful fund raisers in other positions; within some limitations, their reputation was

[1]Faculty antipathy toward development offices seems to be almost a given in Catholic higher education. Faculties object very violently to the salaries and expense accounts of development offices and argued that the school had very little to show in the way of return for such expenses. Interestingly enough, in the three top-growth schools there was practically no such criticism, and the criticism was most intense at two of the three medium-growth schools that we describe.

probably justified, though it is not at all clear whether the kind of fund raising reputation that one can establish as a high school principal is directly transferable to the university milieu. There seemed to be some reason to suspect that these men had been chosen as administrators because they had reputations for getting along well with people ("people" being prominent ecclesiastical and civic leaders in their own city) and for being "safe" men (which is to say that they would not do anything to antagonize the ecclesiastical or political or contributing community). Further, it must undoubtedly have been felt that these men, while being moderately progressive, would not antagonize the older generation within their own religious order. Unfortunately, whoever chose these presidents was unaware that in the cities in question it would have been impossible to build a distinguished university without offending all kinds of people, including members of one's own religious order. We are not condemning the three men in question; they were sincere and dedicated individuals who were doing the best they could in a job they did not understand. But at least two of them did not know what a university was and were not able either to project an image of the goals of the university or to rally enthusiasm of the faculty and lesser administrators for such goals. They lacked both the academic experience, the personal confidence, and the charismatic touch necessary to be the kind of president that could push the university into a great leap forward.

Although two of the three presidents had reputations for being strong administrators, we could not escape the impression that their strong administration meant two things: (1) they centralized most decisions in their own hands; and (2) they avoided most of the minor mistakes that might have occurred in the absence of such centralization. But, in both instances, it did not seem to us that they were strong enough or decisive enough to prevent their institutions from making mammoth mistakes or at least to divert the schools from mistaken paths down which they had been directed in years gone by. Both of the schools were overextended in the vast variety of their commitments to professional education as well as in the tremendously rapid increase in enrolment.

In such circumstances, a strong administrator would not be one who would hoard power or would refuse to make decisions, but rather one who had the vigor and the courage necessary to resist or to terminate unwise expansion and overcommitment. In one institution we were told about a professional school program which had already been enormously expensive and boded well to consume time, money, and energy for decades to come, "Of course, we'd like to get out of this but we've already told the people of the city that we were going to build the school, and now it doesn't look like we have much choice." In other words, a past administration had made a mistake and there was nobody with the vigor or the courage to end the mistake. In two of the three medium improvement schools, it appeared that the growth and development was almost out of control and that the university administrations were being carried along by decisions of the past that were defined as both irreversible and uncontrollable. None of the three schools was faced with disaster, but we did not see how, in the absence of major and dramatic restructurings, they could ever expect to be anything more than they were at the present time.

Curiously enough, in two of the three schools there were more laymen in high administrative positions than there were in two of the growth schools. We were not at all sure that these lay administrators would have earned such positions in comparable non-Catholic universities. Indeed, it seemed that they had frequently been promoted to such positions rather early in their careers and, in return, had greater loyalty to the religious order that was administering the schools than would members of the religious community themselves (a loyalty not incompatible with some minor criticisms and complaints).

Only one of the three schools had an adequate library, though this library was surprisingly good compared to most Catholic university libraries we encountered. There was at none of the three, as far as we could determine, an effective recruiting campaign, and the admissions standards in two of them were virtually nonexistent, while in the third, they were very low. At one school it was something of a joke among students that anyone could be admitted as a freshman of the school provided he had the money to pay his first semester tuition. At another school faculty investigation revealed that a very substantial proportion of the students had a college entrance board score much lower than the published minimum score required for admission. There was a suspicion that the schools were caught in what they took to be financial binds because of overexpansion of facilities and were forced to accept as many students as they could simply for financial reasons. The faculty of these schools was well aware of this admission policy and found it most demoralizing in their own work, arguing that if they wanted to teach at a junior college or at a state university that must accept every applicant, they would have chosen such a school.

With admission standards this low, it is quite possible for a reasonably intelligent group of students to get through the school without any major effort at all because the course demands are necessarily geared for the average or lower-than-average students. One young man told us, for example, that he had gone through one of the three medium improvement institutions for four years without ever reading a book or without ever reading the student newspaper (which, curiously enough, was a relatively good paper).

In summary, we would conclude that the administration at these three schools had proceeded only to a moderate extent along the path toward a professionalization in which their administrative standards would be the same that would hold in most American higher educational institutions of some reputation. They were still run essentially as educational arms of the religious order that owned the institution, and the values and norms of the religious order were much more important than were those of professional educational administration. Similarly, the fact that secular administrators would be considerably less than impressed by the way the school was being run would not be of so much importance because the crucial reference group was not a body of professional colleagues but rather the superiors of the religious order. Just as the three rapid improvement schools had, on the administrative level, pretty clearly entered the mainstream, albeit in some instances hesitantly, the administrations in the three medium improvement schools had just as clearly not entered the mainstream and really saw no need to do so.[2]

FACULTY

As can be imagined, the faculty of the three medium improvement schools was nowhere near as competent as the faculty of the three rapid improvement schools, but at least at two of the institutions there were some surprisingly competent departments. The explanation for the existence of such departments is an interesting one. Given the large amount of overcentralization in these institutions, presidents tend to be very "strong" and deans to be very "weak." With a weak dean and a strong president it is quite possible for there also to emerge strong departmental chairmen. Such men, usually of considerable ability, manage to gain the confidence of the administration and receive full support in building their own departments. The administrators realize that these particular academicians do know how to build a department. Since there is nothing in the administrator's creed against academic improvement he's only too happy to give free reign to somebody who combines academic competence with the political skills necessary to keep the religious order happy. In these circumstances, a very powerful departmental chairman can bring in promising young men, obtain for them adequate salaries and, as one put it, protect them from the administration. Such departmental chairmen consider themselves as go-betweens in keeping their promising younger colleagues from angering the administration and keeping the administration from doing anything too incredibly stupid as to drive the young faculty away. While such a method of building a strong department does not guarantee that the strength will be permanent, it does permit certain departments to assemble a faculty that is much better than either the administration or the student body of the school. However, as younger faculty become dissatisfied with strong control from the chairman and begin to demand more participation in the governance of the

[2]We had the impression that at least some of the middle-level administrators at these schools were trying to persuade themselves that they had entered the mainstream in every way that was crucial, but if they truly believed such an idea they succeeded only in deceiving themselves.

school, the strong department built by a strong chairman will tend to become obsolescent.

Sitting in a car by the shore of a lake, one departmental chairman (having been assured that the senior researcher was not a young priest writing a master's paper) confided that he felt it was the role of the chairman to create an atmosphere in which the younger members of the department could devote practically all their time to serious professional work and not be taken up with the concerns of faculty politics. The chairman in question, a kind, competent, fatherly person, was obviously quite good at creating this atmosphere for the members of his department. And there was no point in denying that academic politics often serve as an escape from scholarly productivity. Nevertheless, the benevolent paternalist as a departmental chairman is an anachronism, and those respectable academic departments in the medium improvement schools that rely on such chairmen to maintain their responsibility may shortly find that survival is much more difficult than it was in the past.

With the exception of these departments and a few men in other departments, the faculty at the three medium improvement schools is not research oriented, though at least it does aspire to do research and some of the members are engaged in research projects. However, because of the vigorous activity in the strong departments and the occasional activity in the other departments the university can persuade itself that it does have something of a research faculty.

Two of the schools did not publish salary information in the AAUP bulletin, while the third school's rank was C. (Salaries for assistant professors at this school had risen to B.) Fringe benefits are somewhat more adequate than salaries, though there is need for considerable improvement. While the teaching load at the rapid improvement universities was never more than nine hours, it tended to be amorphous at the medium improvement universities, with loads ranging anywhere from six to fifteen hours, depending upon the person and the department. Sabbaticals, of course, were extremely rare.

We would routinely ask faculty members if they intended to stay at the school they were at and, if they did, why. At the rapid improvement schools and the low improvement schools there seemed generally to be a tendency to stay—at the low improvement schools because the faculty members could go no place else, and at the rapid improvement schools because there was rarely any point in going somewhere else. But at the middle improvement schools faculty members seemed much closer to leaving. Mass exodus had not started yet and might never start in at least one school with a very favorable metropolitan location. In the other two institutions, faculty stayed partly out of lethargy, partly because of family commitments, and partly because they still entertained diminishing hope that the school might begin to move. As one man said to us, "You know, this could really be a great place. It would take so precious few changes to put it on the road. But they aren't smart enough even to see that they wouldn't have to change very much."

While, as can be imagined, the complaints at these schools were vigorous and indeed almost all-inclusive, there were few charges of direct violation of academic freedom. Those faculty members who might be outspoken on political or social questions beyond the confines of the university were well aware that they inspired considerable nervousness in the administration, a nervousness which might in some vague way affect their career, but there was no concrete evidence cited to show that there had been any direct attempts on the part of the administration to restrict freedom of expression in the faculty. Faculty participation in two of the schools was fairly extensive with academic councils, faculty handbooks, and faculty committees operating, but in none of the institutions was faculty participation particularly satisfactory and in none of the schools did the faculty feel that whatever participation was permitted to them had much effect on the determination of school policy. The faculty was quick to affirm that the administration had absolutely no confidence in them and to indicate that this lack of confidence was a mutual thing. While the AAUP existed in all three schools and was active in two of them, it was also bitterly resented by the administrations in two schools where joining the AAUP, much more holding office in it, was viewed as a sign of some sort of disloyalty to the university. In two of the three schools the possibility of a furious battle between the AAUP and the administration seemed imminent.

All three schools had fairly standard policies on promotion and tenure though the exact norms governing promotion were not altogether clear. It seemed to us that frequently they came to little more than duration of service in the school and perhaps completion of the doctoral dissertation (since large numbers of the faculty of the schools were still finishing their degree work). The faculty seemed to feel that the administration completely controlled the promotion mechanism, though there was no evidence that this control was ever used to punish obstreperous faculty members. While research was not required for promotion, it was surely a help, and an ambitious young professor who did publish fairly frequently could be assured of relatively rapid promotion in at least two of the three schools.

Recruiting at all three schools tended to be a haphazard affair with departmental chairmen frequently hamstrung in making salary offers, in signing contracts, or even in choosing new faculty members. At two of the three schools there were some fairly incredible stories of how procrastinating deans had offended potential recruits to the faculty. At one of the schools the treatment accorded to visiting candidates for appointment by the deans was almost unbelievable. In several instances which the researchers were able to check, promising young people were needlessly offended, it seemed to us, by the vagaries of the recruiting process. Thus, one extremely bright social science graduate student was hired to teach one course at night school by the departmental chairman and, having begun to teach, was notified by the dean of the school that his salary would be fifty dollars less than had been agreed on by the departmental chairman. The young man, needless to say, protested loudly and was finally given the full salary that had been agreed upon but with a rather paternalistic letter admonishing him to better manners. Thus, for fifty dollars and the satisfaction of writing one paternalistic letter, the school lost all chances of getting in a year a very excellent assistant professor.

Despite the many difficulties of working in these schools we were still of the opinion that a good number of the faculty were considerably more than adequate in their own professions and that the schools had assets in metropolitan areas that could be attractive to a considerable number of faculty members. One school in particular had some highly competent faculty who had no affection for the school but either could not or would not leave the metropolitan region in which the school was located. One younger faculty member at this school observed that he would have no hesitancy about sending his children to the school because, knowing the faculty as he did, he would be able to choose for his children the courses in which to enrol and guarantee them an excellent education at no cost (since his school had a tuition remission policy). We would suspect that the same comment could be made of another one of the medium improvement schools. But we are not sure how long this situation will endure. Granted the mobility of the younger faculty members, and the increasing demand for competent faculty personnel, the pressures against these medium improvement schools are going to increase and they will find it, we suspect, increasingly difficult both to recruit and to hold even moderately high quality faculty members. In addition, the reputations of these schools are suffering as their better faculty tends to drift away. If the explosions in faculty-administration relations, which we would deem quite possible given the lack of confidence existing in these relationships, should occur, then recruiting of good faculty will become even more difficult. The faculty situation at these three schools does not seem likely to get better and may quite easily get worse. In summary, faculty morale at these schools is very poor indeed, basically because it reflects the lack of confidence that marks the relationship between faculty and administrators and the apparent lack of professionalized standards and behavior at the highest levels of the administration of the school.

STUDENTS

It is very difficult to find much to say that is encouraging about the student life at the three medium-growth schools. At only one school is there a truly free student paper, though that paper is very excellent.[3] Nor is there any evidence at all that student groups have freedom to invite controversial speakers if, as seems very unlikely, they should so desire. In all three schools the annual retreat is a requirement for graduation. While there are many commuting students in the schools, those who are residents are subjected to rule books that contain extraordinarily detailed regulations. Most of the regulations are unenforced and unenforceable but we were assured by the deans of students at the schools that the regulations existed in the book so that if occasion arose, the university could "protect itself" by pointing to the regulations. They further argued that the students understand that these regulations exist only for that purpose and, hence, realize that they are not to be taken seriously unless they are caught violating them. What this sort of attitude about rules does to the students' development of ethical and moral standards remains an open question.

The students in these three schools were rather limited in their scholarly concerns, and social awareness and commitment were meager. While at least some of the students were bright enough, many seemed to be interested in little more than tests, athletic contests, and social activities. As far as we could determine, few of the students paid much attention to student government activities or indeed to any activity in the school. The religious and liturgical life of the schools were quite inadequate, and the counseling services were unimpressive. While there is an inarticulate but profound resentment among the student body toward much of what goes on in the school, we would not estimate that there is much revolutionary potential in the student body, at least not in the foreseeable future. Students have little or no respect for the religious order and not much for the school, but they have reached an accommodation with the institution that will enable them to get their degrees and to continue with their professional or their life plans. Student life at these three schools is not any less exciting than it is at a vast number of American institutions of higher education. But it is unfortunate that a religious institution which is supposed to provide some kind of meaning and purpose in the

[3]One school had a lively paper but its freedoms have been severely restricted in recent years.

life of a young person is so singularly incapable of doing it as these three schools seem to be.

Our student interviewer commented that at the three medium improvement schools the student body tended to be "blah." This is not to say that there were no concerned, interested individuals in the school; there surely were, but they tended to be isolated individuals and not to be part of any particular group, much less a group that would have influence. The vast majority of the student bodies seemed to find the principal locus of their effort to be the student union, where they would meet between classes in their various groups (the Negroes, the Poles, the law students, the business students, the sorority and fraternity types) and spend the first two days of the week talking about the last weekend's pleasures and the last three days of the school week planning the coming weekend. Visiting such student unions was a demoralizing experience, at least for the older researchers who could take such milieux only in very limited amounts.

CONCLUSIONS

The three medium improvement schools were obviously very different from the three rapid improvement schools, though in physical appearance, ownership, and basic structure they were not dissimilar. The differences were of tone, style, quality, and goals. As a matter of fact, it seemed to us that the three rapid improvement schools had goals and the three medium improvement schools did not, but it does not follow that they were not improving; they surely were. The quality of faculty, the level of faculty salary and participation, even the skill of the administration and the intelligence of the student body, is somewhat better in these three schools than they were a decade ago, but the improvement that has occurred has occurred almost by accident. The schools have been carried along by the great weight of forward movement in all of American academia and Catholic academia in particular. They are better than they were but through no fault of their own.

The difference between the top-level and the medium-level schools is essentially a difference of leadership. The fate of the three schools which we have described in this chapter was decided by provincial appointment. It was sealed on that day that the provincial appointed to the school a man who had a reputation for being a good administrator, a capable fund raiser, and a safe leader but who had little sense of what higher education was and lacked the personal courage and flair necessary for dramatic improvement in an academic institution. At least two of the medium improvement schools are so similar to the rapid improvement schools in age, size, location, composition of student body, past reputation, and ownership that there is little reason to argue that they could not have made the great leap forward if they had had the proper leadership. We could find nothing in the environmental situation that would have precluded at least two of the medium improvement schools from moving forward much more rapidly. As a matter of fact, we would be inclined to estimate that, all things considered, one and possibly two of these schools could have done better than the school that was highest among the rapid improvement schools. The essential difference, then, seems to be in the quality of leadership.

But the quality of leadership affected everything else in the school. The administration was much less professional in its various activities, faculty competence was lower, faculty morale was abysmally low (despite considerable improvements in the salary and work load structure), and student life was severely restricted by rules and by compulsory religious behavior, and was academically and humanly uninspiring.

This last point needs emphasizing once again. These schools were not moving forward at the pace with which they might have progressed, not because they were Catholic schools, but because they were poorly administered. And they were poorly administered because they did not have the right man at the top level of the structure. In this respect they differed not one bit from scores, and probably even hundreds, of other American higher educational institutions.

5

Low Improvement Schools

We contended in the previous chapter that, save for unimpressive leadership, two of the medium improvement schools could have been rapid improvement schools. There was nothing we could find in the environmental situation of the schools that would prohibit academic improvement. However, such an assertion could not be made of at least two of the low improvement schools. One of them, a medium-sized university with very limited graduate activity, and the other, a rather small liberal arts college, are located in geographic regions where, for a Catholic school, impressive academic growth would be very difficult. All of the schools are more than a half-century old. Two of them belong to one religious order and one to another. None of them has any lay trustees on its board of directors. None of them has a national enrolment, though one of them has something of a national reputation because of its athletic teams. One of them has a fairly extensive professional school program, including graduate work; the second has only a very limited graduate program though it calls itself a university; and the third has no graduate program. We would not say that any of these schools were experiencing an identity crisis because we had the impression that at none of them had the identity question ever arisen. The three schools were firmly placed in the backwater of Catholic higher education, and the changes in attitudes and concerns that have occurred in other schools since the end of World War II were hardly noticeable at the three low improvement schools. For one school, the geographical situation made growth and academic improvement almost impossible. For the second, a combination of geography and incredible concentration on physical expansion (on a pay-as-you-go basis) turned administrative attention away from qualitative improvement. In the third instance, a combination of an extraordinarily conservative ecclesiastical background as well as a curious structural flaw in the religious community that administered the school made it impossible for the university to benefit from the fairly favorable geographic location that it enjoyed. The three low improvement schools had very little going for them, and even with strong leadership they might not have moved forward very rapidly. In the rapid improvement schools leadership and environment were both favorable, and in the medium improvement schools the environment was favorable but not the leadership, but in the low improvement schools it would appear that neither variable was favorable.

ADMINISTRATION

It is much more difficult in this chapter to generalize about leadership problems of the three schools under consideration. In one school a conscious decision was made to concentrate on physical expansion for a fairly lengthy period of time before turning full attention to qualitative improvement. Given the particular physical location of the school such a decision might, in the long run, prove to have been a sound one. The school has a new president now who seems firmly committed to qualitative improvement but who has yet to display a firm grasp of what would be necessary to accomplish such improvement. The second school, although it is a small liberal arts college with a very poor geographic location, has resources available that might make it possible for it to become a reasonably distinguished liberal arts college. However, under a previous administration no attempt was made to tap these resources, and the school stagnated. Here, too, a new administration speaks boldly about qualitative improvement and in this instance the new president seems admirably qualified for his job.[1]

The third school is caught in a peculiar latent dysfunction of the democratic processes through which its parent religious com-

---

[1]Indeed, this man, whose academic and personal credentials are impeccable, was one of the most impressive of the college presidents we met on the grand tour, and it is most unfortunate that geographic accident will prevent him from ever becoming a president of a major Catholic university.

munity governs itself. Lay faculty members describe the school as being a political football which is awarded to the winning party in the provincial election. Apparently, the religious order has something of a highly developed two-party system with a narrow balance of power that shifts back and forth in each election so that every time there is an election the administration and the administrative powers of the school shift completely. As far as we can determine, there is little in the way of ideological differences between the two parties, both of them being rather conservative; apparently, whatever differences there are have to do with financial policy with one party favoring retrenchment and the other favoring expansion. In this situation, continuity of administration becomes impossible and planning beyond the duration of the provincial terms is out of the question. In addition, the provincial counselors who elect the president of the school also elect the chief assistants to the president so that the president has no guarantee that those who are selected to be academic vice-president or dean will be men with whom he would care to work or in whom he has any confidence (or who have any confidence in him). Furthermore, as a part of maintaining the consensus which must exist in the order between provincial elections, representatives of the defeated party are often installed in some positions in the university to balance the influences of the representative of the victorious party who is named as president. The only continuity that exists in the school exists in the financial officer, a member of the religious community, who is committed to the most careful and rigorously conservative kind of financing with every modification of the school's physical layout or academic development being on a rigorously pay-as-you-go basis. As a matter of fact, it is one of the great sources of pride and joy to the university administration that it is absolutely free of debt. Unfortunately, it is absolutely free of almost everything else that a higher educational institution ought to have, but this is apparently another matter.

This school was perhaps the most dismal of any we visited. There was no vitality or enthusiasm to be found anywhere—in the faculty, the students, or the administrators. We had the impression, confirmed in several conversations, that the personnel of the school are merely going through the motions, waiting for the next provincial election and the resultant overthrow of everything that had been going on in the school in the present administration. One faculty member remarked, "Fifteen years ago there wasn't much difference between this place and Notre Dame, but Notre Dame had Ted Hesburgh and we have had nothing but a series of non-entities who hold things together between elections. It's all very nutty because we have more things going for us in terms of our location and the potential financial resources than Notre Dame does, but unless they make up their minds to end their silly political squabbling within the community, we are never going to be anything but fifth rate."

The tight financial control and the overwhelming power of the financial officer is typical at all three of these schools. The financial officer of a Catholic college, since he is in some sense a representative of a religious order, has far more power than financial officers would at most educational institutions. While he may in fact be appointed by the president, in most instances he is really the provincial's agent rather than the president's and has the sanction of going to the religious superior if the president's administration of the school is a cause of concern to him. In some instances the treasurer, while he may be subordinate to the president in the college, actually is the president's superior in the religious community, a role-conflict situation whose negative effect on the administration of the school can be well imagined. We see no way for this anomalous influence and power of the financial officer to be corrected in the existing structure of the relationship between the religious order and the higher educational institution. Until this relationship is rethought the financial officer's power will be limited only by the courage and political skill of the president of the school.

As can be imagined, none of the three schools show much élan or dynamism. The administration feels no confidence or optimism itself and radiates none of this to the faculty and student body.[2] None of the presidents are deeply involved in educational and

[2]The liberal arts college with the new president is quite different now though it was a very recent change when we visited the school. In this chapter we are describing the school as it was before the dramatic transformation with the appointment of the new president.

civic affairs beyond those in the Catholic ghetto or those which are purely ritualistic. However, the absence of such involvement is not entirely unfortunate since it is to be feared that the top administrators would have have projected a very forceful image of Catholic higher education. Surely they were unable to do so to their faculty or administrative colleagues. While one man was concerned with building up the physical plant of the school, it seemed that the other two, one because of extraordinarily conservative orientations and the other because of the impermanency of his position, were concerned with maintaining things the way they always had been, in the marvelous immutable world of pre-Vatican Roman Catholicism, and always would be. The recruiting, admissions, and planning operations in all three schools were unimpressive and the development offices seemed to be quite mediocre. There was, however, little communication strain to be observed in the schools because there was little in the way of communication. Nor was there any doubt as to where responsibility was to be found (as was true in the middle improvement schools) because in two of the schools the responsibility was totally in the hands of the president and in the third school, given the anarchical composition of the religious community, responsibility was virtually nonexistent—or was located in mysterious actions within the religious order which the laity could not understand and about which the clergy would not talk.

To say that the administration of these three schools was unprofessional by the standards of American higher education would be to verge on the fulsome. We are not asserting that there is not mammoth unprofessionalism in many American colleges and universities. There are, in all likelihood, a number of non-Catholic institutions that are every bit as poor in their administrative behavior as are these three schools and probably there are a fair number of non-Catholic schools that are worse. What we are affirming simply is that compared to even the medium improvement schools the administrators of the three low improvement schools could charitably be described as amateur.

FACULTY

The faculty of the three low improvement schools was very

mediocre though there were at least some members of the religious faculty in all three schools who were quite competent and one or two who were outstanding. The proportion of Ph.D.'s was low, and those who did have Ph.D.'s generally were trained either in Catholic universities or had acquired their degree at a local non-Catholic university while teaching on the faculty of the Catholic school. The faculty was almost entirely local in its orientation and had little in the way of either professional or research interests. Faculty members tended to view themselves essentially as teachers and at least some of them were probably pretty good teachers. There was in each school a handful of conscientious and reasonably able men who were sincerely interested in improving the school and aiding both the students they taught and the religious order for which they worked. We felt that there was a great deal of personal tragedy for these people in the fact that rarely if ever were their intelligent and appropriate suggestions listened to. However, it would be a mistake to say that the faculty morale was poor, because it was our impression that most of the faculty members were not mobile and did not particularly wish to be mobile but were quite content with living in the region of the country in which they had settled and found their major satisfactions outside the classroom and the university atmosphere.

At one of the schools the salary level was C; at the other two it was D; though at all three schools the beginning salary for an assistant professor was either B or approaching B in the AAUP ratings. These salary scales, admittedly very poor, nonetheless represent dramatic improvement in all three schools over past salary scales, so that the faculty seemed generally quite satisfied with the recent improvement in their compensation. The twelve-hour teaching load was standard and a good number of faculty members were teaching fifteen hours.

There were some faculty committees at all three schools, but they did not seem to have much to do. There was no such thing as a faculty senate, though at the liberal arts college the new president showed every sign of establishing one as quickly as he could. At one of the schools the faculty handbook was being revised (by the president's secretary); at the other schools there was no such thing in existence. The AAUP was quite vigorous at one of the schools and was bringing pressure to bear on the administration, but the issues in case could generally be described as bread-and-butter ones. Disputes regarding academic freedom were almost nonexistent, though at one school a professor was apparently in trouble with the departmental chairman over some obscure question of philosophical principle. However, the problem was resolved without an academic freedom charge being raised. At none of the schools did there seem to be a notable infringement of academic freedom, largely because there was no occasion for such infringement. Faculties were docile and were not likely to make too much trouble and the administration was not terribly concerned about revolution in the ranks. However, at least at two of the schools there was enough intelligence somewhere in the administration to realize that what happened in a major Catholic university on the East Coast in the course of the winter could happen at their own school unless great care was taken. Thus, we would suspect that there would be great reluctance to be involved in an open fight on academic freedom with the AAUP. There was academic freedom at these three schools but more by default than by anything else.

All three schools had standard policies for promotion and tenure, with tenure being almost entirely a reward for duration of service. Morale was not bad, in fact it was much better than at the three medium improvement schools, largely because the lay faculty at the low improvement schools had much less optimistic expectations for either their own future or the future of the institution as a whole. But at all three of the schools the religious members of the faculty exhibited the lowest morale found anywhere on the grand tour. As one man put it, "I hate to think that I've dedicated my whole life to the awful mediocrity that this place represents." It was quite embarrassing to the interviewers to hear members of the religious community speak of the grave doubts of their own vocations which the depressingly low quality of the schools had engendered in their minds.

In conclusion, we would note that in both their faculties and administrations the three low improvement schools were far in the backwaters of Catholic education and distressingly unprofessional and unpromising, though the new president at the liberal arts

college might conceivably change the situation of his school completely. However, we should also make clear that while the schools
were by most standards bad, they were not nearly so bad as the
conditions indicated by the well-publicized incidents that occurred
at a major Catholic East Coast university during the winter. Indeed, in many respects it could be said that these—the poorest
of the schools we visited—still had more in common with the best
schools than they did with the school censured by the AAUP.

STUDENTS

Curiously enough, the student situation at two of the three low
improvement schools was less depressing than that at the medium
improvement schools. While the young people were quite apathet-
ic socially, religiously, and intellectually, they were charming,
docile, well-behaved, provincial young people who liked their
schools and their teachers and were quite incapable of the cynicism and disillusionment that made student life so dismal at the
middle-range schools. However, the extent of student cynicism,
bitterness, and alienation encountered at the third university was
equalled nowhere else on our tour. This cynicism probably arose
from the combination of the extraordinarily conservative religio-
ethnic condition of the metropolitan region in which the school
was located and from the singular ineptness of the university's
administration. The young men and women who attended the
school were by no means unsophisticated provincials. Many knew
what was wrong with their school and what was wrong with the
Church in their own diocese, and they seemed to choose, deliberately and consciously, not to care about either, or indeed to care
about much of anything. Only at this school did the situation
seem to be ripe for a student uprising, but an uprising of the far,
far right rather than of the moderate left—and by far right, we
mean neo-fascist.

At one of the schools the student paper was free; at another it
was apparently becoming free under the new administration.
Compulsory retreat was required at two of the schools; outside
speakers were subject to review at all three; student regulations
were narrow and restrictive in all three and apparently rigidly
enforced at two. All three schools were coeducational, but in two

of the three, coeds seemed to be distinctly unwelcome by many of the senior members of the religious community; and in the third, if they were not unwelcome, they were at least viewed with some suspicion and mistrust.

Communication between the students and most of the religious faculty was virtually nonexistent, though at least at one school some of the religious faculty apparently did have fairly close relations with the students. The liturgy, counseling, and student religious life at all three schools was uniformly poor, but just as the faculty was less troubled because their expectations were not as high, so we felt that at two of the three schools student morale was relatively high simply because the kids had no notion that things could be any better. At none of these three schools did there seem to be any strong possibility of student unrest for the foreseeable future.

There were in at least two of the schools a handful of young people who seemed dimly to perceive the possibility of change and at least one alert and vital student editor who was creating some stir on the lethargic campus. Ideally, these are the kinds of students who should receive encouragement from the faculty and administrators because they are the ones who are most likely to think and presumably thought is the legitimate result of higher education. But, while these students are not creating enough trouble to be repressed, there was surely no attempt to reinforce their enthusiasm. At some of the medium improvement schools the handful of restless and articulate student critics had begun to frighten some of the more insecure members of the religious order, but at the low improvement schools, the complaints of the critical students were so muted as to leave the powers-that-be quite undisturbed.

CONCLUSIONS

Our visits to the three low improvement schools were instructive because they indicated to us what Catholic higher education might have been like in the 1930's. While the three schools certainly did not replicate in every detail the situation in the 1930's (since they have had to change in some respects simply to continue in existence) it was our judgment that the provincialism of these three schools was essentially unchanged from the 1930's. By provincialism we mean the total lack of concern over the differences between the way the school operated and the generally accepted norms for higher education existing outside the American Catholic Church, or indeed presently existing even within a number of schools in the Catholic educational system. The leadership of these three schools was only marginally less narrow than it would have been thirty years ago; there were no goals other than survival, and, in some instances, physical expansion. The faculty and administrators of the school had no more sense of movement or direction than they would have had in the 1930's. Nor did the members of the religious community in control of the operation of the school (as distinguished from some of their colleagues on the faculty) have any sense that the basic educational philosophy that had guided the school thirty years ago needed any major updating to the present time.

We observed at the beginning of the chapter that environmental and structural factors made it unlikely that any of these three schools could have been rapid improvement institutions. It is interesting to ask, however, what would have happened to them if a competent and charismatic administrator had been appointed president. It is our judgment that such a president would have had to use bold experimentation to overcome the environmental obstacles and could not have followed the path toward academic improvement that had been chosen by the three rapid improvement schools. But dramatic innovations in curriculum, student life, and faculty participation of the sort that could put any of these schools on the map, would have been subjected to tremendous counterpressures within the local environment or the religious community. It is highly likely that these pressures would have broken the enthusiasm of even the most charismatic of presidents. It would have been much easier for the middle improvement schools to have broken into the "big time" because less innovation would have been required and less counter-pressures from ecclesiastical sources would have been generated. But at the low improvement schools the environmental obstacles to growth were such that only dramatic and controversial measures would have succeeded in initiating improvement processes. The liberal arts college may provide a classic laboratory case of whether a poor school located in the wrong place can, with competent leadership and fairly good financial resources, become an impressive higher educational institution. On *a priori* grounds we would be inclined to bet against it, but the new president of this school is a very charismatic individual indeed, and he may be able to pull it off.

In conclusion, the low improvement schools are schools that really never had a chance and probably would not have improved academically even with the most brilliant of leadership. Their leadership may have been no worse than that at the medium improvement schools, but they did not have the environmental or structural variables in their favor that carried the medium improvement schools forward with the rest of Catholic higher education. The environmental situation of the low-grade schools was such that they could not even take normal advantage of the long-run trend.[3]

[3]One Catholic educator who read this report commented that two-thirds of the schools we described (in the preceding two chapters) are not impressive institutions and only one-third are. He argued from this that the quality of Catholic higher education is rather poor. Two comments are in order: First of all, the last two chapters are not meant to be quantitatively representative of Catholic higher education but rather representative of the three kinds of schools we visited—those that were improving rapidly, those that were remaining in the more or less fixed position, and those that were being left behind in the surge of progress. We make no assertions that Catholic higher education could be divided into equal thirds according to these categories. But, furthermore, we would also observe that high-quality schools are a rarity in any educational system, since by definition only a limited proportion of any aggregation of institutions can be at the top. Most American higher education is not "high quality," and the Catholic schools are no exception to this statement. We are not speaking to justify the failures of the schools described in these last two chapters. At least in some instances the failures are inexcusable and even intolerable, but we are asserting that such inexcusable and even intolerable failures are by no means a uniquely Catholic phenomenon in American higher education.

6

Analytic Summary

It has been the principal contention of this report that academic improvement in Catholic higher educational institutions is dramatically related to the professional competence of the administrative leadership of the school. When the president of an institution combines understanding of the purposes of a higher educational institution in the United States and the means by which such institutions can achieve their goals with a minimum of interference from the religious community, then the college or university can improve academically—at least if the geographic situation is not totally unfavorable. Our rank-order correlations on the professional competence of the leadership of the school correlated very closely with a rank ordering of the schools based on objective measures of academic growth.

Implicit in this analysis is the notion that other variables, which might be expected to lead to academic improvement, are relatively unimportant when compared with the intelligence and political skill of top administrative leadership. In this chapter, we propose to demonstrate that such variables do in fact correlate only weakly with academic improvement.

The analysis in the present chapter will be based on rank-order correlations between the ranking of the schools on these other predictor variables and on the objective ranking prepared by Messrs. Bradburn and Treiman. It should be noted that this procedure lacks the mathematical precision found in other kinds of sociological analysis. But such rank-order correlation analysis is an extremely useful method of ordering and understanding data about a relatively small number of formal organizations whose degree of adjustment to a given problem is under consideration.

Table 6.1 presents the rank-order correlation between the Bradburn-Treiman rating of the schools and the school's rank on the number of other variables that might be expected to predict academic improvement.

The first two items in the table are concerned with the economic resources available to the school. As might well be expected, the academically improving schools have more money in their annual budgets and are more likely to receive grants from federal agencies or private foundations. Furthermore, as we noted in the previous chapter, development offices of the improving schools are more effective in their fund-raising efforts than those at other schools. However, the fact that more funds are available to improving schools seems to be a result rather than a cause of their improvement. Even though the complaint about financial shortages was heard almost universally on Catholic campuses, the relevant question is not how much money a school has at its disposal in fact, but rather how it can best realize the resources that are potentially available.

It might be argued that well-to-do parent and alumni groups should provide the financial resources to facilitate growth. However, the first two items in Table 6.1 indicate that there are only rather weak correlations between objective rank ordering of the academic growth of schools and rank orderings based on proportion of students who came from families with annual incomes over $10,000 or from families where the father had had a college education. Thus it would seem that the availability of well-to-do constituencies is not in itself a predictor of academic growth for the school. Affluent parent and alumni groups can be a big help, of course, but the potential of such groups will only be utilized by intelligent administration. In the absence of such administrative leadership, the alumni and parental resources are likely to go untouched. Indeed, the fact that such resources are not used in many instances suggests that the complaints we heard about lack of money were excuses rather than explanations. Finances are a problem for any educational institution, no matter how affluent it is. The problem for a great many Catholic schools is not that they do not have money but that the monies they have are not used intelligently, and the available financial resources are not utilized in the most appropriate manner.

The next two items in Table 6.1 have to do with geographic

location. It might be expected that if a Catholic school has a more or less exclusive situation in a given area, the absence of competition would enable the school to focus its development and exploit the Catholic financial resources that are available in the area. Unfortunately if a school has such a monopoly, the reason in almost all instances is that there are simply not very many Catholics in the area. Thus a negative correlation emerges between academic improvement and exclusivity of the market. If, on the other hand, the schools are ranked according to an estimate of the proportion of Catholics in the area in which they are located, there emerges a moderate positive rank order correlation between Catholic population concentration and academic improvement. As we suggested in the last two chapters, it would appear that a favorable geographic location is a necessary condition for academic improvement of higher educational institutions. At least none of the schools with unfavorable geographic locations has moved forward very dramatically.

The next four items in Table 6.1 are concerned with the social organization of the schools. There are weak to moderate correlations between complexity of graduate programs, faculty partici-

Table 6.1 Rank-order Correlations with Academic Growth

Academic Growth	Rank-order Correlations
Income of parents[a]	.25
Education of parents[b]	.12
Exclusivity of market[c]	−.22
Concentration of Catholic population[d]	.40
Size of school	.02
Laymen in administrative positions	.34
Student freedom	.52
Complexity of graduate program	.50
Faculty participation	.25
CUES scales	
Scholarship	.10
Awareness	−.23
School loyalty	.73
Evaluation of research team	.84

[a]Proportion with annual income over $10,000.
[b]Proportion college graduate fathers.
[c]Number of Catholic schools within twenty-five miles.
[d]Proportion Catholic in metropolitan region.

pation in academic affairs, the number of laymen in administrative or departmental chairmen positions, and the liberality of student rules with academic improvement. However, none of these correlations is nearly as strong as our predictions based on our evaluation of the competency of the administrative leadership of the school. In other words, it seems far more important that an intelligent and dynamic man be president than that he have lay vice-presidents, deans, or academic chairmen working for him. Similarly, the amount of faculty participation, the complexity of the graduate program, and the liberality of student personnel policy are not themselves strong predictors of academic improvement. Indeed, these sorts of improvements are likely to result from intelligent academic leadership rather than to create the conditions necessary to make such leadership possible.

In a good number of schools, the faculty felt that the administration should permit them to be responsible for promoting academic development. We had the impression that the faculty thought that they could promote improvement. However, the experience of non-Catholic universities suggests that the opposite is the case—that faculties tend to be conservative educationally. The élan for growth must come from administrators if it is to come at all. Thus faculty participation, as well as other organizational variables, may be signs of academic improvement, but they are not the principal predictors of it.

Neither socioeconomic, ecological, nor social organizational variables proved to be particularly strong predictors of academic improvement. However, questionnaires administered to the students reflect an atmosphere in the schools that correlates with such improvement. For nine of the schools in our analysis, there are available CUES scores based on the instrument developed by Pace described in the second chapter of the present survey. However, as Table 6.1 shows, there is a negative correlation between Pace's "awareness" measure and academic improvement and an extremely weak positive correlation between his "scholarship" measurement and the rate of improvement. As a matter of fact, the school that scored lowest in academic improvement had the highest score on Pace's "awareness" measure, and the school that scored the second lowest had the highest score on his "scholarship" measure. The explanation of this rather peculiar phenomenon seems to be that students at the poorest Catholic colleges had no readily available referent by which to judge their faculty or the atmosphere in their institution. Thus, an overwhelming proportion of the women at a small and stagnant Catholic women's college believe that their faculty is of the highest competence and that the intellectual atmosphere of the school is quite intense. At the same time, the students at one of the best of the Catholic universities with a reasonably impressive faculty and fairly intense intellectual concern among the students compare themselves to one of the nation's great non-Catholic universities located in the vicinity and judge their atmosphere in scholarship and awareness to be very poor. This phenomenon suggests that the CUES instrument can be very useful by taking into account this referent-comparison evaluation.

On the other hand, a rank ordering of nine of the schools according to the proportion of the students responding that they liked their school very much shows that there is a fairly high correlation between the students' loyalty to the school after graduation and the academic improvement of the institution. It may be that something in the atmosphere of an improving institution generates a particular kind of loyalty in the student. The accuracy of such student perception might explain the extremely high rank-order correlation obtained by our student interviewer. In any event, there is some indication that students are much more sophisticated about the rate of improvement of their college than either faculty or administrators would think. But it is somewhat dismaying that a year's interviewing and observation produces rank-order correlations only somewhat higher than the rank-order correlations that could be produced by simply tabulating the loyalty of students to their institution.

However this may be, the evaluation of the competence and independence of the administrative leadership of higher educational institutions is clearly a much stronger predictor of academic improvement than are institutional or environmental variables, such as those presented in Table 6.1. Favorable geographic location is apparently a necessary condition for academic improvement. The availability of parental financial resources does not seem to be too relevant. The school's size has no little bearing, and student freedom, participation of faculty, complexity of graduate program, and prevalence of laymen in administrative positions seemed more likely to be consequences of academic growth than conditions for it. We conclude this more analytic chapter as we concluded the previous three descriptive chapters: The difference between the improving schools and non-improving schools is largely determined by the competence and independence of the presidents. It would therefore seem to follow that the crucial problem for American Catholic higher education is recruiting competent and charismatic administrators and obtaining for them the freedom they need to do their work well. If there were more such administrators, there is every reason to believe that Catholic higher education would be substantially better than it is today.

7

Faculty

At one time the faculty of a Catholic college was virtually indistinguishable from the religious order that constituted the "college community"; there may have been a few lay "helpers" but they were almost part of the religious order. However, by the time of World War II, there were large numbers of lay faculty members in Catholic colleges and universities, and at the present time approximately two-thirds of the faculties are made up of lay men and women, including an increasing number of non-Catholics.[1]

The lot of the lay faculty member in a Catholic college has been the object of much complaint, speculation, and discussion, especially in more recent years. It was often said that even though the lay faculty member did not take the vows of poverty, chastity, and obedience, the financial and administrative organization of the school forced him to keep those vows. More recently, there have been signs of considerable improvement in the situation, but evidence of this has been quite uncertain until now. Much less is known about, and much less interest has been shown in, the working conditions of the religious members of the faculty.

The present chapter is concerned with both the lay and the religious members of the faculty. The origins, freedom, academic citizenship, working conditions, and morale of the lay faculty will

[1]The exact proportion of non-Catholic professors in Catholic colleges is difficult to determine, especially since some of the schools which are most likely to have non-Catholic faculty members very often do not inquire about the religion of a perspective appointee—although in American society, it is not too difficult to guess what a faculty member's religion is. However, there are several schools that report that at least one-fifth of their lay professionals are not Catholic. Virtually all the schools we visited had at least one or two non-Catholics on the faculty and they were, in almost every instance, included on our interview list on the premise that the interview team would be interested in how "satisfied" the school's "non-Catholic" was. Indeed, it must be admitted that they seemed on the whole considerably more satisfied with their lot as teachers in Catholic colleges than did many of their Catholic colleagues.

be discussed. In each section, we shall give both observations and recommendations based on these observations.

ORIGINS

There are two quite different kinds of faculty members on Catholic campuses. We shall call them the "old professors" and the "new professors." While the "ideal types" are models for the examination of reality rather than a statistical description of reality, and while there are many faculty members who would have one foot in both camps, the "old professor–new professor" distinction is very helpful in understanding what is happening in the Catholic faculties at the present time. Although "old" and "new" are chronological terms, it should be noted that there are some senior faculty members whose behavior would clearly place them among the new professors and at least a few junior faculty members who are already old professors.

The old professor is essentially a college teacher. He is a product of the Catholic system, in many instances attended the college at which he teaches, and in most instances received his M.A.—and his Ph.D., if he has one—from a Catholic university. Indeed, if the school at which he is teaching is a university, it is quite possible that he has had all his undergraduate and postgraduate training at that school. He is a "local" rather than cosmopolite and is intensely loyal to the school—indeed, at times almost mystically loyal. His background is working class or lower middle class, and when he entered college he had little notion of going to graduate school or becoming a college professor. Hence, he is profoundly grateful to the religious order that enabled him to achieve a status he would not otherwise have planned for himself. He does little, if any, research, though at times he will speak wistfully of research plans that he hopes to implement if he ever gets the time. He tends to feel subservient to the clergy in the faculty and at times even to act like "a medieval serf"—to use a description of one young liberal college president. He is very poorly paid, even though he may have associate or full professor rank, but still is receiving a much better salary than he did ten or even five years ago. He is greatly pleased with the progress being made in improving faculty salaries. (His full professorial salary may rank as D on the AAUP scale.)

When he does criticize the school, the old professor does so in terms that express great concern about the school's future. In most instances, he does not have the slightest intention of ever leaving. Gratitude to the religious order that runs the school is sufficient to prevent him from feeling that the school would be even a better place if the administrators had more imagination and vision.

The old professor tends to be different even in his physical appearance from the new professor. The tweed suit, the pipe, the harassed and nervous face, the somewhat anxious manner all betray someone as an old professor even before the conversation begins. Further, the conversation, if left to itself, is much more likely to be personal, to recount the old professor's struggles in graduate school, his difficulties in making a living when faculty salaries were much lower than they are now, and the frustrations he experiences in trying to work with the religious who administer the school.

John Donovan has written about these old professors (1964). For reasons not altogether clear, Donovan did not anticipate an increase in enrolment in Catholic schools and therefore postulated an unchanging composition of the faculty. He felt that the "old professors" who joined the faculty at the time of great expansion immediately after the end of World War II would continue to give tone and style to the Catholic campus for years to come.

The new professor is a professional, mainly oriented to his professional colleagues rather than to his school. He is much more likely to be a graduate of a secular school, and he has either finished his Ph.D. or is in the process of doing so. Unlike his older colleague, he will finish his degree work. He is interested in research and is highly mobile professionally. While he may be quite idealistic about helping his school, he hardly plans to spend all his professional life there. He is quite impatient with what he thinks are the mistakes and the incompetencies of the administration but his impatience is frequently based more on professional standards than on any kind of emotional anti-clericalism. This is especially true if he is not the product of an all-Catholic education. He is not inclined to cultivate the clergy as friends nor does he display toward them the amount of respect that some of the older faculty members think is proper. His mobility, his professionalism, and his aloofness easily mark him as being "disloyal" to the school and "not being a happy member of our family here."

The new professor does not like this reaction on the part of the clerical faculty and administrators, especially because he feels that those who are "happy members of the family" are frequently dull and unambitious. He is the first to admit that his primary loyalty is to the profession and to his own professional career, but he feels that this does not mean that he is not interested in the school or not doing a good job with his students. Indeed, he is inclined to argue that his professionalism is a more important contribution to the academic performance of the school than the emotional loyalty he observes in some of his seniors. While the old professor is likely to stay at the school and grow more bitter and frustrated, the new professor is much more likely to shrug his shoulders and go elsewhere. Because of his deep attachment to the school, the old professor's criticisms have a profound emotional tone to them. The new professor, on the other hand, is quite willing to work hard for the improvement of his school as long as there are signs that the administration is seriously and intelligently concerned about this improvement. When these signs are absent, he simply returns to his research projects and begins to look for another school.

The appearance and behavior of the new professor marks him just as clearly as do those of the old professor. While on occasion the new professor may wear a beard, he is usually inclined to dress as a conservative professional man and indeed to view himself as a professional rather than a teacher. His conversation is less agonizing, he talks less about himself, shows less concern about the school, and puts more emphasis on his own personal work and interests. If you ask an old professor what work he is doing, he is more likely to stumble around and explain why the lack of time makes it impossible to pursue his interests, and it takes some persistence to get him to tell you what his interests are. But with the new professor one merely has to ask the more or less standard question, "What are you working on now?" and the floodgates are open. It may be merely that the new professors are, on the whole, somewhat younger than the old professors, and the age difference would explain the difference in enthusiasm. But it is dubious whether, even ten years ago, the old professor had the bright expectations of making important scholarly contributions that the new professor has.

The administrators of the Catholic colleges are quite skeptical about the new professors—or at least they don't know how to understand them or how to relate to them. Despite the school's commitment to the necessity of faculty research, they cannot comprehend either the mobility or the research interests of the new professor. The new professor's willingness to seek employment elsewhere is deemed to be a sign of disloyalty, and his involvement in research is viewed as a sign of his lack of interest in his students. While some of the younger generation of academic freebooters are totally unconcerned about anything but their own research careers, the vast majority of the new professors we encountered are loyal to the schools and concerned about their students, but in a very different way from their predecessors. Unfortunately, the administrators of Catholic colleges are frequently not sensitive enough to perceive this. We could not escape the very strong feeling that the administration of a good number of Catholic colleges and universities will soon be hard put to prevent a rapid turnover rate among its younger faculty. Even though these men are well paid—at the assistant professor level, many of them have A or B+ salaries on the AAUP scale—they are still likely to find greener fields elsewhere and to depart in considerable numbers each June. They do so, at least in part, because in the early years of their professional career, mobility is a good thing. But they also leave because they find the attitude of some Catholic college administrations to be unimaginative and oppressive.

ACADEMIC FREEDOM

Philip Gleason (1966) succinctly summarizes the problem of academic freedom on the Catholic campus:

[A]cademic freedom is a new idea to Catholic educators because they have only recently arrived at the point where it has a vital bearing on the activity of their colleges. But all the while that Catholic educators had other things on their minds, the notion of academic freedom was developing outside the sphere of their interest. Now, at the time of change and new beginnings in their own thinking, Catholic educators are not confronting an inchoate idea which is only at the threshold of its course through human history, an idea in whose mature shaping they will from the very outset play an important role. Rather, they must come to grips with an idea which has already been evolving in this country for a century or more, and has been evolving not only apart from the influence of traditional religious institutions but in contradiction to them. Consequently, academic freedom has become intimately associated with a weltanschauung which tends to look upon religion as an outmoded relic of an intellectually benighted age and which regards the traditional churches as obstacles to the progress of scientific knowledge, weltanschauung which has in fact taken on the character of a quasi-religion itself.

There is something of an irony in this since, while the immediate ancestors of the academic freedom movement in the United States were the German universities of the nineteenth century, the more remote ancestors were surely the Christian universities of the Middle Ages. One suspects that if the medieval scholastics could be born once again they would be horrified to discover that freedom for scholarship was not being passionately defended on Catholic campuses.

On the other hand, it would be a mistake to assume that the Catholic schools' recent conversion to principles of academic freedom are some centuries behind the rest of American academia. Academic freedom as a commonplace in American academic higher education certainly does not date back beyond the 1930's and, as the witch-hunt of the late forties and early fifties demonstrates it was by no means assured even in major universities during the post–World War II era.

But, as Gleason remarks elsewhere, academic theory often lags far behind academic practice. While a good number of faculty handbooks of Catholic schools do not even mention the question of academic freedom, and several others enter qualifying clauses when they subscribe to the AAUP statement on academic freedom, it is still safe to say that academic freedom in the strict sense of the word is violated but rarely in Catholic colleges and universities. Indeed, we were rather surprised to discover how much academic freedom there really was in the Catholic schools. Only one Catholic college (a small women's school) was on the AAUP censure list when our research began. Another school (a large Catholic university) has since made the list in a fashion which can be characterized only as spectacular. The AAUP reports that the number of complaints from Catholic schools has gone up in recent years, though the feeling in the AAUP national staff is that this increase in complaints comes from an improvement rather than a deterioration in the situation, since only when faculty members begin to discover that they have rights are they likely to protest their violation. Since the Catholic Church has for one reason or another become front-page news in the United States, the incidents that do occur are very likely to receive national publicity, and since certain elements of the Catholic press are actively hostile to Catholic education, wide publicity is given to any incident that even remotely sounds like an abuse of academic freedom. While we certainly deplore these well-publicized incidents, we can conclude that such incidents are exceptions.

While the faculty members we interviewed in our survey were very critical of their school administrations in many respects, there was a general insistence that the Catholic professor today enjoys a complete and total freedom in the choice of texts, in his lecture notes, in his grading, and in the kinds of examinations he gives. We were also assured that the faculty member's personal life[2] or political beliefs were not subject to scrutiny by the school.

[2]There is still some question as to the effect of divorce and remarriage on a Catholic faculty member's position. At some schools it is very hard to judge exactly what the practice is on this problem, since cases arise only rarely. At one or two schools it was clear that the marital life of a faculty member was deemed quite irrelevant by the administration. At another school divorce was not an obstacle either to being hired or to having one's contract renewed, but remarriage after divorce was an obstacle even if the given faculty member was not a Catholic. This is not to say that anyone in a tenured position would lose his tenure because of a divorce and remarriage, nor even that someone would be refused tenure on such grounds. However, at least at this school, divorce and remarriage were obstacles to being hired and would create considerable nervousness about promotion to tenure. As far as we could determine, this rather strange procedure was a doing, not so much of the administrators of the school, but of the higher superiors of

Indeed, some of the faculty members (and some of them not
Catholics) insisted that they encountered greater classroom and
personal freedom than they had had at non-Catholic colleges
where they had previously taught. A number of the non-Catholic
faculty members admitted that they had considerable doubts and
reservations about accepting an appointment at a Catholic college
because of the image that they had of the absence of freedom at
such schools, but each one agreed that this image was distorted.
We are inclined to agree with them. Academic freedom, at least in
the strict sense of the word, is the rule rather than the exception
at the Catholic colleges, and the impression that Catholic faculty
members do not enjoy academic freedom is based on information
that is either inaccurate or sadly out of date.[3] No claim is made
that there are not problems of academic freedom in Catholic universities. Indeed, we rather suspect that there will be more problems in the future than there are at the present time since, as the
quality of the faculty improves and as faculty members become
more sensitive to their rights, the freedom and privilege of faculty
is likely to be more jealously guarded than before. But friction
over academic freedom is hardly a monopoly of Catholic institutions, and by and large their problems do not seem to be very
different from those to be encountered at any American college
or university.

Nevertheless, there still persists an atmosphere of "unfreedom"
in a fair number of Catholic schools. This unfreedom may not

---

the religious order who were defending this rampart as one of the last that remained to their notion of what a Catholic university ought to be. We suspect that
while administrators would do everything in their power to avoid a showdown
on what they would consider particularly Catholic moral questions, they would
not be above informally suggesting to a faculty member who, for example, had
divorced and remarried, that he might be happier somewhere else. Again, we could
uncover only a rare wisp of a rumor that such an event had occurred. It is very
clear, of course, what is behind such attitudes. Some of those in key positions in
the religious order still consider the lay faculty to be, in some fashion or another,
members of the order, and they are terribly concerned about the impact on the
order's reputation on behavior of faculty members that someone outside the university community might judge to be immoral.

[3]Some departments (philosophy and social sciences) are viewed by some Catholic administrators to be "sensitive," and academic freedom problems are somewhat more likely to occur in these fields. We will comment on this later in the
chapter.

impinge directly on the faculty rights and privileges, but it still contributes an unhealthy atmosphere to the schools that is an obstacle to faculty recruitment as well as academic respectability. Thus, for example, the well-publicized cases where foreign theologians are forbidden by religious or diocesan authority to speak on Catholic college campuses, the occasional interference of a chancery office in a campus activity or complaint from the chancery office about some outside venture of a faculty member, the summary transfer of a religious who is involved in a project that is unpopular with local civil or ecclesiastical authorities, the suspicions that certain senior members of the religious faculty or administration hold regarding some of the young turks in the school, the occasional high-handed attitude of a dean or vicepresident toward a faculty member—all these contribute to an atmosphere of distrust and suspicion which, while it is not generally an impediment to freedom, still makes faculty members skeptical of how real their freedom is.

As one faculty member commented, "These people say they believe in academic freedom and they've written it into their handbook, but I am not sure that deep down in their hearts they really believe it, and that in a difficult case they would not back off from what the handbook says and toss one of us out, especially if the order didn't like what we were doing. They have so little freedom in their own lives, I just don't think they're inclined to give it to us in our lives." The incidents at a major East Coast Catholic university during the course of our tour reinforced the fears of some of the faculty members. As one noted, "The men who are running our place now are not dumb enough to do that, but how can we be sure that the next administration won't change its mind and do something even more stupid."

It is easy for an outsider to point out that such fears probably are groundless and that whether or not the religious administrators really believe in freedom is a theoretical question. The practical pressures are such that they must behave as though they believe in it. Nonetheless, the uncertainty, suspicion, and distrust on the part of the lay faculty are too obvious a phenomenon in Catholic colleges to be overlooked or ignored. This atmosphere of suspicion and distrust is reinforced by the inferiority complex of

American Catholics, mentioned in a previous chapter, by the fact that anti-clericalism is fashionable among the intelligensia, by the strong heady wine of the vast increase of discussion within the Church of Rome brought on by the Second Vatican Council.

Some administrators still are tempted to fall back on the iron fist approach and to feel that academic freedom and due process are a threat to their authority and their control of the school. A few Catholic college administrators are frightened of academic freedom and do not understand it. Others live in mortal terror of the AAUP and would much sooner give in on a case that they could probably win rather than run the risk of unfavorable publicity or even of setting up an investigative committee which the administration would not be able to control. More sophisticated faculty members surely are not above using this fear for their own purposes.

For all the fears and criticisms of faculty members, they are still inclined to concede that their situation is not basically different from that to be encountered at many other colleges, if not at most. One of the more militant AAUP officials we spoke to was a bit taken aback when we asked whether he thought that the incompetence, distrust, and suspicion that characterized his own institution were a rarity in non-Catholic higher education. He remarked, "No, of course not. There are all kinds of places that are at least as bad as ours and I suppose hundreds that are worse. What frosts me is that those guys [the administrators] are supposed to be men of God and, damn it all, from them we have the right to expect better." Such attitudes are not infrequent among Catholic faculty members.

It should be noted that in the previous paragraphs we have spoken always of "some" schools. Let us emphasize two points: (1) On virtually all the campuses we visited the fact, if not always the spirit, of academic freedom was in evidence; and (2) While the atmosphere at some of the schools indicated that neither faculty nor administration was secure in their academic freedom, in a number of other colleges both the reality and the atmosphere of

academic freedom were as much in evidence as in any university
in the country.[4]

On the other hand, non-Catholics on the faculty, especially
those who have taught in other colleges, are much more sym-
pathetically disposed toward their working conditions than are
some of the most critical faculty members. As one Jewish associate professor remarked to us, "There's a lot more freedom at
this school than at the state university I taught at previously.
They don't tell you what books to use or what outlines to follow,
they don't impose departmental examinations on your students,
they don't warn you about not offending trustees, they leave you
alone. They may leave you alone because they don't know any
better than to leave you alone, but at least they leave you alone,
and they didn't at the state university."

ACADEMIC CITIZENSHIP

While academic freedom in the strict sense of the word does not
seem to be a major problem for most of the Catholic faculty members we interviewed, academic citizenship—that is to say, the participation of faculty as respected partners in the academic
enterprise—is a major problem. We heard much more criticism in
this area than we did in any other area of discussion with faculty
members. Several observations are in order:

1. Most Catholic schools have some kind of faculty body—an aca-

[4]One Catholic college president who read this section of the report commented
that he felt our treatment of academic freedom in the Catholic colleges and universities was rather "grudging." On re-reading the pages we fear that we cannot
agree with this comment. We are inclined to feel, in fact, that compared to the
treatment that academic freedom on the Catholic campuses receives in certain
sections of the Catholic press, our description is extraordinarily favorable and
gracious. We also happen to feel that it is accurate. There is relatively little direct
abuse of academic freedom in the Catholic colleges and universities but still a
good deal of suspicion and uneasiness. We assume that such suspicion and uneasiness will disappear with passage of time, and there were some indications in our
research that disappearance was beginning. But that it was only a beginning
seemed so obvious as to hardly be subject to question.

demic council, a university senate, faculty committee, faculty welfare committee, or periodic meetings of the faculty as a whole.

2. Most have AAUP chapters; the majority of Catholic administrations have learned to live with the AAUP and, in some instances, actually to welcome it. At least in one case that we know of, the AAUP was formed at the recommendation of the college president. In other cases, faculty members have received warm encouragement from the president to join. A good number of the better presidents themselves have been members of the AAUP before moving into the presidential office. We are only aware of one of the schools we visited—and that a large urban university—where the administration is extremely reluctant to deal with the AAUP and avoids such contact whenever possible.

3. Most of the Catholic schools have faculty committees on which laymen are represented and, in many instances, in which laymen have the controlling vote.

4. Faculty handbooks are becoming more and more frequent on most Catholic campuses. During the year of our grand tour it seemed that almost every school was preparing a "revision" of the faculty manual—a revision which in some instances was the equivalent of producing a faculty manual for the first time. We were tempted to believe that faculty manuals had suddenly become quite fashionable on the Catholic campus, since in past years there were no manuals in some schools, and in other schools manuals existed, but the faculty could never seem to find copies of them.

Having made these observations, we are forced to comment that they represent only the bare skeleton of academic citizenship for most faculty members at Catholic colleges and that faculty participation as academic citizens generally leaves much to be desired in the Catholic schools. The faculty senate is often appointed rather than elected, or is loaded with administrators, or is organized in such a way as to be not truly representative of the majority of the faculty.[5] Furthermore, these faculty bodies, as imperfect as they may be in structure, are also quite limited in their jurisdiction and authority and can only make recommendations to the administra-

[5]One favorite form of gerrymandering is to insist that each of the constituent schools of the university have the same number of representatives. Thus, the nursing school and the law school will have two representatives as well as the liberal arts college. The arts and sciences faculties, which are more likely to be liberal, are outvoted by the professional faculties, which are more likely to be conservative or uninterested and, indeed, to have less faculty members than do the arts and sciences school.

tion. It does no good for an administrator to say that he has never vetoed faculty senate recommendations. As long as the senate powers are purely advisory, it is difficult for the faculty members to take it altogether seriously.

The same criticisms can be leveled at the faculty committees. They are frequently appointed by the administration, composed in a way that does not accurately reflect faculty opinion, and safely controlled by the administration. Nor are their decisions and recommendations anything more than mildly consultative. With some notable exceptions, the faculty senates and faculty committees at Catholic colleges do not give the lay members of the teaching staff confidence that they are participating in the direction of the school or that they have any substantial control over their own destination as part of the college or university community. Nor are most faculty handbooks very impressive. They are frequently petty, detailed, and legalistic. Even though the new faculty handbooks represent considerable improvement over past efforts, they are still, it is to be feared, the kind of document that would frighten away a prospective recruit to the faculty rather than attract him to the school. One faculty member noted, "If only, when they sit down to put a handbook together, they'd remember that it is not necessary to adopt the tone that sounds like a cross between the Code of Canon Law and the Criminal Code of the United States. That tone might be all right for the constitutions of the religious order but it frightens the living daylights out of somebody who is thinking of coming here to teach."

There are a few Catholic schools where faculty participation is an accepted principle in theory and an honored custom in practice. Some outstanding smaller schools count many decades of this kind of participation, but there is no escaping the fact that in many schools, particularly some of the Jesuit schools, formal faculty participation is quite new and extremely inadequate.[6]

[6]In at least some schools we visited this lack of formal participation did not present a serious problem to faculty members because the informal participation seemed to be sufficient to their needs and demands. In such schools—and some of them are rather large and important—the challenge of the present moment is to institutionalize and rationalize faculty participation which previously had been effective, if informal. Nonetheless, these schools where informal participation made up for the absence of formal structures are a minority.

The reluctance on the part of many Catholic administrators to concede faculty participation in the decision-making process of the school can in part be attributed to fear that "the faculty wants to take over the school." Many of the older religious members of the faculty are especially skeptical of the ambitions of their younger lay colleagues. In one school, the complaint was frequently heard from the older religious members of the faculty that the president was selling them out to the laity. It was our impression that the vast majority of lay faculty did not want to take over the administration of the school but felt that effective and binding participation in the establishment of policy about curriculum requirements, grading, and admissions was a legitimate faculty prerogative and would not involve any invasion of the authority of the school administration. Admittedly, it is a difficult question to decide when faculty participation becomes so great that it hamstrings the growth of the schools. At one non-Catholic liberal arts college, the faculty power is so great that the school has stagnated for at least a quarter of a century, since, whatever their political positions are, faculties are extremely conservative when it comes to curricular and academic reform. But the Catholic colleges and universities have a long way to go before they will be generally faced with this danger. The present demands of faculties for participation in administrative decision-making are minimal. Yet, given the insecurity of the religious orders vis à vis the university and their fears of a slow deterioration of their control over the university's destiny, it is understandable that some people in positions of responsibility would fear the encroachments of faculty power.

The Catholic University of America is a relatively unique institution in its faculty participation. For example, the rector, the deans, and the departmental chairmen are elected by faculty members—the rector for a five-year term and the deans and the chairmen for two-year terms. While these elections have to be approved by the trustees, they nonetheless represent, at least by the standards of American universities, an extraordinarily democratic procedure. Apparently, The Catholic University's statutes in this matter are a reflection of European and particularly Roman schools.

It is often contended by administrations that the canonical regulations governing Catholic colleges make it impossible for them to delegate decision-making power to faculty committees. As one administrator pointed out to us, "Sure, we'd like to deal the faculty in, but canon law and the constitutions of our religious order simply won't let us do it." However, Poorman's doctoral dissertation on the subject establishes conclusively that such a claim is not a valid one. Indeed, one often suspects that certain Catholic administrators use canon law the same way they use the local chancery office—as a mysterious bogey man on whom to blame decisions that are unpopular with the lay faculty. In some instances the reluctance to admit the faculty to participation and partnership may stem from the fact that administrators are insecure in their own positions, have not been trained for administration, and are afraid that they are not competent at it. In such situations of fear and hesitatancy, the administrators do not want people whom they suspect are more competent to be sitting in judgment of their activities. While such fears and insecurities are understandable, it nevertheless remains true that the biggest single complaint we hear from faculty members is the absence of adequate channels for faculty participation.

It does not seem to us that greater faculty democracy is the answer to academic improvement in the Catholic colleges. On the contrary, faculty democracy and faculty citizenship are much more likely to be a consequence of rather than an antecedent to academic improvement. Those writers who feel that greater faculty control is a solution to the present dilemmas of Catholic higher education would do well to examine the impact of powerful faculty influence at other American universities, where the faculty acts as a major veto group on educational reform and innovation. Some friendly critics outside the Catholic system have suggested that, while there certainly must be more democracy and faculty citizenship in Catholic colleges, it would be a mistake for the Catholic schools to blindly imitate the procedures at non-Catholic schools.

COMPENSATION

There have been major and dramatic improvements in faculty

salaries at Catholic colleges and universities in recent years. While not all Catholic colleges make reports to the annual AAUP census of faculty salaries, fifteen of the schools that we visited did make such reports. Of these fifteen, in 1955 one school's rank was B+, nine ranked C, and five ranked D. In 1966, seventeen Catholic schools of the thirty we visited reported their salary structure to the AAUP. Of these seventeen, two ranked at the E level, four scored D, eight scored C, and three scored B. While such salary scales would hardly indicate that Catholic faculty members are being exorbitantly paid, they do, nonetheless, indicate that the salary of Catholic faculty members is approaching the average for American professors. An investigation of the salaries at various levels indicates that this trend is a strong one. Thus, the junior members of Catholic faculties are likely to receive compensation at the A or B norm, while at the higher levels of associate and full professor compensation slips to C and D. This lag in compensation between the assistant and full professor ranks could be found at many major American institutions of higher learning five to ten years ago, and the present situation at the Catholic schools is simply one more manifestation of the "catching up" phenomenon that has been typical of Catholic higher education for most of its existence. It is also worth noting that while junior professors may well be worth the A or B rank salaries that they are receiving, a good number of the senior faculty could not command this kind of salary in the open market. Indeed, as some of the Catholic schools begin paying A and B rank salaries for the senior men, there will be a period of time when they are paying some faculty members more than they are worth, in terms of the marketplace.

To say that salary levels have improved and that there is less dissatisfaction than we would have expected about compensation does not mean that all is well in the salary scales of Catholic colleges. There are still some faculty members who are severely underpaid, and while uniformity and rationality of payment have notably improved, there is still room for progress. Summer and night school employment is often necessary. At some schools— and not all of them unimportant ones—moonlighting is the rule and not the exception, and a whole infrastructure of academic employment has grown up. Thus, faculty members are able to maintain a fairly comfortable standard of living only by editing textbooks, teaching at night in community colleges, and engaging in wholesale consultation and research outside the college or university environment. Some of the consulting and textbook writing is legitimate activity for an academician, but much of what goes on is ugly and degrading and leads to a deterioration of morale and academic productivity among faculty members. In some instances the administration's behavior in this area is hypocritical. University statutes forbid moonlighting without permission, and permission is given with a show of reluctance and disapproval that is often humiliating to the faculty member. Yet, the administration justifies its salary schedule by observing that faculty members are able to improve their income by outside work. Administrators also argue that since outside work is often restricted to a given metropolitan area, it will increase the "hold" that a school has on its faculty members.

The course loads of Catholic faculty have been improving rapidly. In the smaller schools, while technically and theoretically the load may be fifteen course hours, for all practical purposes most of the lay faculty teach only twelve. At the major universities, while the load may still in theory be twelve, it is in practice down to nine, and for some faculty members engaged in research it has gone down to six. The tendency toward nine class hours of teaching seems to be very strong in almost all Catholic colleges because this is the only way the young faculty can be attracted. The fate of the religious faculty, as we will note in a later section, is often not nearly so happy.

Despite the improvement in course load, there are still many Catholic faculty members who report that the pressure of committee meetings, night schools, and summer school teaching give them little time for scholarly activity beyond the classroom, much less for research of their own. For some faculty, this is an excuse for not doing research that they would not do in any case. But it seems to us that a nine-hour maximum course load and free summers are generally imperative for any kind of scholarly activity.

Fringe benefits at Catholic colleges tend to be rather good, or at least adequate. Most schools have pension and insurance programs of the standard TIAA and CREF variety, although a few schools still have programs in which a faculty member has no vested right for a number of years under the pretext that this is a way of maintaining "faculty loyalty." While the pension-insurance programs are generally adequate, they are often not quite as good as the administrators think they are, especially in comparison with other schools that are rapidly improving their benefits. Some Catholic college administrators thought that once a pension-insurance program was set up it was supposed to persist in its given form for the next millenium and were shocked when the AAUP began to agitate for improvement in the program. We had the impression that some administrators felt that once they had adjusted faculty salaries and had improved fringe benefits they could consider their faculty compensation problem to be "solved." As one administrator complained, "We gave them everything they wanted three years ago and thought we'd have them out of our hair and now they're back wanting more." The administrator can bet on it, the faculty will continue to want "more."

On many of the campuses we visited, the question of tuition remission for faculty wives and children was a vigorously debated issue. Some schools make no such provision; others provide for partial remission for faculty children at the given school; still others grant full remission for children and wives at their own schools; others have arrangements with neighboring schools so that the sons of faculty members of a women's school can go to a neighboring men's school and vice-versa. We would assume that Catholic colleges will eventually provide tuition for a college education of the offspring of all their faculty members. But in some quarters there is still considerable resistance to such trends.

Organized sabbatical policies are a rarity in Catholic academia, and in some of the places where sabbatical leaves are granted, they are not a matter of right, but each application must be considered and approved by administrative decision. Some faculty members feel that one reason for the reluctance to grant sabbaticals is the suspicion that the year of free time will be used to "goof off." There may be an element of truth in this, but there also may be a misunderstanding of the purpose of the sabbatical—to improve the teaching skills of a faculty member or to grant him the time for research activity. Some religious superiors who think that it would be "almost immoral" to give their faculty members a "year off" may be unprepared to accept the idea that a man can be trusted to use a year of freedom in a constructive and creative way. As one administrator remarked, "We were going to give Joe a sabbatical, but we were afraid that if he had the year off he'd get a lot of articles written and then, having used our time and money to get the articles written, he'd leave us and we would have nothing to show for the year we gave him." A rational sabbatical policy is an inevitable development in Catholic higher education. It would be much better if it were granted graciously than if it were a result of conflict.

Finally, the faculties of Catholic colleges and universities are, like most faculty members, given to complaining about the poor office facilities and the lack of adequate meeting places and recreational facilities for faculty members. Here, again, there is some progress being made. At least three of the Catholic schools we visited—all of them notably improving schools—had brand new and impressive faculty office facilities.

In summary, the compensation and working conditions of Catholic faculty members seem to be considerably better than they were as recently as half a decade ago and they seem to be rapidly improving. We heard much less complaint about these matters than we expected to hear. There is still dissatisfaction and room for further improvement, but the more realistic and moderately optimistic Catholic faculty members expect the existing improvement to continue. In this area, at least, the Catholic colleges are catching up very rapidly.

Of the thirty Catholic colleges we visited, twenty-nine had established policies for promotion and tenure. (The thirtieth school is an experimental and highly innovative institution where tenure and promotion—and indeed all faculty ranks and titles—were abandoned on very progressive rather than conservative grounds.) Recommendations for promotion and tenure generally pass through faculty committees of varying degrees of independence and authority, though the president still makes the final decision on promotion and tenure. In a good number of colleges, the president's approval of a decision of the committee is considerably more than just routine procedure. Many of the lay faculty contend that there is a double standard of promotion, with one existing for the religious faculty and another for the lay faculty. At other schools, promotion and tenure seem to be routine awards for length of service, with little or no other requirements specified or taken seriously.

At some major universities now formalizing serious requirements for promotion and tenure, the tenure policies of the past are a considerable embarrassment, especially when seeking grants from government or private funding agencies. The sociology department, for example, with a number of full professors who have published nothing in their careers, is rather unlikely to convince a funding agency that it is qualified for a training grant.

Firm and professional standards for promotion are emerging at some of the major Catholic universities, though such standards are not always rigorously enforced and, on occasion, the faculty objects violently when they are enforced. Erratic enforcement of standards is probably even a worse mistake than not having standards. If scholarly productivity is to be required as a prerequisite for promotion, then it should be a prerequisite for promotion for everyone—including critics of the school and including religious members of the faculty.

Occasionally, we observed situations where administrative decision-makers used promotion and tenure as a means of rewarding the "loyal" and punishing the "disloyal." Only in rare instances did we suspect that someone was discharged because he was "disloyal"; but we did have the impression that some administrators are not above "making him wait a year" for promotion on grounds that have precious little to do with professional standards and a lot to do with personal animosity and resentment. "Look," said one faculty member to us, "they punish members of their own community whom they think are disloyal by transferring them out of here. There's no reason to think that they're not going to use the same tactics on us." This faculty member could not cite any example of the tactics being used, but the point is not so much that they were used but that his fear that they might be used was very real indeed.

FACULTY MORALE

Intellectuals are notoriously morose characters, and the academician who has no complaints about his institution has probably just emerged from electroshock therapy. If, indeed, a college administrator hears no complaints from the highly trained band of prima donnas who have been assembled to push his school forward on a journey toward excellence, he should be deeply upset because either the faculty is planning to decamp, or the Day of the Revolution is nigh. Especially in the present transitional era within the American Church and within American higher education, ferment, friction, and conflict ought to be taken to be routine. But, as a religious faculty member pointed out, "While ferment and conflict are the expected thing in academia, they're not expected at all within a religious community where, at least in theory, we're supposed to have harmony and peace. Of course, this harmony and peace is on the outside and may often cover up serious troubles on the inside, but at least we're civil with each other. Thus, a lot of our men simply don't know what to make of all the criticism and violent discussion we have around this campus."

Furthermore, it is our impression that the basic problems in faculty-administration relationships are not different at Catholic universities from other universities. The faculty complaints we heard at some of the major non-Catholic schools had a remarkable similarity to those we heard within the hallowed walls of Catholic academia. Both in the Catholic and non-Catholic schools, we discovered that the better the school, the more likely one was to hear faculty complaints—so that, at least from one point of view, faculty dissatisfaction could be interpreted as a measure of institutional improvement. (The two best Catholic colleges we visited combined very high morale and great confidence in the administration among the faculty members with extremely articulate criticism.) Thus, criticism and high morale, far from being mutually exclusive, seem to be quite compatible.

Yet, with all these preliminary qualifications, we are still compelled to note that morale in most of the Catholic schools we visited is poor. There are some very notable and impressive exceptions—either because the school has just received a new and very promising president or because the long-term improvement pattern of the school inspires great confidence in the faculty, but the exceptions are very clearly exceptions.

As far as we could determine, the principal reason for the rather low state of faculty morale is the basic distrust, on the part of the lay faculty, of the religious order that administers the school. Communications between the religious administrators and the lay faculty are frequently very bad, and often the poor communication is not merely the result of misunderstanding but the product of a basic difference of opinion about the nature of the university in general or of a particular academic discipline. (As we shall note later, there are some Catholic deans who have concepts of what sociology is that are quite at variance with the concepts of the sociologists about their own discipline.) Catholic faculty members do not think that the administrators trust them or are willing to accept them as partners in the academic enterprise, and on their part, the faculty have precious little confidence in the administrative competence or leadership ability of the administrators. They often feel—and in our judgment quite correctly—that those who have been appointed to administrative positions have received their posts either because of the internal politics of the religious order or because they are considered "safe" by their religious superiors and not because they understand in the slightest what a university is or how academic excellence is achieved. As a matter of fact, after we had visited a number of Catholic schools, we approached each new institution with the assumption that the faculty had no confidence in the leadership of the administration until the contrary of the assumption was proved. Lamentably, the assumption was proved wrong only in a limited number of instances. "In the final analysis," we were told by a lay faculty member, "they own the school and it's theirs to run the way they want. They may give us some power and privileges but it still depends on their ownership and if we don't like it, the only alternative is for us to leave and go someplace else. We may cover this up by all sorts of polite conventions, but it still is inescapable."

In addition, some of the faculty members, especially the older ones, feel they are "stuck in Catholic higher education." Their professional colleagues in other schools look down upon them as being second rate, and the clergy or religious who administer the school are not willing to accept them in full partnership. While neither of these assumptions may be true, it is nonetheless easy for the academician to feel sorry for himself. Some of the lay faculty become "trouble makers." And on a few occasions, such troublemakers are professional malcontents.

But others of the troublemakers—especially the young idealists among the new professors—are genuinely interested in the welfare of the college and make trouble for the administration only because they think in the long run such trouble will be a distinct help to the institution. Some of them obviously have the academic credentials and the professional skills that would enable them to be at much better universities and when pressed for the reason, admit with some embarrassment, "Sure, I could have gone to Yale, but Yale doesn't need me and X does. It may be silly of me, but I want to make a contribution to someplace where my contribution will be really important." But then he added, "When I get to the idea that this place isn't really interested in the kind of contribution I can make toward improving it, then I'll get out of here as quickly as I possibly can." The particular institution the young man is from is not likely to make that mistake. Nonetheless, it is appallingly true that the average Catholic college administrator seems to be unaware of the latent idealism found among many of the instructors and junior assistant professors just recently recruited into the faculties. Admittedly, this idealism is sometimes hard to discover beneath the veneer of mobility and professionalism—at least in part because to some extent the young people feel awkward about their idealism. Nonetheless, the idealism is surely there, and for the administrators to continue to be unaware of it would be a disastrous mistake.

Despite the idealism found not only among the junior faculty but throughout the entire range of faculty members in Catholic schools, bitterness and frustration continue to be a serious problem. Those who, for one reason or another, cannot leave feel trapped, and those who can leave will do so as quickly as they possibly can, especially when the collapse of confidence in the administration becomes complete. While, at some of the schools we visited, we thought that confidence in administration was strong and growing rapidly, we would be less than honest if we did not report that in several schools we felt that the confidence was deteriorating to such a point that mass exodus in the very near future was highly probable.

RELIGIOUS FACULTY

As we indicated before, the problem of the religious faculty is in many ways more serious than that of the lay faculty for, while the lay faculty may come and go, the religious faculty is clearly the core of most of the Catholic institutions of higher education, and a collapse of morale or a loss of nerve in this core could well signal the effective demise of the school.

There are a number of reasons, it seems to us, for the low morale of the religious faculty:

1. The religious community is of declining importance in the school. While it still may be the inner core, it no longer controls all administrative offices, all the departmental chairmanships, and no longer can view the school simply as a reflection of itself. While this may be viewed, and quite legitimately, as an improvement for the institution, it also can create serious problems for the self-image of the religious on the faculty, especially the older religious.

2. The religious orders themselves are going through severe internal strains and "identity crises" in the current renewal within the Church. It is no longer clear to everybody exactly what a religious order is or what it ought to be doing. A combination of this transition and the declining importance of the religious faculty of the college has led many religious to ask themselves whether they ought to be in the higher education business at all—a question we heard repeated with great frequency during our survey. One young priest who was the only member of the "new breed" in the religious community of a small liberal arts college commented, "If twenty years at this place makes me as stuffy and narrow-minded as my older colleagues I want to get out now."

3. Many religious, both young and old, are going through a personal identity crisis in which the meaning of their religious vocation in a changing world and changing Church is very much in doubt. This identity crisis seems to be especially difficult for the younger religious and those with professional training in the secular graduate schools. There can be

no denying that the strain has been very great for many of these young people, and at least some of them have decided that although they are still Catholics, their religious and priestly vocations seem quite irrelevant in the modern world.[7]

4. Many of the older religious faculty see everything they stood for in Catholic higher education going down the drain; the implication of much of the renewal of the Vatican Council and the modernization of Catholic higher education is that the old forms were a mistake. It is difficult to accept the fact that most of your life has been dedicated to that which is now considered a mistake. A religious faculty member at a major university commented to us somewhat wistfully, "This was really a marvelous place in the days before the war. It was small, most everybody knew everybody else, we had great relationships with the students, everything was warm and friendly, pretty much like a family. Now, all we've got here is a great big faculty for turning out degrees."

5. The younger members of the faculty, on the other hand, see the utter frustrations of trying to do what they take it the Vatican Council wants the Church to do in the face of almost insurmountable opposition from older faculty members who simply refuse to accept the post-Vatican renewal.[8]

6. Those in between—those who are neither new breed nor old breed but, like the senior reporter in this survey, lamentably half-breed—see time running out on them. Especially those who were long marked as liberals, though they now feel quite conservative in comparison with their younger confreres, and who felt that the Vatican Council was the legitimation of all they stood for, now wonder if the implementation of the Council is going to reach the grass roots while they are still alive. These members of the half-breed who have had their hopes frustrated so many times before are in many instances not prepared to see it happen once again. Indeed, they are often the most articulate of the critics and

[7]The senior researcher in the present study could not be in more complete disagreement with these younger colleagues of his. Indeed, he suspects that their feelings of irrelevancy are a result of their subscribing to intellectualist fads as well as succumbing to the intellectual temptation of self-pity. As a matter of fact, it seems to him that there have been few times in the course of Christian history when the priesthood could claim to be more relevant.

[8]We were personally quite shocked by the resistance of some of the older religious members of the faculty to even the most minor changes recommended by the Vatican Council, particularly in matters of the Church's liturgy. We found this inflexible opposition to change especially shocking in the religious order which has historically claimed special loyalty to the decisions of the central authority in the Church.

the most vigorous of the rebels against what they take to be the establishment within their religious order.

7. Many of the faculty of all ages are dissatisfied with their involvement in what they take to be pastoral work—that is to say, counseling and other priestly or religious activities with young people. To the younger faculty members with their high professional standards, pastoral work with the students is a major dilemma. They enjoy it very much but are afraid that it interferes with their vocation of scholarship. For older faculty members, this sort of pastoral responsibility is something that they think they do not have the vigor and enthusiasm left to sustain. For yet other priests or religious of whatever age, it has become clear that their main attraction to the priestly life or the religious life was the hope of dealing with people, and their academic and administrative responsibilities deprive them of much opportunity for this sort of contact. One brilliant young priest-scholar said to us, "I want to help the kids who come to see me and I also want to do my research. I find the only way I can do the research is to take the telephone off the hook, but it's pretty hard to live with your conscience when you do something like that."

The whole question of the role of a priest or a religious on a Catholic campus needs to be examined. Our own inclination is to think that once a priest or religious loses his contact with young people it is practically impossible for him to reestablish it once again, but we also have grave suspicions about the celibate scholar who has isolated himself from the human race and produces his research work in the splendid loneliness of an academic ivory tower completely undisturbed by human problems and human love.

8. The decline of religious vocations simply reaffirms what many of the religious faculty have been suspecting—that they no longer have the respect and admiration of their students. This suspicion is quite correct. To be a "Jesuit," for example, is no longer to automatically guarantee the affection and respect of students. Quite the contrary, at least in some institutions, it is enough to automatically guarantee the distrust and suspicion of students. Even those religious faculty members who can personally live with this sort of thing find themselves quite upset that their religious order has so failed in its purpose as to lose the confidence, respect, and admiration of those young people to whose education the members of the order have dedicated their lives.

9. There also is, at least among some religious faculty members, a feeling that they are professionally inferior to the members of the lay faculty as well as increasingly inferior in power, since the lay faculty often has more influence with the administration than do the clerical confreres

of the administrators. We would be inclined to agree with David Riesman's comment that in many, if not most, Catholic colleges the very best of the scholars are still the religious and priests.[9] Nonetheless, it would also seem to us that the average lay faculty member may well be more professionally competent than the average religious faculty member. This is a difficult thing for a member of a religious order to admit, and even more difficult when he knows that both the laymen on the faculty and the students also feel that he is professionally inferior to a lay faculty member.

10. Religious faculty members are also likely to be overworked. It has not dawned on a good number of religious superiors and college administrators that to send a young man to, let us say, Harvard for his academic training is largely a waste of time if upon return he must teach twelve hours of class during the regular year as well as in summer session, hear confessions and say Mass on the weekend, moderate a sodality, prefect a corridor of a residence hall, give nuns' retreats, teach a special course for a contemplative community, and serve as assistant sexton in the college chapel. This is, of course, an angry caricature. But few things on the study made us more angry than the absurd impositions made on the good will and obedience of members of the religious faculty. It may take a long time for American Catholicism to understand that, although a good man can do one job well, when he is saddled with two or three or five he is likely to do all of them poorly. The burdening of talented people with multiple responsibility is a form of economy which is inexcusably wasteful.

We know of one particular school where virtually all the religious faculty with the single exception of the college president must do weekend work in adjoining parishes, and the "adjoining parishes" are sometimes 150 miles away. One faculty member at this school must leave early Saturday morning to hear confessions all Saturday afternoon and evening in a parish, say two Masses on Sunday, help with counting the money, and then begin his journey back to school late Sunday afternoon, get back well into the small hours of Monday morning, and grab a few hours of sleep in order to be fresh and bright for his first class on Monday morning.

11. The religious faculty member is not particularly confident that his community will protect him from oppression by outside authorities. While interference in the administrative affairs of the college is relatively rare, it is nonetheless true that one nun was exiled for several years from a college at the request of a local chancery office which objected to Salinger's *Catcher in the Rye* being on a reading list. (This despite the

[9]Personal communication.

fact that almost every American young person has read the book by the time he or she has graduated from high school.) Indeed, the failure of the Jesuits to protect some of their distinguished scholars such as John Courtney Murray, Joseph Fichter, or Albert S. Foley hardly brings credit to that community.[10]

12. The religious faculty member knows he has no rights vis á vis his administrators. Even though he may be promoted, he certainly has no tenure in his department and can be removed or sent to a high school half-way across the country without ever being consulted. Of course he can also be appointed to a department without the chairman of the department being consulted. Thus, a lay chairman of an academic department can never be sure when the provincial of the religious order that administers the school is going to remove one of the members of the department or indeed assign another man to the department without the chairman being given any right to examine the man's credentials. We know of one religious with a Ph.D. from a prominent graduate school who wrote asking for employment to the departmental chairman of the university to which he would surely be assigned. The chairman was only too happy to have this young man since his credentials were admirable. The correspondence was a bit of a game because both knew that the man was going to be assigned to the department in any case, but at least the young priest could feel that he received his appointment on his own merit and not simply because his provincial assigned him to the department.

13. Finally, there is the phenomenon of early retirement of a religious with adequate or excellent academic training who never produces anything in the way of scholarship after his doctoral dissertation. Several reasons for this widespread phenomenon have been advanced. First of all, there is the censorship barrier. Many religious orders assume the right to judge not only whether a given piece of work is opposed to faith or morals but also whether it is prudent or wise to publish it. This gives the censor extremely broad powers if he wishes to use them and, at least in some provinces of certain religious orders, this power has been used in an indiscriminate and destructive fashion. Thus, a social scientist has had five consecutive scholarly volumes banned by his censor merely on the grounds that their publication was imprudent. It does not take

[10]One very distinguished Jesuit administrator has taken issue with this statement by arguing that Jesuits have given tremendous assistance and encouragement to their scholars in the physical and biological sciences. Unquestionably they have, but it is no particular virtue to give support to those for whom support requires little in the way of courage. It is precisely those scholars who are under strong and unfair pressure from outside the religious order who, if the religious orders mean anything at all, have the strongest claim on support and protection.

very many such instances to dissuade scholarship. Second, we have been informed that within the closely knit familial life of the religious order there are strong but subtle pressures toward conforming to a general level of mediocrity, and the priest or religious—especially the young one who "singularizes" himself by impressive scholarly effort—is viewed with some suspicion and distrust by the older members of the community and by his religious superiors. There is always the fear that scholarly success will give rise to "pride" in the young religious, and this is a vice that his superiors deem must be avoided at all costs. Unfortunately, in the minds of many religious superiors, pride and self-respect seem to mean the same thing. Further, the responsibilities with which the religious faculty members are saddled frequently makes it impossible for them to squeeze in any time for scholarly activity. Finally, in many instances there is no motivation for a religious to engage in scholarship. As one religious put it to us, "We don't even have economic motivation to produce; our lay colleagues have to do something respectable if they're going to be promoted, if their careers are going to be successful, if they are going to be able to support their wives and family in any dignified fashion. But no matter what we do, our all-providing mother will take care of our every need. We had tenure on the day we took solemn vows."

In the absence of external motivation for scholarship such as a lay faculty member has, it would appear that the religious faculty member must be guided to scholarship by very powerful internalized norms. We would suggest that these norms probably ought to be developed at the time of the formation of the religious, especially during the novitiate. It seems to us that at the present time the spiritual training undertaken during the novitiate places little emphasis on professional respectability or on the standards of academic scholarship. It is then imperative for those orders that intend to engage in scholarly works to view such professional training as an integral part of the development of the young religious.

Certain qualifications need to be added to the comments made in the previous paragraphs. Many religious scholars have high morale. Some orders seem to be permeated by much more optimism than others. And, indeed, within given religious orders there are some provinces with much higher morale than others. Second, there are some colleges where the spirit of the religious faculty is considerably higher than in other schools. Third, some individual religious have been able to maintain excellent morale and academic orientation in the midst of almost impossible conditions.

Thus, there are still a good many outstanding and productive research scholars among members of the religious communities. Nevertheless, we can only comment that we found the condition of the religious members of the Catholic colleges and universities frighteningly bad, and we could not escape the conclusion that many religious orders are frustrating not only their own purposes but also the lives of their most talented members.

COMMENTS ON SPECIFIC DEPARTMENTS

Theology

If there is any justification for Catholic higher education at all, it is that the Catholic schools provide a place where the Catholic theological tradition can be handed on and where relevant research in the tradition can take place. Because of a variety of circumstances, the Catholic theology departments are, with several exceptions, either the poorest or almost the poorest on the Catholic campus. Until relatively recently theology was viewed as a static discipline that could be taught by anyone who had had seminary training. It was merely necessary that certain principles be memorized and that certain answers be internalized. For example, a Catholic school faculty member might distribute at the beginning of each course a list of thirty-four propositions selected from various pre-Vatican conciliar documents and inform the students that if they memorize these statements they will know what Catholicism is. The theological revolution which went on in Europe before the Vatican Council and was legitimated and furthered by the Council has its impact on few American Catholic theology teachers except the youngest. Unfortunately for the Catholic colleges, many of their students are more aware of the new theological currents in the Church than are faculty members.

Since many schools have a requirement of a theology course every semester, or four or five courses during the four years of college, a large staff is needed in the theology department. Frequently the theology department is not staffed by the best people a religious community has to offer but by some of the poorest—in some instances, people who have been unsuccessful in either high school or parish work. While one generation of students was prepared to put up with and suffer through poor theology courses, the present generation clearly is not and the periodic outburst against the theology departments in Catholic student papers is a forceful sign of the student dissatisfaction.

At the present time, virtually all Catholic college administrators are willing to pay lip service to the need for upgrading theology departments, and a good number have taken concrete steps to do so. But, it will take many years before a sufficient number of theology instructors competent in modern developments can be trained to take their places in theology departments on the Catholic campuses. In addition, the graduate schools of theology that will make a distinctively American contribution to Catholic theology as well as train the theology instructors of the future are virtually invisible on the American Catholic scene. Only one graduate department of theology has now achieved any sort of respectability. The chairman of another theology department, who has been given carte blanche by his president to spend as much money and hire as many people as needed to construct a good department confided to us that, even with this almost limitless resource at his disposal, it would still take him five years to build an adequate department. It is to be feared that other schools will have even more serious difficulty in bringing their theology courses into line with the renewal of the Second Vatican Council, to say nothing of the needs and demands of their students. While there is general awareness of the problems of theology departments, there does not seem to be enough vigorous concern on the part of Catholic college administrators with what surely must be their most serious problem.

Philosophy

For a good number of years, philosophy was at the very core of the curriculum of the so-called "liberal" or "humanities" education in Catholic colleges and particularly the Jesuit schools. Thus, forty-four hours of theology and philosophy with twenty-eight of these hours in philosophy was by no means unheard of in some Jesuit institutions until recently. This "philosophy" was in many cases merely textbook translations of what was alleged to be

Aristotelian-Thomistic philosophy. Thus, in courses on "ethics," "natural theology," "metaphysics," and "rational psychology," the Catholic college student was expected to learn (i.e., memorize) a Catholic philosophy of life. This dry, ritualistic, and often stagnant process was justified on the grounds that it was at the core of an "integrated," organic view of life. In reality, many of the classes were not nearly as bad as they might seem because imaginative instructors were able to stimulate the students to constructive and vigorous thought of their own. Unfortunately, what occurred in these courses, at least formally, had precious little to do with what contemporary scholars think of as philosophy and, many would allege, precious little to do with what either St. Thomas Aquinas or Aristotle meant by philosophy. If philosophy is defined as the search for meaning and truth, one scarcely does philosophy when one presents truth and meaning already defined and circumscribed.

Philosophy, of course, has fallen rapidly from eminence within Catholic higher education, and philosophy and theology requirements are now being substantially reduced. Furthermore, younger philosophy faculty members are much more inclined to a historical or an eclectic approach to questions concerning the ultimate being than to repetition of a static version of Aristotelianism or scholasticism. Again, it seems that practice is ahead of theory. In a good number of the larger Catholic universities, the old course titles are still used, but the academic approach to "rational psychology" or "ethics" is vastly different from the traditional scholastic approach. (It should be noted that "traditional scholasticism" is the scholasticism of the philosophy manuals and not the philosophy of the scholastics of the Middle Ages.) In some Catholic philosophy departments, the historical or eclectic approach to philosophical questions now rules supreme with the departmental chairmen being committed officially to such an approach. In other departments latent and occasional open warfare rages between the "Thomists" and the "historicists" (sometimes called existentialists). We could find few instances where the academic freedom of the antischolastics had been infringed, though in one or two schools there were rumors of anti-Thomists who had left because the departmental chairman had made life unpleasant for them. At least in one school we visited, however, there was a major and open conflict between those who favored a historical approach to philosophy instruction and those who favored a more sophisticated version of the traditional teaching of scholastic principles. In this department it was argued that, at least in ethics, psychology, and natural theology, it could be required that a faculty member teach certain stipulated conclusions— e.g., free will, the existence of God, and the immortality of the human soul. Lay faculty members who did not feel that these propositions could be rationally demonstrated beyond all doubt were not dismissed from the faculty but were not permitted to teach these particular courses. The religious members of the administration could not understand the problem because, as they observed, "These things are true; why can't philosophers teach them?" It is not our intention at the present time to enter into a long discussion of the possibility of a "Catholic philosophy," a problem that has agitated Catholic thinkers since the early Middle Ages. But it is our observation that modern academicians and students (including Catholic ones) do not think very highly of a philosophical system in which the answers have been stipulated before the inquiry begins. They would contend that simply because one believes in the existence of God, one is not committed necessarily to a philosophical system that argues for the possibility of the strictly rational demonstration of God's existence. Those Catholic school administrators who insist on keeping philosophy a slave of theology are doing grave harm to philosophical inquiry and to the healthy morale of their faculty and student body.

However, open conflict on this question has been relatively rare, and the traditional scholastics are grudgingly but increasingly giving way to newer trends in philosophy teaching. Time and natural evolution will resolve this question, and the only places where conflicts will emerge will be where one side or the other think it can gain an advantage by bringing the conflict out into the open. As part of the curious world in which we now live, a good number of Catholic administrators would much sooner hire a philosophical historian or an existentialist than they would someone whose specialty is Aristotle or St. Thomas, and this despite the fact that in certain European centers, especially Oxford, the careful study of Aristotle is an extremely popular form of philosophizing.[11]

Physical Sciences

Just as we had a general rule of thumb that the theology department would be nearly the worst in any Catholic college we visited (and we were rarely surprised), so we had a rule of thumb that the chemistry department would be one of the best. It is our impression that in general the physical sciences in Catholic colleges tend to be in much better shape than the social sciences. There are several reasons for this: First of all, professional accrediting agencies like the American Chemical Society have very rigid standards of accreditation to which a department must live up or find itself without any professional recognition. Second, while every man can expect to be his own philosopher or historian or social scientist, the average Catholic administrator knows precious little about chemistry and, hence, is not inclined to interfere in the administration of this department but to leave it to the professionals. Furthermore, the physical sciences are not considered to be nearly as "sensitive" as the humanities or the social sciences. Hence, they are less immediately connected with what might be taken to be religious views of the nature of man and of reality. Finally, research moneys are much more likely to be available in the physical sciences, and especially in chemistry, than other disciplines, so it is easier to attract young Ph.D.'s, since they can be paid better salaries and promised shorter teaching loads. Thus, the Catholic colleges, which could be expected to have achieved some sort of excellence in those things most directly connected with religion and the nature of man, have actually done much better in areas that are somewhat more remotely connected with

[11]Professor Ernin McMullin of the University of Notre Dame has recently prepared a mimeographed report on *Philosophy of the U.S. Catholic College, A Survey*, an interesting and extremely helpful analysis of the present state of Catholic philosophy departments. Professor McMullin's most significant comment is that even though there is some considerable shift away from strictly orthodox Thomism in the Catholic philosophy departments, this shift is not necessarily in the direction of the characteristically American "analytical" approach to philosophy found in most non-Catholic universities and colleges.

human life. Some of the best Catholic college administrators we encountered were men who had been chairman of one or the other of the science departments. We also were inclined to think that in many instances those whose background was in philosophy or theology were considerably less adequate as administrators. There is here more than just a little bit of paradox.

Social Sciences

The picture of most Catholic social science offerings, and particularly sociology departments, can only be said to be dismal. While Catholic psychologists, anthropologists, and sociologists have long since abandoned the idea that there was a specific sociology different from the kind practiced in other universities, there are some Catholic administrators who have not been disabused of this notion. The residue of past suspicion of social science continues to have its impact on a good number of Catholic social science departments. Psychology departments have done somewhat better, if only because the clinical psychology programs have proved quite successful and generally quite uncontroversial, but sociology is still considered to be a "sensitive" discipline in which one's values can be expected to have some impact on one's research or classroom teaching. Indeed, at one Catholic university every potential candidate for the sociology department is asked whether he believes in values, whether he thinks values can influence his teaching, and whether he has read the Papal Social Encyclicals. There are some Catholic sociology departments that are adequate and one or two that are moving toward a fair amount of excellence. But we could not escape the conclusion that Catholic sociology departments were in sad shape and were having a terribly difficult time recruiting new faculty members, especially since the young Catholics in graduate school who are studying sociology are all too aware of the persistent suspicion of sociology and are strongly disinclined to expose themselves to this suspicion.

On the other hand, it is still fair to say that while suspicion of sociology, the notion that it is a "sensitive" or "value" discipline still persists, this suspicion is on the wane, and a very considerable number of Catholic schools have exorcised it completely. It will, however, take some number of years before the evil effects of such misguided notions are no longer felt.[12]

SUMMARY

To summarize this lengthy chapter, we have discovered much progress in faculty status in Catholic colleges and universities, indeed, in some instances, more progress than we expected to find. In such areas as salary, teaching load, and classroom and personal freedom we concluded that progress in the Catholic schools, though far from perfect, has been reasonably adequate. There has also been some progress in developing faculty participation, professional standards, and faculty research competence, although the progress here was frequently much less than satisfactory. Third, we felt that there had been all too little progress in establishing relationships of trust and confidence between administration and faculty in Catholic colleges, and that this is a problem of extremely high priority for the Catholic schools. Fourth, we observed that the morale of the religious faculties tended to be very poor and that, in the absence of a dramatic improvement, the Catholic colleges could be said to be in dire straits. Finally, while we advocated certain changed attitudes with regard to the philosophy and the sociology departments, we thought that the major curricular problem on Catholic campuses was the inferior and extremely unsatisfactory state of the theology departments and that there is not sufficient awareness of this problem.

[12]The whole question of values and scientific research is, of course, by no means a completely settled one. In the judgment of many social science scholars, values may indeed play a role in choosing the subjects on which a scholar will focus his research interests and also on the policy recommendations that may be implicit in the way he reports his findings. It is difficult to see how one can be a human being and behave in any other fashion, but these value influences either precede or follow the research itself which, at least according to the most common opinion now, can and ought to be value free.

8

Administration

As was indicated in the last chapter, the relationship between Catholic colleges and faculty personnel is becoming increasingly professional. The demands of the marketplace have forced schools to abandon the modes of behavior of the religious community in dealing with lay faculty members. Relationships between faculty and school administrations still leave much to be desired, but even in the low improvement schools, there is a modicum of professionalization in faculty-administration relationships. However, the religious community still exercises considerable influence on the style and behavior of academic administrations, even in the rapidly improving schools. As we note in the next chapter, it has proven even more difficult to pry loose the supervision of student life from the grip of traditionalist religious orders. Thus, the administration of the Catholic colleges stands somewhere between the faculty and the students in the level of professionalism that can be observed.

It is clear why religious orders are reluctant to see the administration of the school function independently of the religious community. In their view, the religious order "owns" the school, and the administrators merely "run" it. If the administration were independent of the religious order, then those who "run" the school would presumably be independent of those who "own" it and could make decisions that would be unacceptable to the religious order or to the controlling groups within the order. As we noted previously, the single largest obstacle to a more rapid improvement in Catholic higher education is the reluctance of the religious communities to appoint creative and sophisticated people to key administrative positions. This reluctance permeates virtually every level of Catholic higher education. If administrative posts are filled by men or women whose values are derived from the community of professional colleagues rather than from the traditions of the religious order, then, it is feared, the school will not be true to the values of the religious order and there will be no point in the religious community's assuming financial responsibility for it.

Implicit in such an argument is the notion that there is a conflict between the best of the traditions of the religious order and the highest standards of American college and university administration. A good number of priests and nuns insist that there is no such opposition, but the fact remains that many religious superiors and not a few of the older members of the orders are firmly persuaded that there is a conflict and are, therefore, very eager to exercise veto power over the policy-making decisions of educational administrators.

The power of the religious order is often so strong as to "tune out" messages that may come from other evaluative groups. If a given judgment is made often enough within the religious community it may be taken as true even though to an outsider it is ludicrously false. Thus, if members of the order say often enough and with enough conviction that Father Y is a veritable financial wizard, then not only will the members of the religious order believe it is true, but Father Y himself will come to believe it, even though an outside observer might judge that Father Y's financial outlook is more suitable to 1936 than to 1966.[1] Similarly, if one hears it said often enough that Father Z is a great fund raiser and builder than one may come to believe it, even though an impartial observer would judge that the fund raising is badly mismanaged and that the buildings are either unwisely constructed or the money improperly spent. In the final analysis, the college administrator who is a religious can fall back on what he takes to be an unanswerable argument, "It's our school and we run it our way, and if you don't like the way we run it you can go somewhere else."

Catholic college administrators are often accused of paternalism, and the charge is a valid one in many instances. If one defines

---

[1]We were assured that one such financial wizard had vast experience in the business world before he came into the religious community. Further research indicated that this experience consisted of working in his father's delicatessen.

paternalism as a tendency of an educational administrator to control as many decisions as possible and to delegate as little responsibility as possible, then Catholic college administrators are paternalistic. If one defines paternalism as the mistaken notion that holding a rather high educational post makes one wise, then Catholic administrators surely tend to be paternalistic. If one defines paternalism as the temptation to arbitrary, eccentric, and, at times, vindictive modes of behavior, then Catholic administrators are surely paternalistic. But they are not the only ones. We found as much paternalism in the non-Catholic schools we visited. The most paternalistic institution we visited was not a Catholic school, but a very famous non-Catholic university in which, if the school were Catholic, open revolt would have occurred long since. At no Catholic school that we are aware of did the president personally determine the increment each year for every individual faculty member, solely on the basis of the extent to which the faculty member was assumed to have supported the president's policy. But at the non-Catholic school in question, composed of an extraordinarily illustrious faculty, this sort of behavior was taken for granted. Paternalism is merely tough-minded administration pushed a little bit too far, and since, in the present state of American society, no college is going to improve without tough-minded leadership, the temptation to paternalism is a given in higher educational administration. Catholic administrators are often tempted to envelop their paternalistic tendencies in the religious mystique, complete with quotations from the popes, canon law, and the gospel. But mystical rationalizations are by no means absent from the non-Catholic campus either, and the president who views a higher educational institution as a projection of his own personality is anything but a rarity in non-Catholic colleges. The Catholic colleges have one advantage in that the members of the religious community are in a much better position to make their complaints against tyranny felt at higher levels in the order, and that it is somewhat easier to pry loose an autocratic president from a Catholic school than it is from a non-Catholic university. The real problem in Catholic colleges and universities is not paternalism but incompetence, and not merely the incompetence which is inevitable in any large corporate bureaucracy where there are more problems than there are people who are able to solve them, but rather an incompetence that is magnified and emphasized by the peculiar nature of the relationship between a religious order and a school.

A Catholic president observes:

I doubt very much that in the future provincials and higher superiors will be allowed to choose less than dynamic administrators for their institutions. Provincials and other higher superiors will be forced, because of the tensions among faculty and students, to be more daring in their choice of administrators. I think it is safe to say that at least among the Jesuits we find more and more provincials who are familiar with universities and coming more frequently now from university ranks rather than from seminaries.

ADMINISTRATIVE OFFICERS

The result of such an orientation is that those appointed to administrative positions in many Catholic colleges and universities are often "amateurs." They are either religious with mediocre talents and little training or laity of the sort that would be content to work for people with mediocre talent and little training. The amateurish administration of many Catholic colleges and universities may be no worse than that found in many other American educational institutions. Furthermore, one of the reasons for the mediocrity of non-Catholic colleges is precisely the desire of the ruling clique, either the administration or the trustees, to preserve their schools from change and professionalization. What is unique to the Catholic situation is not the opposition to professionalization or the fear of loss of control, but the fact that the opposition and fear are concentrated in a highly visible and closely integrated structure—the religious order. For the administrators of Catholic colleges to obtain independence from some of the restraints imposed upon them by the religious communities is not so terribly different from the task of other administrators to free themselves from the restraints imposed upon them by less than progressive trustees. But the principal source of the amateurism in the administration of Catholic colleges seems to be the attitude of religious superiors and of substantial elements of the religious community toward the "Americanization" and professionalization of higher educational administration.

Such a statement should not be taken as an indictment of the religious orders, either in general or in particular. Most of the good administrators in Catholic colleges are members of religious communities, and easily the most articulate critics of administration are members of the religious community. As one extraordinarily competent priest put it to us, "The situation here is nobody's 'fault'; it's what happens when you spread yourself out so thin that the man in charge has to be an expert on four or five different kinds of human behavior. The provincial means well, but he simply doesn't know enough about how colleges operate, and he's got a hundred and one other worries in addition to the school. So it's not his fault; it's not anyone's fault. But unless we can do much better than we are doing now, we should get out of the business."

While there is as yet no definitive sociological study of the Catholic religious orders, it is clear that they are extraordinarily powerful reference groups for their members. The intimate and diffuse nature of the relationship among the members of the religious community creates a situation in which, for many of their members, the only reference group of any major importance is the religious order. Judgment passed on a given member of the order by people outside the order is not only irrelevant, it is not even heard. It does not much matter what outsiders think of the competence of a given administrator. If, by the standards of the religious community, he is a "good man," then there is no reason why he cannot be assigned to be a college president or, indeed, to hold any other office in the religious order. This is not to say that the religious orders are completely capricious and arbitrary in assigning people to responsible positions, though at times appointments do seem to be almost arbitrary. Generally speaking, the appointments go to "qualified" individuals, but the qualifications are those judged appropriate by the superiors in the religious community and are not necessarily the same as qualifications that would be judged appropriate by others. Often such qualifications would be deemed very inappropriate by others.

From the point of view of many religious superiors the ideal person to be a president, an academic vice-president, or a dean would be a man who gets along well with other members of the community, who is not likely to disturb the ecclesiastical authorities of the area, who can be expected to present a good image to well-to-do Catholics, who will take good care of the other members of the community working under him, and who will not risk serious financial problems for the order. Since these qualities are not all likely to coexist either with an innovative personality or with experience outside the religious order of how to run an American university, it is likely that the man who would make a good administrator from the point of view of the religious order would not make a good administrator from the point of view of the educational institution.

Somewhere between three-fifths and two-thirds of the college presidents we interviewed would fall into the category of being good administrators from the religious order's viewpoint but not from the educational institution's viewpoint. The proportion of lesser administrators who demonstrate professional competence would probably not be any higher. We would further estimate that of those presidents and lesser administrators who are professionally competent, about half were chosen deliberately for this reason, and the other half were chosen out of sheerest accident.

We met only one provincial in the course of the study, and that by mere accident. Unlike his colleagues in the religious order who were administrators of the college, he was distinctly unfriendly and suspicious, and made no pretense at hiding these reactions. He did not even know enough about college administration to realize that when there are visiting scholars around studying your institution, you should at least pretend to be friendly so that they don't know you are suspicious. Curiously enough, the school in question was one of the better schools that we visited, but the provincial apparently was not sure of that fact.

The good Catholic administrators are very good indeed. At least some of them could be college presidents even if they were working outside the Catholic educational system. The very best of the Catholic colleges are as competently administered as are most comparable American educational institutions, and there does not seem to be any necessary conflict between either Catholic affiliation of a college or ownership of the college by a religious order and efficient, intelligent, imaginative administration. The reason so many administrators are poor is that they were chosen during a period when the religious orders were struggling out of a traditional outlook and American Catholicism out of the immigrant ghetto. There are not enough really good higher educational administrators to go around either, but there are far more able Catholic administrators available than are being used.

One of the results of the way college administrators are chosen is that the men who are picked for the jobs are unhappy in them. A good college administrator should enjoy the use of power. If he does not find rewarding the obligations, responsibilities, and headaches—the "rat race" of educational administration—he does not belong in it. But, unfortunately, those who do enjoy the use of power and would find college administration thoroughly rewarding are precisely those people whom a religious community would judge to be too deviant. It is axiomatic in most religious orders that he who would enjoy the use of power should not be trusted with it. Thus, those more frequently chosen as college presidents and administrators are those who are "good religious," who have learned well the lesson of the novitiate that the use of power is an obstacle to holiness, and who will therefore be most likely to hate their job and to count the days until they can be released from it. Most of the Catholic college administrators to whom we spoke assured us that they did not like their role and could hardly wait until they got back into the classrooms again.

The fate of the typical Catholic administrator is, then, not a happy one. He has no particular training for his job (in some cases, he has not even been inside a classroom), he does not like his work, he senses that he is something less than competent at it, and he finds that the faculty—both religious and lay—do not respect him and that the students are unfriendly or contemptuous. He fears outside agencies (such as accrediting associations and the AAUP), he is worried about the financial status of the school, and he is so overwhelmed with the need to make all kinds of decisions (since he reserves most decisions to himself) that he has no time to plan for the future. Attempts at innovation that he may approve of are likely to be strongly resented by the older members of the community, and often he finds his regulation of the school efficiently supervised by a kitchen cabinet of such senior members who actually have more power than many of the formal officials of the institution. It is a thoroughly miserable job and, under the circumstances, one can hardly blame the administrator for wanting out of it as quickly as he can.

Two points need to be emphasized before we progress to more detailed comments. In the remainder of the chapter we will speak primarily about institutions that were administered with a relatively low level of efficiency. If we imagine the thirty Catholic institutions spread out on a continuum of efficiency, we would say that one-third are administered reasonably well (and some of this one-third, brilliantly), another third adequately (though in many cases barely adequately), and the final third so poorly as to raise serious doubts about their viability if there were not a seller's market in higher education. Most of what we will say in the remainder of this chapter will be true of the lower two-thirds, and especially of the lower half of the schools on the continuum. It is necessary to remind the reader that we are not speaking about all Catholic colleges and universities, that some schools will be free of all the strictures that we level against Catholic higher education, and that many of them will be free of at least some of the weaknesses that we note. Thus, what we will describe will be the most serious kinds of administrative problems in Catholic higher educational institutions.

Second, inefficiency is a relative concept. None of the schools that we visited were so bad that they were faced with loss of accreditation, though in two or three instances it seemed reasonably clear that the accrediting agencies had recommended major changes in the institution. Thus, while by the standards set by the best American colleges and universities, as well as by the improving schools within the Catholic system, many of the schools were run in an amateurish fashion, they were still not so incompetently administered that they were below the acceptable threshold for admission into the "club" of American higher education. In other words, if the administrators were pretty poor in many of the Catholic colleges, they were no worse than many a non-Catholic educator, at least some of whom we encountered in our visits to non-Catholic schools. It may not be reassuring to Catholic critics that "their guys are no worse than the other guys," but the bitter truth is that most corporate institutions are poorly administered and survive because of inertial force, or the expanding economy, or the hardihood of any corporate institution, no matter how degenerate, or perhaps because of a kind Providence that does not abandon all hope in the possibility of renewal.

TRUSTEES

In addition to the legal trustees who, in almost all instances, are members of the religious order and have nothing more than nominal power, virtually all Catholic educational institutions have advisory boards of trustees, regents, counselors, or whatever other fancy name is attached to an office that has neither power nor responsibility. These boards are generally composed of prominent Catholic business or professional men whose major function from the point of view of the university's administration is to aid in fund-raising ventures. While some of those assembled for such tasks know very little about education, others are men of considerable competence and skill who could be a tremendous asset to the institution if they were given a chance. We interviewed some of those men, who take seriously their responsibility to offer advice, and found them to be frustrated at the difficulties in communicating with the school administrators. While they are listened to politely and their suggestions are often agreed with, virtually nothing ever comes of these suggestions. Indeed, the attitude of many of the long-suffering trustees toward the religious educators is the attitude of a patient parent trying vainly to communicate some notion of the nature of the real world to stubborn, willful children who simply will not listen and will not look. Why laymen would continue to play such a role is an interesting question, though it must not be overlooked that membership on the board of trustees of a university is a fairly prestigious role and may impress those who do not realize how empty it is in the majority of instances. As one trustee put it, "They're nice men, but after awhile you get the impression that you're talking to a brick wall."

Of course, some Catholic universities make far more intelligent use of the abilities of their trustees, and at least two institutions have turned over legal control of fund-raising foundations to such boards of trustees. As one very wise and very experienced high-level lay administrator observed, "This was the best thing that ever happened to our school, because the order does not dare to come up with a president who cannot face these very competent business and professional men with the same skills in his field as they have in their field." From a sociological viewpoint, such an innovation creates for the university a new and powerful reference group whose values may be very different from that of the religious order.

The most far-seeing Catholic educators are aware that unless the renewal of the religious orders rather quickly places people in levels of provincial responsibility who do understand what it takes to run a decent American college or university, the only hope for improvement within the schools will be increasing power of various boards of trustees who are in some sense independent of the religious order. In the final chapter of this report we will discuss at some length these suggestions, which we heard at virtually every Catholic college we visited. At this point, we will content ourselves with observing that the mere fact that such innovations are so widely discussed is evidence that many people in Catholic higher education see quite clearly the problem of the relationship between the religious community and the college.

FINANCES

The authors of this report are not financial experts and do not propose to engage in a detailed commentary on the fiscal practices of Catholic colleges and universities, though we would note that a careful study of financial problems of Catholic higher education is long overdue. But, from the point of view of social researchers, we must observe that nowhere was the amateurism of Catholic higher education more evident than in their fiscal affairs. We could not escape the impression that in all but a few exceptions, the approach of the religious order to matters financial was colored by an abiding fear and distrust of the outside world. That the fear was justified by past financial mistakes—some of incredible proportions[2]—made by the religious orders is undeniable, but it does not seem to follow necessarily that the answer to past mistakes is to put the most conservative and careful members of the community in the financial offices of the colleges. Even in this day of affluence and increasing enrolment, it is possible, of course, for an American college to get itself into an impossible financial situation, but this possibility would not seem to justify the overriding fear of bankruptcy that obsesses many Catholic administrators. Debt is a horrendous evil. The administrator who can keep his school out of debt or notably reduce the debt is viewed in the religious community as being a great man. The fear of risk taking is bad enough in itself, but it becomes even worse when it is compounded with the proclivity to start expensive new projects—at least in part as public relation gimmicks—or to maintain expensive old projects on the pretext that an inescapable commitment has been made.

With financial control of the school in the hands of frightened amateurs, one can reasonably expect that administrators will frequently see the school's problems as being essentially financial. Time after time after time we were told that the biggest problem the school had to face was money. In some sense this is certainly true. Higher education is expensive and growing more expensive. The Catholic schools, with little in the way of endowments, must rely to a considerable extent on tuition to pay their expenses and financial shortages, which can become quite serious. But no higher educational institution has enough money—not even, we suspect, Mother Harvard. We would have been more impressed with the financial plight of the Catholic colleges, however, if we had seen greater evidence of a professional approach to the raising and budgeting of funds. But in perhaps half the schools we could not escape the feeling that the alumni and development officers were inefficient and that the institutions' relationships with govern-

[2]Millions upon millions of dollars have been lost in overeager expansion into certain branches of professional education. At least some of these losses occurred and continue to occur at schools, where we were assured that the major problem was financial. In reality, the major problem was that there was not enough courage to get out of what was clearly a disastrous adventure.

mental agencies and foundations were poor. People were assigned to positions of responsibility because they were acceptable to the religious order; they were safe religious or laymen who would not be viewed as a threat to the order's control of the university. But only rarely would people who fit these qualifications have the ingenuity, the alertness, the vigor, and the imagination to mount effective fund-raising campaigns. When a college president tells us that his financial problems are serious and his alumni secretary tells us that the school has a very poor list of the current addresses of alumni, we are inclined to believe that the basic problems of the institution are anything but financial.

The relationship of many of the Catholic colleges with the large private foundations were marvelous examples of amateurism combined with a peculiar blend of arrogance and defensiveness. The grants of the Ford Foundation, for example, to a number of Catholic institutions are proof both that the Ford Foundation is not anti-Catholic and that intelligent and vigorous proposals do gain a sympathetic hearing in the world of the large foundations. Yet, in several institutions, we were assured that Ford had turned down their proposals in a rather brusk and summary fashion. Usually, there was some dark hint that Ford executives were discriminating against Catholics. But our feeling at these schools was that the Ford decision was a wise one, that the school had very little to offer, and that, if its presentation to Ford was anything like the other aspects of its financial operation, it had presented its own rather poor case even more poorly than necessary. Again, it must be noted that fund raisers who combine intelligence, integrity, and drive are rare, but the difficulties of working in the atmosphere of fear and distrust that characterizes the financial operations of many Catholic institutions are probably obstacles to the procurement of good development personnel.

We do not intend to make this book a litany of horror stories; yet, one example of how a foundation grant was handled will illustrate the problem that arises when administrative and financial decisions are made by those who have little concern for evaluations outside of the reference group of the religious community. One rather small and not terribly impressive Catholic women's college with a reputation that exceeded its actual worth managed to obtain a foundation grant that was supposed to be matched by contributions from other sources. The purpose behind the program of which this grant was a part was to enable small schools to develop new financial resources not hitherto available to them. The administration of the school, instead of trying to find new sources of funds for its matching grants, proceeded to level an assessment on all the parishes where nuns from the religious order teach, a method of fund raising as traditional in the Catholic Church as it is objectionable to the pastors who feel that they must either provide funds or run the risk of losing some of the sisters who teach in their schools. The decision of the administrative officers of the school, whether consciously or not, directly frustrated the purpose the granting agency had in mind. It will be some time before this institution gets another grant from the foundation, and the foundation executives may be suspicious in the future of small liberal arts colleges run by orders of nuns. Those outside the college would consider the behavior of the administrators in question as being unethical, but in the strange never-never world in which this community of nuns lives the question of the ethics of their behavior did not even arise.

Let us affirm once again that we are not speaking of all Catholic colleges. There are enough financial operations which are intelligently administered, and enough fund-raising programs which border on the brilliant to show that there is no necessary conflict between Catholicism and intelligent educational administration, or even between ownership by a religious order and intelligent educational administration. The conflict is rather between the traditional notion of the relationship between the religious order and the school and intelligent administration.

THE LIBRARIES

One suspects that the faculty at Harvard may be satisfied with Widener Library, but, if they are, they may be the only college faculty in the country that is not complaining about the collection and facilities of their library. Thus, complaints from faculty and students about the inadequacies of libraries in Catholic colleges and universities were not particularly surprising. Nevertheless, it is surprising that the Catholic Church, which preserved written literature for a millenium or so through the Dark Ages, has not been able to inspire its higher educational institutions to strive for excellence in their libraries. Chemistry labs, football fields, gymnasia, dormitories, nursing buildings, administration offices— all seem to take preference to library construction and even greater preference to the improvement of library collections. During the year of our visit, the subject of libraries had become a very controversial one on Catholic campuses and most schools were either beginning construction of new libraries or making firm commitments about doing so in the near future. Such commitments have of course been encouraged by the fact that the federal government is now willing to invest money in library construction. But in only a few of the schools was the amount of the budget alloted for improvement of libraries close to, or in excess of the 5 per cent taken to be a rough rule of thumb of how much of the school's budget should go into its library collection. Even some of the very top schools had extraordinarily poor collections, and instructors were forced to arrange reading lists based either on paperbacks available in the college bookstore or in the collections of the nearby public library. One faculty member remarked to us, "The public library is a favorite place for me to meet my students. There they are getting the books they need for the course, and I'm there getting the books I need for my research." There were a few excellent libraries and some more very good ones, with the small women's schools often doing better not only proportionately, but in absolute number of books than much larger male or coeducational institutions. One of the poorest (economically) of the women's schools we visited had more books for its five hundred students than did a coeducational university in the region for its twenty-five hundred students, even though the coeducational institution was engaged in building a splended new library and the women's school had its collection in all sorts of odd corners around its small, cramped campus.

With the exceptions above noted, until very recently, libraries were not important in the judgment of Catholic higher educational administrators. They were not unimportant, of course, but there were other things that diverted the administrators' attention and funds.

The Catholic librarians we interviewed by and large seemed to be more competent than most other educational administrators and to have some professional training though, generally speaking, they were bitter and frustrated men. Many suggest that the reason their administrators were not interested in improving the libraries was that they rarely read anything anyhow. This is too harsh a judgment. The administrators are hardly opposed to good library facilities, but the mandate given them by their religious community for safe, conservative development of the college simply precludes the possibility of spending very much money on libraries. Some of the newer presidents of Catholic colleges feel acutely embarrassed by the library situation. As one of the best of them said to us, "I built a new library at the last college I was in, and before my six years are up here, I'm going to get a new library here, one way or another. I'm so ashamed of what we have now that I don't even have the courage to look at it when I walk by."

One question that inevitably arises in a discussion of Catholic higher education is the question of the Index of Forbidden Books. In the course of our year of research, Pope Paul VI mercifully put the battered and beaten Index out of its misery. But even before this happened, it seems to us that the Index was a relatively minor problem in most Catholic colleges. Either it was ignored, or permission to read various forbidden books was easy to come by. A few schools had horror stories about faculty members taking Salinger's *Catcher in the Rye* off the bookshelves and burning it, or about nuns being transferred because of the reading lists they assigned to their students, or letters to superiors about the kinds of books a lay professor was discussing in his English class. However, all of these stories referred to what had happened in the past, and it seems that present norms have changed to such an extent that, even though libraries may not yet be terribly important, at least book censorship has become relatively unimportant.

COMMUNICATION
One of the distinct advantages of life in the religious community is that it is informal and relaxed. Everyone is on the first-name basis with everyone else, and there is a high premium placed on

friendly, familial behavior. It would be wrong to minimize the profound human needs that such diffuse, warm, and informal relationships serve. The primary group relationships existing among members of the religious community can provide strong emotional support in time of trouble as well as great encouragement in time of opportunity and challenge. Unfortunately, the informal, casual styles of communication that exist in a religious house are not always appropriate in running a more formalized educational institution. In a religious community, one can conceivably discuss future plans in a chance meeting in the corridor, ask a person whether he will accept an assignment in a casual recreation room conversation, or even hash out a knotty problem over the lunch table or by the icebox late in the evening. But such casual and informal methods are something less than effective in a larger organization and are frequently bitterly resented not only by the laity but even by the clerical faculty of Catholic colleges and universities. The criticism heard in perhaps half the institutions was that the channels of communication and decision making were so casual and informal as to be obscure and, at times, invisible. One was never really sure how decisions were made or who made them. One could never really be confident that a casual conversation in the corridor might not take on far more importance in the mind of the religious administrator who initiated the conversation than would be attributed to it by the faculty member who participated. The cult of informality and friendship persistently pursued by a good number of Catholic administrators is considered to be unprofessional, if not dishonest, by the laity who are willy-nilly brought into the cult. Informal lines of communication are most helpful in any social organization, but when they become so important that one can never be sure that the formal lines have any value at all, the resulting confusion and chaos will almost certainly be demoralizing.

One member commented, "I don't give a damn whether they call me by my first name or not, but I wish they'd stop pretending that friendliness is a substitute for professionalism. They may be able to get away with it in the order, but when they make a stupid mistake or ask me to do something that's well nigh impossible, the first name doesn't make it one bit more sensible." Many of the religious who are administrators in Catholic colleges cannot really understand this criticism. The informality, and the relaxed atmosphere (sometimes authentic, sometimes phony) of the religious house seems to them to be an excellent thing, and they cannot understand why outsiders resent it and even suspect (usually completely without foundation) that most of the really important decisions made in the college are made in the community room of the religious order.

The informal style also gives some plausibility to lay suspicion that there are unseen powers in the religious community who conspire to control the school and for whom the president and the other higher administrators are often merely fronts. In some instances, the suspicion was, in our judgment, perfectly justified, but in most cases it was not. However, in the absence of businesslike, formal, and serious channels of communication this suspicion is likely to persist.[3]

The second problem of communication in Catholic colleges seems to be that many of the top-level administrators are, in the judgment of lower-level administrators as well as faculty, "indecisive." This is to say that they both centralize the decisionmaking power in their own hands and then procrastinate over making the decision. From what we said previously, such behavior will not be at all surprising. If a man who does not feel in his heart of hearts that he is qualified for a job and finds himself in a position of grave responsibility for which his colleagues and superiors in the religious community hold him accountable, he will be both afraid of making a decision himself and also afraid of letting others make decisions for him. He will neither delegate nor decide, but put off decisions as long as possible in the hope that by not deciding, the necessity for the decision will go away. Of course, in many instances it does, but the results for the institution are quite frequently disastrous.

A third aspect of the communications problem in the less professional colleges is that there is a basic distrust between the laity

[3]On the other hand, many of the members of the religious community insist that the community recreation room is the last place to find out about important decisions that are made which affect the school. At one school, where a new executive vice-president had just been appointed, several members of the religious community bemoaned the fact that the first they heard of it was from the students.

and the clergy, and sometimes among both laity and clergy. The religious order and its appointed administrators in many instances still have grave suspicions about whether it is a good thing to have lay people teaching on its faculty, even though there obviously is no longer any choice. Furthermore, they are suspicious that somehow or other the laity are trying to take the school away from them (and, in at least one or two instances, their suspicions are quite reasonable). On the other hand, some of the religious on the faculty are gravely suspicious of their own confreres in the religious order whom they feel to be incompetent and seeking an opportunity to deprive them of their academic freedom as professionals. Everyone is suspicious of the laymen who have been coopted by the administration to serve in some kind of subordinate role in administrative affairs. The lay executive vice-president or assistant dean is a man who is suspected by the religious order of not having quite as much loyalty as the religious he has replaced, by the religious faculty of being someone whom the administrators have hired to spy upon them, and by the lay faculty as being a fink who has sold out to the enemy. This not to say, of course, that some lay administrators do not overcome these suspicions by vigorous, independent, and imaginative activity, but in a number of schools, the position and status of the lay administrator are ambiguous and threatening .

This suspicion is not founded merely on fantasy and will not be improved merely by opening channels of communication. What is at issue are basic differences of values concerning the purpose and goals of higher education and the idea of who should have decision-making authority in a higher educational institution. The faculty is inclined to think that they should have such power; the religious order is tempted to feel that such power must be jealously guarded for itself. The luckless administrators are caught in between, but the successful ones are able to satisfy both the faculty and the religious order, as well as some of their own assistants, and at the same time run the school the way they know it ought to be run. Presumably, the present situation is transitional, though we would note in passing that if the veto power of the religious community is transferred to the faculty it may well be that the last state of the Catholic colleges will be worse than the first and that the possibility of creative innovation and growth will be permanently precluded.

ADMISSIONS, RECRUITING, AID, COUNSELING

In the next chapter we will comment more directly on the nature of policy regarding students in Catholic universities insofar as it affects the life of the students on campus. Of all the amateurism displayed in Catholic higher educational institutions, we found nothing more amateurish, more unprofessional, and more incredibly naïve than the regulation of student life. The various services that could be grouped together under admissions, recruitment, aid, and counseling—both vocational and psychological—at the Catholic colleges and universities run the full gamut from quite good to poor with the median being unfortunately somewhat below the average in American educational institutions. Some of the schools are extremely impressive in these areas and others are so amateurish as to be almost beyond belief.

In most of the improving schools, admission standards are high and going higher, recruiting is carried on vigorously at a national level, an increasing proportion of the school's budget is allowed for scholarships, and the counseling services are intelligent, sensitive, and popular with the students. On the other hand, some major universities, have almost no admission standards. At one such institution it was a joke among students that anybody who had the tuition to pay for the first semester could get admitted to the school. In other institutions, where there are published standards of admission, the faculty discovered that one-fifth of the students who were admitted the previous year had college entrance board scores lower than the published minimum. Still other institutions simply refuse to reveal what their entrance standards are, though they claim that they do have them. Recruiting, counseling, and aid programs in some schools are carried on by incompetent mediocrities, either lay or clerical; at other schools they are carried on by skilled professionals. There is frequently no relationship between the size and presumed importance of the school and the professionalism of these student relations offices. Some of the small schools—both women's colleges and coeducational institutions—were quite good in these services, and some of the larger and better known of the universities were intolerably poor.

One of the best institutions we visited had a fantastically effective recruiting program that was attracting some of the best Catholic high school students in the country. The president of the school told us with great delight how he had "stolen" the top graduates of several high schools in different parts of the country that were attached to universities where his own order also taught. "Alas," he lamented, "some of the other schools are beginning to catch on to what we're up to and they're going to try the same things. I'm afraid we'll have to come up with some other clever tricks." But such aggressive recruiting still seems out of place to a good number of administrators who have persuaded themselves that their schools are so good that they really need not seek students. In one sense, they need not, of course, since there are long waiting lists in many Catholic colleges. But high quality students are harder to come by. In the absence of aggressive recruiting, they simply will vanish from many a Catholic campus.

The explanation for the rather chaotic nature of these student services is not hard to find. Many members of the religious community do not feel that such activities are particularly important in a school that has so much to offer in religion and philosophy courses, as well as in its religious life. These things must be done, of course, because the accrediting agencies insist on them and because parents and students increasingly have come to expect them. There is no ideological opposition to doing them well, but since they are relatively unimportant in the religious order's frame of reference they are either done by members of the religious community who are not qualified for much else or by laymen working on low salaries and lower budgets. If a school is amateurish in its choice of a president it is not very likely to be professional in its student aid, admissions, registration, or counseling policies. Sometimes, of course, there are exceptions to this generalization, and through some happy mistake a rather poor school does have one or another of the student services run by a competent professional. But in general, in all but the rapidly improving schools, the harassed administrator simply does not have time to think of such things as counseling or student aid.

PLANNING

The eight or nine rapid improvement schools all had detailed, comprehensive, and realistic plans for their future development. On the other hand, the lowest third of the schools seemed to have no plan other than bumbling ahead just as they had bumbled since the memory of man. In the middle range of schools (which included a fair number of large urban universities) there were some kinds of comprehensive plans, some good and some not so good, but usually quite secret. At one institution, a major crisis occurred when one member of the research team accidentally revealed in conversation not what the comprehensive plan said but merely that he had had a chance to look at the plan. It is understandable, of course, that a fear-ridden administrator would be afraid of letting anybody—faculty, student, or even religious superior—know what the future might hold because the future is filled with so many threats and dangers. But in several cases the "comprehensive plans" in middle-level schools were little more than projections of the present situation based on assumptions that costs and enrolment would continue to increase in the future as they had increased in the past. While such projections are useful models, they seem almost by their very nature to rule out the possibility that a higher educational institution can be master of its own destiny, can choose to develop in some areas and not in others, or, indeed, can even choose simply to cut off its enrolment at a given level.

Many Catholic colleges have consistently tried to keep their enrolment at a given point but have been unsuccessful largely, it seemed to us, because of pressures of financial officers who were persuaded that government-financed dormitory construction made it possible to admit more students and thus to increase the annual revenues of the school. Since Catholic institutions must finance their work largely out of tuition, the prospect of more tuition is a tempting one. Although more students mean more expenses, more overhead, and more financial problems, at perhaps as many as a third of the institutions we visited there was considerable faith that increased enrolment would mitigate current financial pinches.

But the principal problem in planning in the Catholic educational institution seems to be the identity crisis concerning which we quoted Philip Gleason in the previous chapter. A good many of the institutions we visited were not really sure what they were doing or what Catholic education was; there were no clear norms to guide their development. Vague references to the education of the whole man and the spiritual and moral development of the young Christian are admirable ideals but hardly furnish precise goals against which new construction or expanded movement can be evaluated. In years gone by, the goals of Catholic higher education in the United States might have been much clearer—the schools existed for the training of future clergy and the protection of the faith of young Catholics. Since it is now clear that, by and large, the faith is not being corrupted at the secular universities, and the negative function of the Catholic schools has been pretty much eliminated, there is still considerable obscurity about what the positive function is. Until Catholic educators become much more hardheaded and realistic in stating what they can expect to accomplish and why they think these accomplishments are worth the effort, it would be unreasonable to expect that institutional planning will contribute anything but interesting statistical tables.

Self-studies are fashionable in American higher education, if only because the accrediting agencies seem to think that they are a good idea. Thus, Catholic institutions engage in periodic self-study projects which manage to keep a fair number of faculty and administrators out of harm's way for a good number of their waking hours in the course of the year. Many of these studies are quite good and some are excellent. A few of them even have some influence on what goes on in the school, but in many of the middle and low improvement schools it seems very obvious that the self-study is something to be proudly showed to visitors and occasionally used to justify innovation or change but rarely to be taken seriously in day-to-day administration. If the self-study recommendations are not offensive to the religious order, local ecclesiastical authorities, or major contributors, and if they do not cost too much, there is hardly any objection to them. They simply look very impressive on a president's desk.

EXTERNAL AFFAIRS

If fear and amateurism characterized the internal activities of many Catholic schools we visited, they were no less characteristic of their relations with other institutions. We found only very rare occasions where the relationship between the university and the local chancery office could be described as good. The administrators of the school seemed to proceed on the principle that the less the chancery office knew about what was going on, the better, and that all possible effort should be taken not to offend local ecclesiastical authorities. To resist the demands, however unreasonable, of a chancery office official would be unthinkable; and it was a rare university president who would be prepared to defend one of his faculty members against the chancery office's interference. Some of the very best schools seemed to lack the courage and the confidence necessary to warn local ecclesiastical officials that they would tolerate no interference in university affairs. The problem is complicated by the fact that the precise nature of the relationship between the local bishop and the university—at least in the United States—is a matter of considerable canonical obscurity.

Nevertheless, one would hope that the academic administrators would be vociferous in demanding that the canonical relationship between a university and a diocese be reevaluated and modified to suit the needs of the American environment. We could find no evidence of such demands. One very able Catholic president contended that the university simply could not afford to protect members of the religious community to whom the bishop was unfavorable because, as he put it, "the bishop is a higher ecclesiastical authority." He further argued that only in certain areas—especially the social sciences and theology—would a problem arise in any case, and that in other areas the order would certainly support free, untrammeled research by its members. But such support is hardly virtuous, and the defense of members of the community from outside interference seems to be praiseworthy only when it requires effort. The whole question of the relationship between the college and the bishop obviously needs much more careful consideration, and the protection of a controversial

scholar need not, it seems to us, involve any disrespect for epis-
copal authority. Indeed, one suspects that on occasion some
Catholic college administrators turn bishops into bogeymen on
whom they can blame decisions that they themselves have made,
but for which they do not wish to assume responsibility.

Tension between the religious clergy of the universities and
the diocesan clergy from whom most bishops are selected has been
widespread in the Roman church since the Middle Ages and does
not seem likely to abate even in the post-Vatican renewal, but
such conflict is quite dysfunctional for Catholic higher education.
Most bishops are far too busy with other responsibilities to interfere with universities in their dioceses. And a typical situation is
not open conflict but peaceful, if at times suspicious, coexistence,
with the university only too happy to stay out of the chancery
office's way, and the chancery never thinking that the college or
university really could be of any help to it in solving its own problems. It is not at all surprising, therefore, that when the American
bishops went to the Second Vatican Council they brought few, if
any, university faculty along as consultants to advise them during
the conciliar sessions. Not only did the bishops not think there
was anybody at the universities who could have been a help to
them, it never occurred to the university administrators (nor,
probably, to most of the university faculty) that the universities
should concern themselves with what was going on at the Council
or that they could have actively offered to make their assistance
available to the hierarchy. We did not find evidence of limitation
by chancery offices of academic freedom at universities, contrary
to the image frequently portrayed by Catholic writers. But the
existing detente between the university and the chancery office is
worse than constant interference. We saw no signs that the situation is likely to improve.

If the lack of cooperation between university and chancery office is unfortunate, lack of cooperation among Catholic higher
educational institutions is at times criminally stupid. The St. Louis
University study, which was carried on in the same year as ours,
will provide careful documentation about interinstitutional cooperation in Catholic higher education, so we will limit our
comments to the very strong impression that there is no such

cooperation. In more recent years there has been cross-registration in some institutions and occasional joint ventures of one sort or another, but these projects are pathetically unimportant when one considers that there are over three hundred institutions purporting to provide Catholic higher education and that some of the large metropolitan areas have more than a score of various Catholic seminaries, colleges, and universities. Thus, two schools constructed next to each other have entirely different library systems, with one library on the Dewey decimal system and the other library, scarcely half a block away, on the Library of Congress system. Two Catholic universities in the same city are both pushing ahead to build Ph.D. programs in psychology, not only without cooperating with each other but without even speaking to each other on the subject. Or, again, an institution run by a community of nuns refuses to cooperate in any but the most desultory fashion with a school run by priests of the same religious order a couple of miles away, because one hundred years ago the priest who had founded the neighboring institution had allegedly defrauded them of money, land, or buildings. Furthermore, interinstitutional projects are often hampered by the fact that one of the cooperating schools is firmly persuaded (for no objective reason, of course) that it is far better than the other and that to cooperate in any but the most minimal way would lower its standards of excellence. We take it to be almost axiomatic that the school that thinks it is too good to cooperate with others is one that is very bad indeed.

Interinstitutional cooperation never comes easily, since institutions, like individuals, are very jealous of their rights and privileges and their independence. But given the fact that there has been a dramatic development in interinstitutional cooperation outside of Catholic higher education, the snail's pace of progress made among the Catholic schools requires further explanation. Once again, the peculiar nature and history of the religious orders provides some explanation of the skepticism of Catholic schools about such cooperation. The religious community generates intence pride of membership in those who belong to it. While this élan and conviction of excellence may be very important in sustaining the morale of a religious community, it can very easily lead to the conviction that no other religious community measures up to one's own standards of goodness. It also preserves the memory of offenses commited against the order as long ago as the sixteenth century. One might suggest that after the ecumenical movement has healed the breach between Catholics and Protestants, it might turn its attention to the problem of stimulating some sort of fruitful dialogue among the religious orders within the Catholic Church. This is not to say that individual members of a given community do not have excellent personal relations with members of other orders. But when the independence and sovereignty of the institution, which is the embodiment of the peculiar ethos of the religious community, are involved, no room for compromise or negotiation is seen.

Are there national agencies through which the Catholic institutions can cooperate? The unfortunate answer is that for all practical purposes there are not. There is a college division of the National Catholic Educational Association with a small and competent staff in Washington that tries manfully to keep the channels of communication open and to bring the educators together for discussion at an annual meeting. In addition, some of the religious orders, such as the Jesuits, Benedictines, and Augustinians, have their own national educational associations where the heads of various institutions and members of different provinces can meet to discuss their common problems. But until very recently these organizations have been mere paper associations with no effective national cooperation. Most surprisingly, there is very little cooperation across provincial lines even within the Jesuit order, so that the university in any one of the eleven provinces of the Society of Jesus in the United States might well cooperate with another Jesuit university in a different province, but such cooperation would be quite accidental. We found not only considerable differences in the quality and goals of the various Jesuit provinces, but also considerable rivalry among the provinces and a strong disinclination on the part of educators in one province to make any sort of sacrifice that could conceivably give another province an advantage over their own. So great were the differences among Jesuit provinces that it almost seemed that we were speaking to members of different religious orders and

that within the Jesuit community there was at least as much pluralism as in the whole of Catholic higher education.

If petty rivalries can prevent any but the most minimal interinstitutional cooperation among Catholic colleges, we could
hardly expect the Catholic colleges to engage in much cooperation
across denominational lines. Of course, one would not expect that
a state university would be much interested in what goes on at a
"backwash ghetto school run by benighted relics of another era,"
even if in fact the schools is neither benighted nor backwash.

It is not clear what steps could be taken to ameliorate this situation. If the American bishops could put together a commission
on higher education they might discreetly knock together some
administrative heads and demand that the ludicrous rivalry and
duplication of effort come to an end. However, such a move
could be easily described as interference in academic freedom and
a return to the authoritarian policies of the past. If the bishops
do become seriously enough concerned with Catholic higher education to try to facilitate cooperation, they will probably have to
be more discreet and diplomatic. But somebody surely has to do
something.

The final "external affair" that is notable is the relationship
between Catholic schools and the neighborhoods in which they
are located. Many of the urban universities are located either in or
near the Negro ghetto. For the most part, they have been concerned only with escaping from the ghetto or with keeping the
ghetto from pouring over into the school and making it "unsafe."
In some of the urban universities there have been signs of a beginning of concern about the social problems of the city, and a
few programs dealing with urban problems have been instituted.
But, when one considers the immensity of the inner city problem
and the claims of the Catholic university to be an urban service
institution, the efforts being made by the schools with inner city
problems seems pathetically inadequate. Indeed, the students of
the universities seem to be more concerned than either the faculty
or the administration about the problems of the inner city. Sometimes they become involved in inner city projects not only without
the aid and support of the university, but sometimes in the face

of its opposition, either latent or active. Of course, Catholic schools are by no means the only ones that adopt an ostrich strategy in dealing with urban problems, though one would have hoped that the Catholic ideology would have led to a greater commitment in this area. But apparently minority groups in the inner city simply are not an important focal point for the religious orders, which feel that their contribution to the poor and suffering has been made by sending missionaries to foreign lands. It seems incredible that there are active recruitment campaigns going on in the Catholic campuses for lay volunteers to the foreign missions, while the injustice and misery scarcely three blocks away is conveniently ignored.

With the exception of a few institutions, there is no sign that any vigorous effort was being made by Catholic universities to recruit Negro talent by offering substantial scholarship assistance. There is no discrimination against Negroes; they are not excluded from Catholic schools; and, indeed, the university or college was quite proud of the Negro scholarship winners it had. But only a few institutions seem to feel that there is a social obligation to seek out the talented Negro who might not go to college or who might need considerable preparation before he would be college material. Surely the Catholic educators are not opposed to such a program, but, with the exception of four or five schools, we were unable to detect much conviction that such a development ought to have high priority.

THE TRAINING OF ADMINISTRATORS

It hardly needs to be observed at this point that not very many of the college presidents had been specifically trained for the job, although some of the lesser administrators did have degrees in educational administration. It is not altogether clear what the proper training for a college president ought to be, save that he ought to be a college president before he becomes a college president since there is probably no other job that provides the same kind of experience. It should be possible, given the variety and extent of Catholic higher education, for men and women to obtain experience as presidents of small schools before they become presidents of large schools but, as noted in a previous section, the requisite cooperation among institutions and among religious orders (and even among provinces of the same religious order) is most unlikely at the present time. Whether a president, a dean, an academic vice-president, or an assistant dean ought to be trained in educational administration or in one of the more academic disciplines seems to be an open question. Some of the most gifted presidents we encountered had been successful departmental chairmen. They possessed the academic competence as well as the political skills necessary to build a good academic department within a Catholic institution. Some of the other administrators we encountered, however, had been trained directly in educational administration and did not seem to have been harmed by the experience. We are inclined to suspect that far more important than the school the administrator attended or the courses he took is his demonstrated ability to handle touchy political situations, his knowledge of how American higher education works, and the imagination and courage to balance a number of conflicting forces. The specific field of his educational training is less important than his political experience in an administrative role, such as assistant dean or departmental chairman.

The attributes of a good college president described in the last paragraph and in previous chapters are neither hard to discover nor invisible in a man who possesses them. On the contrary, those who are presidential timber are often painfully obvious on Catholic campuses. It is sometimes equally painfully obvious that they will never be college presidents. In one very large Catholic university we visited, there was a man in the religious order who seemed to have every possible talent required for a president. He was a respected academician, a highly successful department chairman, a skilled diplomat, and a charismatic leader. A body of experts coming from outside to choose a member of the religious community to preside over the university would have taken about fifteen minutes to decide that this man was the one for the job. Yet, when we asked others in the religious community why he had not even been considered for it, the standard reply was, "We couldn't take him away from the department in which he's working." Finally, one more honest member of the community pointed out, "Jerry could not possibly be president here; the archbishop wouldn't sit still for it and neither would a lot of fellows in the religious order." The "Jerry" in question was not a radical by any stretch of the imagination. Indeed, in his own discipline he was considerably more conservative than many others. But he was not "safe"; he was just a little bit controversial. Consequently, there was not much chance of his becoming president of the school, and there was not much chance of the school ever amounting to anything.

In another institution—a fashionable women's college—a charismatic president retired some time ago and has been followed by two undistinguished administrators. When we asked people in the order why another nun—a brilliant, efficient, and nationally famous scholar—was not chosen for the job, the reply was, "Our community isn't ready for someone like her quite yet."

At yet another school, the presidency was vacant and there were several well-qualified nuns who could fill the job. But the president was to be selected by the new mother general, who would be elected at the order's chapter the coming summer. When we were at the school, there seemed to be a universal dread on the part of the religious members of the faculty that the gerrymandered representation in the chapter would preclude election of either an enlightened mother general or a competent college president. As one nun put it to us, "The sisters who are running the old peoples' homes will, in effect, decide who our next president is."[4]

Some of the more influential and successful college presidents have set up training programs for their own successors by appointing bright young members of the religious community as "administrative assistants." Such positions are, in effect, internship programs in which young men can learn about the day-to-day operation of the university as well as have the opportunity of soaking up the wisdom of their teacher. While there is some danger that such a program would lead a president to choose a successor molded in his own image, it still seems to be an intelligent and sensible way of training a future president, especially if the

---

[4]Her prediction turned out to be wrong. On the first ballot, the chapter overwhelmingly elected one of the most enlightened and liberal members of the community as mother general. It seems safe to guess that the college will shortly have a talented new president and will join the ranks of the improving institutions.

crown prince is given experience either at the subpresidential level
or in a smaller institution before being promoted to the top position in a large university.[5]

To say that the administrators of Catholic colleges are not
trained for their positions is only to indicate a secondary element
in the problem. Training is, of course, important. But it is not a
substitute for competence nor a guarantee of it. The man with the
political, personal, and intellectual qualities necessary to be a
great college president will be one no matter what kind of degree
he has, and a man who lacks these qualities will be a poor president no matter how many academic credits he has assembled or
how many years he has spent working in an administrative office.
The problem is not so much that the religious orders do not train
their future presidents (though they certainly have not done that
in the past), but that they seem to be unaware of what the president ought to be.

With all these criticisms having been made about the choice of
presidents and other administrators in Catholic colleges, we
should conclude by noting that in most recent years there has been
a very dramatic improvement. Nine of the thirty institutions we
visited in the course of the year had new presidents, and in seven
of the nine instances the new man represented a considerable improvement over his predecessor. As a matter of fact, the continuation of the kind of appointment that we witnessed this year
would probably lead to the elimination in the not too distant future of the administrative problem of Catholic colleges and
universities. On the basis of the new presidents who were appointed during the past year, we can see that competence and
imagination are no longer an obstacle to becoming a Catholic
college president, and apparently are becoming a very important
asset. The handful of truly great presidents are rapidly being
joined by a whole host of new members. The replication of the
present survey about ten years from now may show the problem
to be almost solved.

[5]The peculiar problem that the Jesuits have in training their administrators
is that the unduly prolonged period of training before admission means that the
typical Jesuit administrator is only beginning his academic or administrative experience in his middle thirties, perhaps ten years later than his counterpart in the
secular institution.

INNOVATION

Although they do not realize it, Catholic college administrators have a tremendous asset at their disposal. As a number of non-Catholics have pointed out to us, the Catholic schools represent the last substantial body of four-year educational institutions in the United States where there is still wide freedom for innovation and experimentation—free from both governmental control and the veto power of powerful, prestigious and reactionary faculties. Catholic college administrators could begin a brilliant set of experiments and innovations that not only could improve tremendously the education offered on Catholic campuses but also could have a profound influence on the whole of American higher education. Unfortunately, at least until very recently, the Catholic schools were content to follow after the non-Catholic institutions and many times imitate the worst of the current educational fads.

A Catholic president comments:

From my own personal experience I am finding it much harder these last couple of years to move as quickly as we could earlier towards innovation and experimentation. Another problem we find now in Catholic universities as we begin to give more responsibility to faculty for appointment, dismissal, and promotion, is that they are hesitant to accept these responsibilities if it means doing some "dirty work" like firing or refusing to promote. I presume it will take some time to achieve the attitudes of faculty in the prestigious secular universities. I have had a similar experience with students. We are granting many more privileges each year, and lessening the student restrictions so that now we are facing the problems of alcohol and parietals, but seldom, if ever, at this particular time can we get the students to assume a responsibility of setting guidelines. They still seem to want the administration to handle all the nasty things."

It would seem that over the long run the Catholic schools must innovate, or they will become less and less important in the American scene. They simply will not attract governmental or foundation money and, in the long run, they may not attract students unless they can claim that they have something different to offer. But what is different now? Is the faith of Catholic students protected? There exists overwhelming data that the faith of Catholic students is not in any particular danger in most non-Catholic colleges. Are the theology courses lively, distinctive presentations of the best of contemporary Catholic theologizing? On the contrary, in most instances they present dull, lifeless, and pre-Vatican theology which young people are compelled to take and would escape from cheerfully if they could do so. Do they offer an integrated education in which the various strands of Western cultural and intellectual traditions are woven together in some systematic format? Despite claims to the contrary, philosophy courses are usually unbearably dull and have nothing to do with either integration or even philosophy. Are there experiments in the integration of study, worship, and community living, such as one might expect of people who claim membership in a Christian fellowship? On the contrary, the personal touch is as absent from Catholic schools as it is from other schools, with the possible exception that there is a little bit more rigorous supervision of personal behavior at the Catholic schools. With the exception of some of the small women's colleges, the Catholic institutions seem to be as depersonalized and as inhuman as any of the big multiversities. Have Catholic schools acted on the principle that education is most effective when it is integrated into personal experience beyond the educational environment? Have Catholic schools made any attempt to integrate volunteer service in the inner city or in foreign countries into their educational curriculum? On the contrary, with some notable exceptions, the possibilities inherent in the multinational religious body for the integration of education and service have been completely ignored. Is there a premium on creative innovation in the Catholic higher educational system? On the contrary, those schools that do try experiments, such as Webster in St. Louis, Missouri, are frequently condemned as having departed from the Catholic educational system. There is no way to escape the conclusion: Even though innovation is a prerequisite for Catholic higher education, there is little of it on the Catholic campuses. Once again, of course, there are some schools that are highly imaginative and innovative and, indeed, in a couple of instances overwhelmingly and excitingly so. But all these schools establish is that it is possible for an institution to be Catholic (and, on occasion, profoundly and magnificently Catholic) and also imaginative, creative, and innovative. Such things are possible, but in the broad panorama of Catholic higher education in the United States, the possibilities are achieved only in a very small minority of institutions.

One is forced to face the question: Why not? By now, the reader will be prepared for our answer. Catholic administrators do not innovate because they are afraid to. They are afraid of going into debt. They are afraid of offending bishops. They are afraid of antagonizing the power structure within their own religious community. They are afraid of losing control of what is going on in their school. They are afraid of proving false to the traditions of their religious order, afraid of the faculty, afraid of the lesser administrators, afraid of a thousand and one nameless demons and ghosts that haunt their waking and sleeping hours. It takes courage and sometimes herosim to innovate. The Catholic schools that we rated as improving schools were administered by people who did have this courage, and their schools were splendid, exciting, and at least on occasion, joyous places. But the main reason the Catholic schools have not been innovating is that the people who are responsible for the appointment of the top administrators do not want innovation in their institutions. Only when the religious orders, and particularly the superiors who determine policy for these orders, are convinced that without innovation Catholic higher education in America will not in the long run survive, only then can we expect that the great potential for innovation which is surely latent in the Catholic higher educational system will be actualized.

CONCLUSIONS

We have reported in this chapter that the administration of Catholic schools is somewhat less free than is the faculty from the traditional constraints and limitations imposed by the relationship between the institution and the religious order that owns it. We concluded that in those instances where the administration had managed to obtain some degree of freedom from the religious order, then professionalism seemed to permeate the administration from top to bottom, but in the other institutions incompetency, amateurism, mediocrity, and indifference seem to result from the fact that the educational leader's important reference group was not professional college administrators but rather the superiors and the governing groups within the religious order itself. We reported that we visited enough schools that were professionally administered to have no doubt that Catholicism, and indeed ownership by the religious order, was not necessarily in conflict with excellence in the administration. We further reported that while the administrative scene at Catholic colleges was relatively dreary, it was probably no worse than that at many non-Catholic colleges in the country, and truly no worse than some of the things we observed in the non-Catholic colleges we visited. The basic problem, as we saw it, was not that Catholic college administrations were so bad, but that they could be very much better if the norms according to which the higher educational administrators were chosen were consonant with the realities of the contemporary academic world.

9
Students

Back in the 1940's, there was a joke that the Taft-Hartley Law was hell for unions, purgatory for management, and heaven for lawyers. A not dissimilar comment could be made about American education today. Higher education is heaven for faculty (especially for those academic free-booters who can live off government and foundation grants), purgatory for administrators, and hell for students. It is not the purpose of this book to engage in a general critique of the horrors of depersonalization and inhumanity that are taken for granted as a normal part of the academic careers of late adolescents. We will refrain from saying anything, for example, about the madness that puts freshmen, who need personal attention, into the most crowded classrooms, with five hundred students presided over by inexperienced teaching assistants, while seniors who need personal help the least have small seminars with associate professors. If we observe in this chapter that student life is the most dreary and dismal aspect of Catholic higher education, we are simply saying that Catholic schools are a little different from other schools. Even though in some respects they imitate the worst faults of other American colleges in dealing with students, the Catholic colleges have a few unique faults of their own and, worse yet, tend to overlook resources of the Catholic tradition for improving the quality of student life.

But in a curious paradox, the religious community can be said to have more influence on the quality of student life in Catholic colleges than it does on the behavior either of faculty or administrators. In some schools administrators have been able to obtain a fair amount of freedom from the traditional norms of the religious orders. And a large number of lay faculty members, in a time when faculty is hard to come by, have obtained even more freedom. But there is no shortage of students and precious little pressure from students for a change in their own situation. On the contrary, there are vast pressures from the religious order to make student life the last desperate battleground for those who reject the modernization of Catholic higher education. The old narrowly ecclesiastical approach to Catholic higher education is slowly dying. However, its death is the slowest and most painful in the area of student life on Catholic campuses.

We are not denying that there has been substantial liberalization of regulation in the Catholic colleges, nor are we denying that at least some universities have become as permissive in dealing with the student as have most of the great secular universities. But we do feel that liberalization and Americanization of supervision of student behavior has proceded at a much slower pace than have the changes in either faculty or administration. Trust in and respect for the dignity of the student seems to be an important part of student personnel policy in only a relatively small group of Catholic schools—perhaps no more than five or six of those that we visited. (Some of these were very small but good women's colleges.)

THEORY

There are several theoretical propositions which we take to underlie the attitude of the religious communities toward the students who attend Catholic colleges. First, it is the role of the college to develop virtue in the student, and virtue is something that can be obtained by a repeated performance of obligatory actions. This is a rather curious notion from the viewpoint of educational psychology as well as from the viewpoint of scholastic philosophy, which considers that virtue is acquired by the repetition of free acts. Compulsory daily Mass is now extremely rare in Catholic higher education (though one rather good college still requires it for a couple of months from its freshmen, not so much because the freshmen need it, or profit from it, but as a last final concession to its own old guard). In years gone by, however, even some of the great insitutions brought major pressure, formal and informal, on their students to get them into church every morning and to confession every week, under the pretext that this is the way habits would be developed that would stay with the young

people in later life. Unfortunately, there never was any attempt
to collect data other than anecdotal to prove that this sort of compulsion was effective, but the crowds of students in chapel each
morning was surely reassuring to the clergy who thought that they
had responsibility for the souls of the young men entrusted to
their care.

Even though compulsory church attendance is now relatively
infrequent, the compulsory annual retreat is still common in
Catholic higher educational institutions. We were assured by
otherwise intelligent and sensitive Jesuit educators that when the
obligatory annual retreat was eliminated, the school would stop
being a Jesuit institution. Despite this, some eight or nine Jesuit
colleges have already eliminated the retreat and still seem to be
securely in control of the Jesuit order. One Jesuit president remarked, "St. Ignatius of Loyola would be scandalized to know
that his Spiritual Exercises have been made a requirement for
graduation." Another Jesuit educator assured us that even though
the retreat really didn't build up much in the way of good habits,
it forced the young men and women to make at least "one good
confession" every year and that this was in itself enough justification for the obligatory retreat. It did not apparently occur to
him that if only "one good confession" a year was all the young
people would make, there might be something drastically wrong
either with American Catholicism or with Jesuit higher education.
Nor did it occur to him that this one compulsory confession might
be obtained at the price of turning the young people against retreats, against Catholic higher education, and against the Church
itself. Finally, it has apparently not occurred to some Catholic
educators (or for that matter, students or parents) that to expel a
young person because he has not attended a religious service
which is not required by the general law of the Church might be
an atrocious and intolerable infringement of the student's human
freedom.

Similarly, it has been argued that the compulsory theology (and
often philosophy) program is imperative if a school is to be truly
a Catholic university. It is not enough that excellent theology and
philosophy programs be offered, but the students must be compelled to accept the offerings or a school, at least in the judgment

of many Catholic educators, is no longer a Catholic school. Even though it is a rare institution that still requires forty-four hours of philosophy and theology, some institutions still require that some twenty to twenty-four hours be spent on philosophy and theology courses. It has not occurred to many Catholic educators that they can legitimately insist that philosophy and theology be part of an academic curriculum in any educational institution which is an heir to the Western cultural tradition. The courses are obligatory in most instances not because they are part of education but because they are part of the religious and spiritual development of the young person. The students bitterly resent both the boredom and the compulsion of such courses. The obligatory retreat and the required theology courses are, in the minds of many Catholic educators, absolutely essential for Catholic higher education, independent of any proof that they accomplish anything, and indeed in the face of massive evidence that they create far more problems than they solve.

The second proposition that seems to be widespread among Catholic educators is that the school acts *in loco parentis,* an assumption that is, of course, shared by many non-Catholic institutions. Leaving aside the question of whether the parental role is a feasible one for any college, we must still ask what kind of a parent a Catholic college thinks it is. As one student put it to our interviewer, "I wouldn't mind if they acted the way my parents do at home. Believe me, my parents don't treat me like this. My parents respect my judgment and trust me. I confide in them. But they don't regulate every minute of my day for me and they haven't for the past ten years. That's why I really think I'm leaving this place right after this semester, because I'm used to ten times as much freedom at home."

It would seem that a good number of those responsible for student life at the Catholic university are not aware of the changes in styles of behavior among young people in the contemporary world. Parents do not snoop into the private lives of their children. They do not closely regulate their activity. They do not lay down rigid and elaborate rules that cover every moment of the day. They do not force their children to be religious. They do not distrust and suspect their children, and they do not refuse to engage in honest and open conversation with them. Parents may and frequently do manipulate their children, but if they do so, it is generally in a way so sophisticated that the child does not realize that he is being manipulated. But the regulation, supervision, and constraints of Catholic colleges (as well as other colleges) are often so obvious, so oppressive, so bizarre, and, from the student's viewpoint, so senseless that for the university to claim that it is acting in the role of a parent is a cruel joke as far as the student is concerned. No parent would ever dare treat a child that way.

The third assumption that we found frequently on Catholic campuses, is the assumption that the primary problem in dealing with young people is sexual immorality. There is no reason to doubt that in the late adolescent years during which the awakening sexual urges become extremely powerful, young people will engage in all kinds of heterosexual behavior, at least some of which will come rather close to the borders and even go far beyond the borders considered legitimate by the tradition of Catholic morality. Unfortunately, many Catholic educators seem to assume that it is their responsibility to prevent such behavior from occurring, forgetting the old dictum that while one can legislate against immorality, one cannot make it unpopular. Some student personnel administrators assured us that when the parents sent the young people to Catholic colleges they entered into a contract by which the university agreed to protect the morality of the child—as though any institution could safeguard the morality of a young person whose moral values had not been formed in the family environment. But at least in contemporary American society if young people are of a mind to sin, then sin they surely will, and there is precious little that any institution can do to prevent this, though it is possible perhaps to make it a little more difficult. On the other hand, one often suspects that regulations which are designed to decrease the incidence of sexual "sins" among young people succeed only in making the sin more attractive and in presenting a challenge to the young person.

It should also be noted that there is some danger that celibates may judge certain behavior to be sexually stimulating on the basis of their own expected reactions, forgetting that young people whose experience, training, and future expectations are different might react in a rather different fashion. Even the most sophisticated and virtuous of young Catholics will not be persuaded that certain kinds of behavior are "sinful" when all his experience suggests that, while exciting and fun, it is not innately wrong. Finally, some young Catholics feel that morality based on tape measures, stop watches, and rigid *a priori* notions is a poor guide for human behavior, and that far more important than any specific act is the general tone of relationship between two people—whether the relationship is leading to emotional growth and development and increasing freedom or whether it is a relationship that creates ever-increasing dependencies, both physical and emotional. Unfortunately both the explicit and the implicit morality embodied in student regulations often overlooks this fact.

In one school a dormitory was raided and the religious community was shocked to learn that four hundred copies of *Playboy* were confiscated in the course of the raid, though apparently nobody was shocked at the thought that such confiscation was a violation of the rights of the young men in the dormitory. Nor does another school think it amiss to turn over copies of *Playboy* that come in the mail to the college chaplain to whom a young man must appeal if he wishes to claim his copy of Hugh Hefner's latest efforts. Presumably it has occurred to no one in the institution that in addition to violating the rights of the students such behavior might be viewed with considerable dismay by the United States postal inspectors. It should be clear that the present writers are not supporters of *Playboy,* but the question is not whether *Playboy* is wholesome reading for anybody, but whether attempts to intercept it and to confiscate it make any substantial contribution, or make any contribution at all, to the moral health of the young person on the Catholic campus.

Sexual Jansenism reinforced in some of the all-male institutions by prolonged isolation from the companionship of members of the opposite sex is one of the most dismal aspects of student life on the Catholic campuses. Even though in some institutions attempts are being made to promote much more positive attitudes toward sex, the existence of reinforcing regulations, restrictions, supervisions, and suspicions seems to inhibit substantially the development of positive attitudes. The student wisely argues that the educators can't mean it when they say sex is a good thing, since the spirit of the regulations of the school suggest that sex is something dirty.

It would surely not be our contention that residential dormitories ought to be so permissive as to become virtual houses of prostitution. On the other hand, there are other sins in the world besides sins against the Sixth and Ninth Commandments. It is quite possible that a display of greater respect for and confidence in young people might lead to more moral behavior in regard to all the Ten Commandments instead of restricted behavior on two and license on the others. (Robert McNamara, S.J., has suggested that students in Catholic colleges are indeed somewhat more moral than students in other colleges in matters sexual, but somewhat more immoral in matters of cheating and stealing, a curious commentary on the emphases in contemporary American Catholicism.)

Closely related to the suspicion of sex—one might almost say the morbid suspicion of sex—is the resentment in some of the recently coeducational Catholic institutions toward the young women students. Many of the older members of the religious orders resent the coeds and think their admission to the campus was one more step in the direction of deterioration of the traditional values of their own style of education. Granted the long tradition in Catholicism of discrimination against women, such antagonism is not particularly surprising. Nevertheless, in view of Pope John's endorsement of the feminist movement, one wonders how long it will survive. We suspect that it will be a while before the swimming pool of one college will be made available to the coeds because of the suspicion that swim-suited coeds would be a threat to the virtue of the lay students of the college, to say nothing of the religious vocations of seminarians. We further suspect that the rule in another college forbidding a female graduate student to visit her brother (also a graduate student) in his rooms may remain in the rule book for the foreseeable future.

The fourth assumption on the part of some educators responsible for the life of students on Catholic campuses is that the world is still essentially a hostile one and that the young person must be prepared to defend himself, his virtue, and his faith against the attacks of the enemy, whoever that enemy might be in this ecumenical age. In some of the schools, even today, the theology a student gets is apologetic; the sermons he hears warn him about temptation and sin; the atmosphere of his school attempts to protect him from the loss of virtue; and his advisers display little confidence in his ability to persevere in goodness and become threatened and horrified when he raises serious questions about "truths of faith." There is no room for serious questions, much less for doubt. Indeed, he who begins to doubt his faith is told that he has already lost it, and little or no value at all is seen in what one religious educator calls a Socratic period in regard to one's faith.

The defensive spirit is waning in Catholic higher education as it is in the whole American Church, but still there are many Catholic educators who feel that it is their job to protect the young people under their care and to prepare them to resist the temptations of later life, forgetting that young people have already experienced all kinds of temptations against which no school can build a protection, and that in our day and age a protectionist approach is ineffective.

The fifth proposition implicit in some Catholic higher educational institutions is that the priests and nuns are "big brothers" or "big sisters" of their students. Given the young person's proclivity to identify at least temporarily with hero or heroine images, it is easy for the charming and attractive religious to temporarily exercise powerful emotional controls over the life of a young person. The use of personality and charm as means of social control is not objectionable in itself, so long as the freedom and the dignity of the other is recognized. Unfortunately the temptation for the religious, especially the young one, to assume a protective, paternalistic attitude toward the college student is not unlike that which the novice master or mistress assumes toward his or her charges and is singularly inappropriate behavior in the college environment. It is also very dangerous from the point of view of the religious growth of the young person because the influence is likely to pass away, and the persistent attempts of the religious to maintain it could turn the young person not only against the religious but against the higher educational institution and the whole Church. This problem can be aggravated by the tendency of some religious orders to put in positions of responsibility over students precisely those people who are likely to be most attractive personally to students (at least in the short run) and also who have the greatest emotional needs for creating dependency relationships with young people.

Furthermore, it is assumed by many Catholic educators that one of their prime responsibilities is to protect the "good name" of the school. One wonders what kind of confidence they have in the reputation of the school to be so profoundly concerned that a scandal of one sort or another will substantially impair its reputation. They seem to be unaware that scandals occur whether there are regulations or not, and an institution whose reputation depends on it being totally free of unruly or scandalous behavior by young people has built its house on shifting sands. Nonetheless, we were told in many institutions that the complicated, detailed regulations, especially about off-campus behavior, were not enforced but were on the rule books just in case the local police should apprehend young people in some form of illicit merriment. Under such circumstances the school would presumably be in an ideal position to wash its hands of the matter by expelling the students involved. Whether this is a particularly charitable approach for students in trouble is problematic, and what it does to young people's respect for law when they are informed unofficially that a certain number of rules will only be enforced if people are caught violating them is equally questionable.

Nonetheless, attempts to minutely regulate the behavior of students even out of the campus situation persist, and in a couple of instances young people were threatened with expulsion for drinking off campus, even if they were over twenty-one. In one instance, women were told that they might not smoke off campus, no matter where they were—apparently including the safety of their parental home. Such enormities are absurd to us, but not to the religious administrator who fears that the good name of his order, and his own reputation, can be smashed by a couple of "wild punks." Massive drinking can be tolerated all over the campus and off the campus too, so long as young people are not caught, but if they are caught, either by design or by accident, and either by college authorities or by the police, then the rule book must be reached for and the young person must be suitably disciplined, if not expelled. Whether such an approach to young people and their maturational problems does far more harm than good to the image of the religious order is apparently a question that has not been raised.

Finally, and perhaps the most basic assumption of all, is the idea that one cannot trust people. Even though Catholic theology takes a rather benign and optimistic view of human nature, by the time this theology is filtered down to the practical operation of student life in many Catholic campuses it has become highly Calvinistic, and the basic operating premise seems to be that all people and particularly young people are wild and evil and that the most stringent regulations, supervisions, and compulsions are necessary to prevent them from becoming even more evil.

The attitudes we have described may sound more like a caricature of a student personnel policy than an accurate description of one that actually exists.[1] Not very many of those responsible for supervising student life on Catholic campuses subscribe to every proposition rather broadly stated in the previous description. Nonetheless, we would judge that somewhere between two-fifths and one-half of the Catholic campuses are governed according to these propositions, and in another one-quarter the proponents of this view are fighting a powerful rear guard action. The younger student personnel people and not a few of the more resourceful college presidents have a very different view of the nature of the relationship between the university and its students. But they have an uphill fight ahead of them if they are to sell their

[1]One Catholic educator thought that our description was a caricature of the truth about the operating assumptions of student personnel and administrators in Catholic colleges. We would note first of all that we carefully qualified our remarks by saying that the comments are true of some or many schools, but surely not of all. Certainly, some of the more impressive Catholic universities and colleges are quite free from most of the assumptions that we have described. Nevertheless, we contend that the description we have given is accurate. If some anger showed through in the text, the reason may be that the research team has very strong feelings on the subject. We concede that the situation is changing, and in some Catholic institutions changing rather rapidly, but to say that a situation is changing does not mean that the problems described have been eliminated.

ideas to their colleagues. In the absence of anything more than disorganized and intermittent student pressures, we would not anticipate that the prevailing view of student life will change in the very near future. However, there are at least some signs, which we will discuss later, that the younger students on Catholic campuses may revolt sooner than even the most optimistic of the progressive student personnel administrators expect.

PRACTICAL POLICIES

From the theory described in the previous section, it is relatively easy to derive a comprehensive student personnel policy—one whose basic premise is that the school must form good habits in its young people by insisting above all else on order, discipline, and obedience. First of all, the school issues detailed student handbooks that provide rules to cover a vast variety of student behavior. It is not advisable to leave the student in doubt as to what he ought to be doing at any given time or in any given situation. (Indeed, a school that provides only a very generalized student handbook with a few regulations is thought to be failing in its duty to provide the guidance needed by the confused and passion-ridden young person.) For the most part, the regulations are non-negotiable. They may be changed or liberalized, but if they are, it is, with some very rare exceptions, on the initiative of the administration and not under pressures of student government.

All the Catholic colleges have some form of student government, but at most schools the students are dissatisfied with the government and student leaders are frustrated in their jobs. Those elected to student leadership positions in Catholic colleges are generally responsible and rather docile middle class youngsters who are eager to behave maturely in dealing with the administration. But we did not very often get the impression that the administration is willing to return the responsibility; in many cases, it seems that the student personnel directors are likely to use interminable discussions, procrastination, and arbitrary decisions as a way of keeping the student leaders at bay. As one personnel director put it, "The student leader is effective here for about two years and then he's gone and a new crop comes along who has to learn the game. In the meantime, we can stall them indefinitely." Such delaying tactics are very effective in turning student governments into "Mickey Mouse" organizations and are by no means limited to Catholic campuses. It does not seem to bother the people who play this game that it is likely to turn the very best of the student leaders into cynics and reinforce the students' suspicion and distrust both of the religious order and of the Catholic Church. Only in three or four schools did we have the impression that the administration was secure enough and open enough to engage in honest dialogue with the students about the problems of student life on the campus. In a couple of schools, student governments had real power and actually legislated and enforced university or college rules. The astonishing success of these ventures in self-government does not yet seem to have persuaded other student personnel administrators that self-government in student life might be a good idea. As one of them pointed out to us, "We simply couldn't trust the kids to make their own decisions."

A logical result of the distrust is considerable restriction on the rights of students to have free student papers or to invite speakers of their own choosing to address student organizations, or even to found such student organizations. We discovered that about one-quarter of the student newspapers in the Catholic colleges were completely free from censorship. Another quarter were relatively free in fact if not in theory, since the faculty member who had been appointed to moderate the paper chose pretty much to leave the students to their own devices, though there was an implicit understanding that if anything desperately went wrong it would be necessary for the moderator to step in and exercise control. The remaining half of the student newspapers of the Catholic colleges were the house organs of the school with various forms of pre-censorship and editorial control remaining in the hands of the administration.

It was argued by the student personnel directors that the school had no choice but to exercise such control because otherwise "the kids might do something that would embarrass us." At one school, where a lively and at times brilliant student newspaper published a column ridiculing one of the prominent benefactors of the university, the columnist was fired (and later quit the school), tighter censorship restrictions were imposed on the paper, and the editor of the paper was denounced for permitting immoral and uncharitable material in his journal. As one of the faculty members remarked later, "That kid could have cost us ten million dollars."

What it cost the school when it restricted the freedom of its student press is not measurable in dollars, nor is it possible to say whether the reputation of the school will suffer from a free student press if it is made clear to everyone in the community that the press is truly free and that the school assumes no responsibility for what its editors say. One wise and witty college president told about going to dinner at a prominent home with the archbishop of the diocese in which the school was located. As they walked in the door of the house, the archbishop said to the president, "Say, Pat, I don't suppose there's anything much you can do about those kids that edit your school paper?" To which Pat replied with a laugh, and the archbishop laughed, and the "kids" on the paper continued to do what they pleased. Such sophistication and humor unfortunately are all too rare, both in Catholic higher education and in the relationship between the Catholic colleges and the various publics that surround them.

Similarly, student organizations are, with rare exceptions, limited in the kinds of speakers they can invite to the campus. As one priest pointed out to us, "If you let the kids invite whomever they want, they would invite every nut that walks down the street." The Williamson and Cowan study (1966) documents in detail the restrictions on speakers in Catholic colleges. The far right and the far left are equally unwelcome, though at one major Catholic university in the not-too-distant past, four very moderate speakers were banned, with resultant national controversy.

Most student organizations in Catholic schools are docile enough so that there is no great danger of them inviting either a Castroite or an anti-Semite to speak at the school. Hence there are few open conflicts between student organizations and administrations on this point. But the fact remains that in almost all Catholic schools, speakers must be cleared with the administration, and the clearance is by no means automatic. The same principle is at work as is operative in the question of student newspapers. University administrations are afraid that if a controversial speaker is permitted on campus, the public mind will identify the views of the speaker with the official position of the university. It does not occur to such administrators that they could educate the public mind to the notion that the university is an appropriate place for controversy and discussion, indeed one of the most appropriate places in the society.

One Catholic school saw no problem in sponsoring a symposium on the dangers of communism, but the following year had to cancel, for reasons of shortage of space, a symposium on the encyclical, *Pacem in Terris.* Another school had no difficulty in inviting a Republican senatorial candidate to speak, but his Democratic opponent was somehow cancelled at the last moment, again allegedly for reasons of lack of space and after complaints had been made by conservative members of the advisory board of trustees. But cases like this seem to be extremely rare. The right and the left are both welcome speakers at Catholic colleges, so long as they are not too far right or too far left, and so long as the administrators of the school have been given the opportunity to approve invitations to them.

In none of the schools that we visited could we find any evidence of due process that guaranteed the rights of students. Often, young people could be expelled for whatever grounds seemed appropriate to the university (since the rule books frequently reserved the right to expel students whose behavior was deemed "inappropriate"), without any right of counsel, cross-examination, or appeal. On some occasions, dismissal was so summary that within twenty-four hours after an offense the student found himself on the train or the plane with his baggage.

The disciplinary boards (which, in a few cases, have student members) are rarely arbitrary or unjust, but the student has no guarantee other than the presumed kindness of the board that his rights will be respected. The attitude at Catholic colleges, seems to be, "This is our school. We own it and we are the ones that determine who can stay and who can't. If we don't reserve to ourselves the right to expel people whose behavior is inappropriate, then our good name is likely to be damaged in the community's eyes." The fear of loss of control and loss of reputation is used as justification to continue the policies of the past. Whether such a summary approach to the question of student rights and freedom is in keeping with Christian ethical teachings is another matter.

The courts have recently ruled that a state university cannot expel a student without following procedures that recognize his rights to an education. In the absence of preservation of due process, it would appear that students can safely sue for readmittance to state universities. Whether the courts will extend such interpretation to include private schools is problematic at the present. However, the AAUP's increasing concern with student rights makes it very likely that faculty pressure will be brought to bear on the private schools to institute such safeguards of students' rights. (Faculties can do this, of course, because such modifications of policy will not cost them any power or control.) Such a development is inevitable in American higher education, and the Catholic schools would be well-advised to recognize the fact.

One of the most dismal aspects of student life on the Catholic campuses is the religious. The old theory of religious life on campus, based on compulsory church attendance, compulsory annual retreats, and compulsory theology courses, is on the wane. In the improving schools, especially, the old policies are being rapidly abandoned. But, unfortunately, it did not seem to us that much in the way of an exciting and meaningful substitute had been found. Despite the dramatic changes made in Catholic worship by the Vatican Council, the general state of campus liturgy was quite discouraging. No more than ten schools had caught the spirit of the liturgical changes of the Vatican Council and provided a meaningful and exciting worship, particularly adjusted to the needs of young people. In some instances, the dull liturgy was blamed on chancel office restrictions, though we could find no evidence that the university had tried to present a very convincing case to the chancel office that campus liturgy ought to be a place for experimentation. At a good number of schools there were still opportunities for young people to attend Sunday Mass the "old way," that is to say, everything was in mumbled Latin, there was no sermon, and the worshippers could get in and out within twenty minutes.

There was enough evidence in the schools where liturgical experimentation was going on that even in its present state the Roman liturgy can be a very meaningful experience for young people. Unfortunately, the majority of Catholic student personnel directors do not seem to be terribly interested in such liturgical developments, quite possibly because many of them are not terribly enthusiastic about developments in the Church at the Vatican Council. At one justly famous Catholic liberal arts college, long a center of liturgical revival, we were surprised not at the poverty of Catholic worship on the campus but that the great liturgical and religious tradition of the school was not exploited nearly as much as it might be with the students. We discovered that most of the students were completely unaware that the abbey attached to the school was one of the great leaders of renewal and reform in the American Church. Here, surely, there was no opposition to reform, but simply no realization that the school had at hand a highly effective substitute for the compulsory religion of the past.

One of the more interesting aspects of many Catholic schools is that a priest or a nun is on each floor of the residence hall. Such availability of a religious functionary could make for a very warm and meaningful relationship between the Church and the collegians, especially if the religious is young and enthusiastic enough to be able to share at least some of the hopes and disappointments of the student. Unfortunately, in many instances the priest or nun is there in a disciplinary role, is expected to enforce rules, supervise behavior, and punish misbehavior. Some of the younger clergy will have nothing to do with such responsibilities, but many others take the disciplinary part of their assignment seriously and find themselves turned into policemen rather than religious functionaries. This mixing of the religious with the disciplinary role seems quite unbelievable to the outsider, but it has been taken for granted for so long in Catholic higher education that it is being abandoned only very slowly. In some instances where it is abandoned, the clergy and religious are pulled out of the dormitory completely, which is the functional equivalent of throwing out the baby with the bath water. In other cases, in addition to the disciplinary and counseling role conflict in which the priest or religious is caught, he is also saddled with full teaching loads and various other duties within the religious order.

Some of the colleges have trained counselors—either religious or lay—available to assist students in a capacity less formal than the official psychiatric counseling center. Other schools have campus chaplains, who are alert to the needs, problems, and aspirations of the young people. Nevertheless, less than one-quarter of the schools we visited were sensitive to the religious or the human needs of their young people, or alert in organizing personnel and programs to stimulate enthusiasm and the search for meaning and significance. There are, as we have indicated before, two reasons for such failures. First of all, the theoretical stance described in the previous section would surely discourage innovation in religious life on the campus. Second, many of the people appointed to student personnel work are unbelievably inept and as a result terribly fearful both of failure and of innovation which might bring discredit upon them or upon the religious order.

Our student interviewer was quite dissatisfied with the state of housing in most of the Catholic schools we visited. The older dormitories—relics of the past—tend to be decrepit and overcrowded, while the newer ones were built in the finest tradition of urban renewal modern architecture with all the homey comforts of prisons or mental hospitals. The interviewer was particularly critical of the lack of places where young people could sit and talk. She argued that there were not likely to be serious discussions of what had gone on in class unless there were rather small, quiet lounges where young people could smoke and converse in some kind of privacy. She also noted that at several women's schools such lounges had been made available, but they were quite empty because the sisters in charge of the schools felt that it would be a shame to mess up such nice rooms with anything as foul as cigarette smoke. Young ladies who wished to be so unladylike as to smoke were therefore exiled to a small room in the basement, which became the overcrowded, very vital center of campus life.

However, the problem in dormitory construction was not so

much a concern either for cleanliness or for discipline, but rather a financial concern—to construct a building as cheaply as possible. In some institutions, new students were being taken in primarily because it was thought that they would ease the financial strain of the school. The dormitories were being constructed as cheaply as possible in order to house as many students as possible, with the result that practically no concern was given for the comfort of the students. Catholic colleges are not the only ones that create massive skyscraper dormitories that have all the personality of the New York Hilton. But, one would think that because of the theological position of the Catholic Church on community and fellowship, the designing of dormitories would have respected values other than economy and that student personnel directors would not be satisfied that theirs was a thoroughly "Christian" dormitory because there was a chapel tucked away in some corner of the building.

There were some impressive exceptions. One school has consistently pursued a policy of having many small, family-like dormitories, housing no more than thirty or forty students and providing the opportunity for integration of living and studying. Many secular universities are just beginning to experiment with this concept.

The most serious weakness of student personnel policy in Catholic colleges and universities was not the inadequate housing, the unchallenging religious life, the minute supervision and regulation, the absence of due process in disciplinary cases, or even the pathetic attempts at development of virtue by compulsion. The most serious failure was rather the failure of these colleges to be that which they claimed to be—Catholic. If Kenneth Kenniston is right that the basic problem of contemporary youth is the search for meaning, then the most serious failure of any university is its failure to provide an atmosphere and resources by which young people can work out a meaning not only for the private sphere of their lives, but also for the public sphere, and for the relationship between the private and the public spheres. If Kenniston is correct that the retreat into privatism and disengagement is the result of the young person's failure to find any system of meaning, then any Catholic college or university that does not give meaning to the private and public sectors of life is proving false to its whole raison d'être.

Such a failure is particularly depressing in a time like the present, when the Roman Catholic Church is engaged in one of the most vigorous periods of ferment that it has experienced in the past thousand years. One may agree or disagree with Roman Catholicism as a way of life, but it is hard to deny that at the present time the Roman Church is engaged in an exciting attempt to renovate and renew its interpretation of reality and to make relevant to the contemporary world its traditional wisdom. It would not be difficult for Catholic higher educational institutions to communicate some of this excitement to their students. But with the exception of a few schools and a few people in other schools, no attempt is even being made to communicate it. In their role as meaning-giving institutions, the majority of Catholic colleges and universities are pathetic failures.

Let us assert once again that some schools are doing a splendid job, and that two or three of them have captured the spirit of the post-Vatican age with almost incredible insight and perception. Furthermore, some other schools, are trying, but whether ecumenical lectures and occasional additions of new courses to the curriculum represent an adequate response to the Vatican Council remains to be seen. Theology programs are being drastically revised in some schools and moderately improved in many more, but the pace of change in theology programs does not indicate that administrators have responded with any sense of urgency to the growing restlessness and dissatisfaction of students. For instance, at one school where a new theology program was offered, lines of students began to form at six in the morning on registration day to get into the new courses. At the same school, a lecture program in theology began in a small classroom and quickly expanded to a large lecture hall off campus, since there was no room on the campus large enough to hold the masses of students who came to hear discussions by famous contemporary theologians. (Our student interviewer argues that, at least among the most intellectually concerned students, there seems to be far more interest in Catholic theology than is found among most of the faculty members.)

While there is therefore no necessary conflict between Catholic higher education and enthusiastic response to the spirit of the Vatican Council, the colleges and universities have failed to interpret the renewal of the Church in such a fashion as to provide opportunities for meaning, explanation, and understanding for their students. There are several reasons for this failure. First of all, not all priests or nuns have accepted the renewal of the Church accomplished at the Vatican Council. (One student personnel administrator assured us that Pope Paul had put an end to all the foolishness that Pope John started—this despite overwhelming evidence that, at least on the level of theory and idea, the present pontiff is extending the ideas of his predecessor.) This die-hard resistance to renewal of the Church seems to be especially entrenched in some religious orders and particularly in the power elites within the orders. Thus college administrators find that their religious superiors or the senior members of the community are likely to be strongly opposed to changes in student life or student education, if they might reflect the renewal currently going on the Church. Second, many of the religious orders themselves are caught in an internal struggle over power between conservatives and progressives, and until the progressives definitely win control of the order, they will not be able to apply their own policies to student life. Third, there seems to be a fear that even if the religious order and the college were in favor of reorganizing student life, the local ecclesiastical authorities would be opposed to such innovations and would somehow or other (in ways not immediately clear) "crack down" on the school if it tried to institute such reforms. Finally, there is an inevitable time lag between any major policy change in an organization and its implementation at the grass roots. Even though there was plenty of advance warning for those who cared to listen to it, the drastic change in Roman Catholic policy of the Vatican Council caught most ecclesiastical administrators off guard, particularly student personnel administrators, who seem in general to be less in touch with what's going on in the world than anyone else. Hence, any attempt to revitalize student religious and social life and provide meaning in terms of contemporary Catholic theological developments is bound to be slow.

In addition, there is often an almost overwhelming problem of lack of understanding. We described to one high-level administrator a program of voluntary theological discussion groups that had flourished and provided stimulating religious atmosphere at another campus. The administrator thought that was an excellent idea, hoped to initiate it in the very near future at his own school, and thought that such a program of informal theological discussion groups would be a tremendous asset to a Catholic college. He then added that as soon as he organized such a program he intended to make it obligatory for every student in the university.

THE STUDENTS THEMSELVES

What does the theory and practice of personnel work that we have described do to students at Catholic colleges? It doesn't do very much to them, either for weal or woe. The students are decent, docile, confused, respectful, troubled, ambitious, lonely, young Americans, like their counterparts at other colleges and universities. With some exceptions, their intellectual involvement is only that required to get through college, and their social and political interests are minimal. Many of them are quite satisfied with the education they are getting, and many others are unhappy with their educational experiences but don't care enough to do anything about it. Others are restless and dissatisfied, but not to such a level as to engage in any organized program for change. Of the minority who might become active campaigners for reform and modification of student life, some are disorganized and in many instances afraid because the college does reserve to itself the right to expel and release students.

The picture is not terribly different from that of most American college students. At only one or two of the large urban Catholic universities was there a left-wing element comparable to left wings at some of the first-rate American universities and liberal arts colleges. Undoubtedly, part of the reason for this is that the Catholic campus atmosphere is simply not the kind of place where radical social movements are likely to find a favorable climate. But the absence of popular radical movements at the Catholic schools can be explained sufficiently by the middle class respectability of the Catholic population of the country. It may well take another generation of affluence in American society before the Catholic middle class begins to produce its Robespierres.

The Catholic university atmosphere probably does no more harm to young people than does the atmosphere of other universities, just as Catholic schools do not interfere any more with intellectual and academic career plans of students than do other colleges and universities (as discussed in Chapter 2).

But two problems must be noted: First of all, with a few exceptions, Catholic colleges and universities are missing a golden opportunity. Given the ferment in the Church, the volunteer movements among students, the complexities of the modern world, and the supernational organization of the Roman Church, it ought to be possible to turn a Catholic college or university campus into a dynamic, challenging, socioreligious milieu, in which young people would see a connection between their beliefs and the problems of the contemporary world. We do not deny that Catholic colleges have some moderate effect on the social attitudes of their students; the data presented in Chapter 2 seem to establish that they do. Nor do we deny the obvious truth that colleges and universities will not change completely the values of the vast majority of their students. But, at a few schools, the ferment and experimentation persuaded us that not only was there no necessary opposition between Roman Catholicism and extraordinarily meaningful higher education but that, properly understood and utilized, the Catholic religious tradition, particularly as it is being interpreted at the present time, can make important positive contributions to young people.

From the point of view of the larger American society, the failure of the Roman Catholic higher education system to utilize the best of its own traditions and to make its own unique contributions to our pluralistic culture is serious enough. But from the point of view of the Church, its higher educational institutions, or at least some of them, are doing a serious disservice to Catholicism itself. The data in Chapter 2 show that the defection rate in Catholicism is rather low among Catholic college graduates, although a more careful analysis of the data reveals that the defection rate is somewhat higher among those who were most successful academically in the Catholic colleges and were planning academic careers. So the Catholic colleges are not driving out of the Church vast numbers of young people, as some of the more sensational Catholic journals claim. Nor is it necessarily dysfunctional to the Church that a number of students go through a crisis of faith during their college years, because such crises of faith are in most instances little more than adjustments of religious beliefs and sentiments from adolescent to adult modalities. The real disservice to the Church is that most alert, intelligent and potentially dedicated students at Catholic colleges are being turned against the organized institutional Church. Some of them will leave the Church; the vast majority of them will not. But almost all of the creative, concerned, committed minority seem to come out of the Catholic colleges with a great deal of suspicion and contempt not only for the religious orders that run the college, but also for the whole institutionalized Church. The words "hypocrite" and "phony" seem to be on the lips of most of the student leaders that were interviewed in the course of our study.

These are not young people who are going to start rebellions or who will lead picket lines or demonstrations against the institutional Church (though from the point of view of the eventual health of the institutional Church, it might be better if they did). They will go through life with the profound suspicion that dialogue, mutual respect, and trust are impossible between Catholic laity and ecclesiastical authorities.

It is a supreme irony that the protectivism and authoritarianism that was designed precisely to keep young people safely within the Catholic tradition and to deepen (by compulsion) their commitment to the tradition has instead produced a profound cynicism about and alienation from the institutionalized expression of the tradition. It is hard to tell whether this represents a major change over the past. But one had the impression ten or fifteen years ago that young people coming out of the Catholic colleges were proud that they had a "Jesuit" or "Benedictine" or "Holy Cross" education. Unquestionably, large numbers of young people still do come out with similar pride. But among the creative, concerned minority, this pride seems to be almost invisible, and to have been replaced by shame, disillusionment, and cynicism. That it need not be so is established by the schools that have drastically changed their student personnel policy and created a campus atmosphere where student morale and élan can be positive and vigorous. It is not the role of social researchers to make policy suggestions. But we cannot resist the temptation to observe that if religious orders are unable or unwilling to drastically reform their relationships with the students in Catholic colleges, then it might be appropriate for someone in higher ecclesiastical authority to start knocking heads together.

CONCLUSIONS

We have suggested in this chapter that the basic problem in Catholic institutions is that their relations with students are determined by traditional attitudes toward human nature that have held sway in the religious orders for the past couple of centuries. Despite the major transformations going on in Roman Catholicism today, some religious orders have not adjusted to these changes with sufficient rapidity to modify their attitudes and behavior towards college students. We visited enough Catholic schools where dramatic changes had taken place (or where the traditional policy was astonishingly enlightened) to persuade us that there was no inherent contradiction between Roman Catholicism and enlightened, imaginative, and humanistic student personnel policy.

We further observed that liberalization of rules and regulations seems to be in process in many Catholic campuses, and in some schools the progress is rather rapid. Nevertheless, only a bare handful of schools have come up with relevant and challenging functional substitutes for the campus religious life of the past. The very best of the Catholic student personnel people, as well as the very best of the Catholic student leaders compare favorably with the best that we saw on the secular campuses, and the worst are no worse than those in non-Catholic schools. On the average, social commitment among the students and professional competence among student personnel administrators tend to be somewhat lower at Catholic colleges than in American higher education in general. But the real weaknesses of student-administration-faculty relationships at the Catholic colleges is that the present policy seems to be alienating from the Church its most concerned and creative leadership and to be depriving American society of the unique contributions to our pluralistic culture that Catholic higher education is capable of making. At those Catholic schools that were most impressive, we found a playfulness, a willingness to experiment, a search for relevance to contemporary problems, an attempt to integrate education and social commitment, a freedom from cliché and pseudo-seriousness, and an integrated view of the meaningfulness of life which are disastrously absent from most American educational institutions. Since some such schools do exist and since some religious orders administer them, it is obviously possible for them to exist in greater numbers and to be administered by orders. But such institutions do not have much chance of becoming typical until the religious communities set their own houses in order and determine much more clearly that the college and university must have their own rights and must have independence. Until this happens, the dreary mistakes will continue; they may decrease, but the rate of decrease will be so slow as to waste the magnificent opportunity of the present moment.

10

Summary and Conclusions

On a steep hill, in a fading district of a large American city, there are to be found the very unpretentious buildings of a small Catholic women's liberal arts college. It does not take long to suspect that St. Mary's College is a poor school. The president's office is the least elaborate of any that we have seen, and one can dimly perceive the smells of the chemistry laboratory next door to the president's office. There is no large assembly hall, nor even small meeting rooms. Discussion groups simply meet in the cafeteria. There is an acute shortage of storage space; boxes are piled in every corner of the school's corridors. Classrooms, offices, and study halls are all cramped and crowded. Young women in the school are anything but wealthy. Their clothes are nondescript; the cars in the parking lot obviously are second, third, or even fourth hand. The hasty visitor would assume that St. Mary's was just one more Catholic women's college that should never have been founded—a little bit more impoverished than the other schools that ought to be "phased out," to use the favorite phrase of the critics of Catholic education.

The poverty of St. Mary's is in some respects more apparent than real. Its budget in 1965-66 was $1.3 million, and there was no deficit. Furthermore, the library was ranked in a recent survey in the top 20 per cent of all liberal arts college libraries. The nuns who administer St. Mary's seem to have made the remarkable discovery that books are more important than buildings in higher education and would apparently much prefer to have a high quality library than impressive buildings.[1]

[1] In reading this chapter, the president of St. Mary's College expressed the fear that her school emerged looking "ragged and funny and even a little silly." We really don't think that our description does this to St. Mary's at all. But let it be

But, St. Mary's College is, to use the words of our student interviewer, "something else." It may not be academically the best of
the thirty Catholic schools we visited, but as a human institution,
it was far away the most impressive. The dilapidated corridors
rocked with laughter. One member of the research team remarked
after the first hour and a half in the school, "Everybody's laughing here—the sisters, the laymen, and the girls. They're laughing
all the time. What in the world is the matter with them?" What is
the matter with students, faculty, and administration at St. Mary's
is something that is not the matter with most other colleges in the
country—Catholic, or non-Catholic. The people at St. Mary's are
happy. As a matter of fact, they are happier than anybody has a
right to be, especially the students.

Imaginative classroom instruction, well-trained sister faculty,
enthusiastic and dedicated lay faculty (many of them with departmental chairmanships, a tradition that goes back fifty years to the
beginning of the school), voluntary "theology workshops" to
which the students swarm, an extraordinarily creative art department, social commitment that brings better than one-quarter of
the student body to inner-city work, a relaxed, playful atmosphere
that affects even the most serious of subjects—St. Mary's is indeed a unique school in American higher education, one that is
difficult to believe even when one is in the midst of it, and even
more difficult once one has departed (and it is by no means easy
to depart).

We tried to discover what the secret was of the magic of St.
Mary's. We were constantly referred to Mother Jeremia (and I
trust that the real-life counterpart will excuse me for labeling
her with a pseudonym). Mother Jeremia was mother general of
the order some time ago and is now presiding over a high school
near the college. Her fifty years or more in the religious order
would span most of the history of the college and the community.
She was the one who, we were told, could tell. It became clear,
after a few minutes of conversation with this remarkable lady,
that only a very special religious order would have made some-

noted that we do not believe for a moment that St. Mary's is a "silly" institution.
Playful and happy indeed, but hardly silly. Or if indeed it is silly, then it is a
silliness of which American higher education is in great need.

body like Mother Jeremia president of the college and mother general. To our question of how St. Mary's had become the unique place it is, she replied, "There are two explanations, Father. First of all, we believe in this religious order that our function is to create an atmosphere in which each of the nuns is able to develop her own talents and personality to its fullest. We don't want to mold our sisters into any pattern. We want them to be themselves in the best possible way. And so we do everything we can to help each sister develop her talents to the fullest. Secondly, we decided fifty years ago that you could either build beautiful buildings or educate young women, and we chose to do the latter."

Such an explanation is not completely sufficient, but at least it reveals enough of the spirit of the religious order to make St. Mary's College relatively easy to understand. Apparently, the Spanish ladies who came to the United States to begin the order were convinced fairly early in the game that they would be successful only if they became thoroughly and completely American. They put off all the customs and attitudes that might have been relevent in one society but were not relevant in the other. The norms and customs that were maintained were those that were relevant to their work of education. And anything that would interfere with doing this work in the most efficient possible way was discarded. Young sisters were sent to secular graduate schools long before most other communities even thought of such a procedure. The mother general of the order has a doctorate from a high quality school. Laymen were moved into key positions in the faculty and administration because their help was needed, and there was no fear that they would "try to take the school away." Younger nuns were trained during the novitiate to be educators primarily and to identify their religious life with the apostolate of education. Freedom and permissiveness, both within the order and within the school, were promoted because they were viewed as sound educational procedures. Pressure from ecclesiastical authorities outside the school was resisted on the grounds that with all due respect for authority the school still had an independence of its own which the order was bound to maintain. In other words, the sisters of St. Mary's College were not trying to maintain the customs and traditions of some past excellence; they were rather interested in focusing on a present excellence and working for improved excellence in the future. The organization of their religious order, far from being a handicap to promoting the academic development of the college, turned out to be a strong asset. The result was not merely an exciting college; it was also a religious order that seems to have no problem in recruiting young women.

When our visit at St. Mary's was over, the senior researcher stopped by the president's office to thank her for her hospitality (which, as might be remarked, was much more casual than that encountered at many other schools). He had facetiously warned her against the plan to move St. Mary's to a campus with several non-Catholic liberal arts colleges.

"You have too much going for you here, Sister," he noted, "don't take the risk of losing it by moving."

"But," Sister President replied, "what is important here is not buildings; it's people, and the people will be the same out there as they are here."

"Yes, but the people out there will be more than just your college, Sister, and a lot of them take higher education very, very seriously."

The Sister President's eyes sparkled. "How much do you want to bet that we change them before they change us."

We tell the story of St. Mary's College not merely because it is a fascinating institution, and not even because it demonstrates that affiliation with the Catholic Church and ownership by a religious community are no obstacles to enlightened and imaginative higher education. St. Mary's college also points out the precise nature of the problem of the relationship between religious orders and colleges.

We have been harsh on religious orders in this report. But it ought to be established clearly that we are not opposed to religious orders, not even opposed to them owning and administering colleges. On the contrary, the religious orders have probably produced a larger per capita number of enlightened, sensitive, and progressive human beings than any other group within American Catholicism and, perhaps, within the whole of American society. The problem is not that the religious orders are bad, nor that the individuals within the orders are not enlightened or competent. The problem is rather that the structure and history of many religious communities place serious obstacles in the way of their work in higher education. And, unless these obstacles can be eliminated, the future of Catholic higher education is not encouraging.

Philip Gleason has remarked that it is not at all surprising that the religious orders became heavily involved in American higher education. Once the decision was made by the American Church to pursue a policy of constructing a higher educational system, the religious orders had the personnel, the resources and the background in education that made it feasible for the early bishops either to invite them to found colleges or to turn already founded colleges over to their administration and control. While the religious orders were in many ways qualified to assume the administration of colleges, they were not completely qualified. Their views of education were, to a greater or lesser extent, in variance with those which were held by most American higher educators. But more seriously, their training, their style of life, their norms and values, and their methods of administration were shaped by a historical tradition that did not come into existence with the problems of American higher education in view. Almost from the beginning, there were inevitable tensions between the historical traditions within the religious community and the administration of the college. The more liberal members of the orders have always held that the spirit of their founder and his traditions permitted them to drastically revise the role relationships and the goals of the religious community to fit new work. But the more conservative members have always held that such adjustments should not be permitted to go too far. The religious community might cease to be that which its founder made it. Furthermore, they argue that the community is not only in the business of higher education, and it cannot restructure its whole life and organize all its plans around the needs of a higher educational institution. Thus, both the values and the other works of the religious order provide serious potential for conflict with the values and the work of the American higher educational enterprise.

It seems to us that so far as the religious community is able to take a "functional" approach to the relationship between itself and its higher educational institutions, precisely to that extent is the college or university likely to be on the path of academic improvement. If the superiors of the religious order are able to say, "At least insofar as our colleges and universities go, we will adhere to those norms and customs of the religious life that promote the school's improvement as an American higher educational enterprise and discard those norms and customs that interfere," then the academic institution will improve and the morale of the religious faculty will be excellent. (The order that administers St. Mary's College has formulated this policy more completely and effectively than any other we encountered.) On the other hand, if the religious superiors maintain that there are some norms, some customs, some methods of administration that are not negotiable, and that there are some compromises with the needs of higher education that the order could not in conscience make and be true to its own tradition, then the school is much more likely to stagnate.

The original hypothesis with which this study began was that the Catholic higher educational institution would improve academically to the extent that its president and his upper administrative colleagues were independent of traditional norms and restrictions of the religious community. The high rank-order correlations obtained in the study suggest that this hypothesis was quite accurate. But an important question remains unanswered. We are still faced with the necessity of explaining for what reasons other than sheer chance (a factor not to be ruled out), one religious community has the imagination and courage to appoint an imaginative, forceful president while other religious communities (or other provinces within the same community) seem to lack this courage. If we are to completely understand the phenomenon of Catholic higher education, there must be more intensive research in the social history of the religious orders in the United States.[2]

[2]Sister Rose Ann Murphy suggests that some religious orders are founded with an orientation toward certain apostolic work to be done, and as the nature of the

But we would still be faced with the puzzle of why one province of the Jesuit order, for example, has a rapid improvement university while another province has a medium or even a low improvement university, in circumstances at least as favorable for rapid improvement. Some Jesuits we interviewed during the course of our study suggested that the differences might be traceable to the ethnic origins of the elite group in the province during its formative years in this country. They observed that certain provinces had ethnic backgrounds oriented toward maintaining the Jesuit tradition with all the detailed rigor possible, while other provinces were much more flexible and functional in their approach. Such an explanation is plausible, but unfortunately there is not nearly enough research data available to validate it.

But whatever the explanation for the decision of the religious superiors to appoint a competent president and then to give him the power and independence he needs to launch the school in a program of academic improvement, such a decision is critical in determining whether a Catholic higher educational institution will improve dramatically, merely slide along, or stagnate. The money available from various constituencies, geographic location, concentration of Catholic population, social class of the students, and the proportion of laity in key administrative positions are not nearly as effective predictors of academic improvement as are the leadership style, independence and ability of the president of the college.

Academic freedom of the faculty, faculty participation and decision making, complexity of graduate programs, and liberalization of student personnel policy seem to be related to academic improvement, but as consequence rather than antecedant. Some institutions, for reasons of geography or the internal condition of the religious order, simply could not improve academically

---

work changes, the style and the ethos of the community changes with it. Other communities are founded not so much with an orientation toward work but rather an orientation toward preserving a tradition of the past. These "traditional" rather than "functional" communities change only very slowly and reluctantly. It would be quite possible, if we were able to investigate the history of the orders, to find a stronger functional ethos in the orders that preside over rapid improvement schools, and a more traditional ethos in those that administer medium or low improvement schools.

under any conditions. But others seem to be similar in every respect to rapid improvement schools save the quality of presidential leadership. In some instances, a visitor fifteen or twenty years ago would have predicted that several of the medium improvement schools would have been rapid improvement schools and vice-versa; as far as environmental circumstances went, a number of the medium improvement schools were much more favorably situated than the rapid improvement schools. But those in the decision-making positions did not appoint the kind of president the school needed.

The president of the rapid improvement school has five critical roles to play. First of all, it is necessary for him to symbolize in his own person and in his activities the goals that the institution has set for itself and to radiate confidence and hope that these goals are achievable. Presumably, the president is in a crucial position to determine what the goals are. Since most Catholic higher educational institutions have only the vaguest of goals, it is most unlikely that a charismatic president would arrive on the scene to find that the goals had been predefined for him. In those schools that are clearly improving institutions, faculty, students, and administrators are virtually unanimous in explaining the improvement of the institution in terms of the presidential charisma.

Second, the presidential leader must be an extraordinarily skilled politician in order to achieve consensus among the diverse and often opposing groups that constitute the university social system. He must placate the older members of the religious community and, in many instances, the religious superior, while at the same time encouraging the young turks in the lay and religious faculty and sustaining the morale of hard-pressed and threatened administrators. He must reassure students that they are not forgotten and parents that students are not being given complete license. He must persuade alumni groups that the finest traditions of the school are being maintained while at the same time persuading government agencies and foundations that the school is undergoing-drastic reform and innovation. It is a delicate balancing act, and some institutions require that the president not be bound by the strictest and most literal interpretation of truth.

Third, the president ought to have the knowledge and the skills necessary to determine what an educational institution is and how his particular school ought to become one. He must be an ambassador to the outside world and from the outside world, a transmitter of the educational values of the larger American higher educational enterprise to the Catholic system. It is necessary for him to persuade his various constituencies that the norms of American higher education are not merely not opposed to the norms of traditional Catholicism but are in fact simply the logical development of Catholic principles and philosophy.

Fourth, the president plays a key role in the selection of the lower-level administrators and faculty because only he has enough prestige and influence in the school to legitimize the necessary professionalization of the operation. The president, in other words, must take an active hand in replacing familial and sacral values with professional and secular values. He must make sure that people appointed to key positions in the faculty and administration have the professional, collegial, and secular values without which a school simply cannot claim to be an American higher educational institution.

Finally, the president is, in most instances, the primary representative of the school to the world of contributors, foundations, and government agencies. All of the presidents of improving schools were masters at this game, and some of them would have been college presidents, even if they were not clergy or religious. A Catholic college president who is not interested in, or is afraid of the role of civic leader, fund raiser, and contact man, whatever his other admirable qualifications, will be a failure as a college president.

When we found a president with imagination and professional orientation, the lower-level administrators of the college were professionally competent, the faculty members were well trained and had high morale, and the students were treated more liberally and in some instances had available to them an imaginative challenging religious life. When the president's main reference group was not in the world of higher education, but rather in a religious community, the lower-level administrators were either incompetent or had no real power, the faculty was undistinguished and discouraged, and the students were restricted and sullen. The president set the tone for the school. If he liked his job and did it well, it was an improving school. If he did not like his job or was more interested in keeping the religious order happy than in pushing the institution forward, then the school would advance very slowly or stagnate.

What does the future seem to hold for Catholic higher education? In at least half of the institutions we visited, there were major transitions going on—new presidents took over the reigns as older presidents prepared to leave office. In such a very fluid situation, prophecy or even projection is risky. There was, we thought, a widespread feeling among the younger (and some of the not so young) members of the religious community, that the time had come "to get out of the business of higher education" or "to give the schools to the laity." The arguments used were that the higher educational institution was an impossible burden for the religious order to support in terms of money and personnel, that the religious order could not produce sufficient talent to administer the school, and that the religious community was incapable of adjusting to the problems of higher education and administration.

The suggestion made most frequently was that legal control of the college or university be turned over to a board of trustees either completely lay or partly lay and partly religious, which would be not only the technical, legal owners of the school but the actual controlling body. Such a board of trustees would make policies, elect officers, and evaluate the performance of the institution. It would be empowered to choose presidents who were qualified for the job, whether religious or laity—the implication being that in most instances the president would be a lay person.[3]

It is not our intention to criticize such a plan. At least one, and possibly two, Catholic higher educational institutions are apparently going to institute such experiments in the very near future. Experimentation in this direction is probably very well advised. Furthermore, the inclusion of laity in boards of trustees and their eligibility for the highest administrative positions in Catholic

[3]It would be a mistake to underestimate how widespread is this notion of "getting out of the business of higher education." We heard of it on almost every campus and almost every level of university and college faculty administration.

schools would represent great progress. It seems to us that such moves would demonstrate most clearly that the "traditional" approach to the relationship between the religious order and the higher educational institution was being abandoned in favor of a "functional" approach.[4]

But whatever benefits might arise from such experimentation, it did not seem to us that such drastic measures were absolutely necessary to assure a selection of the most competent college presidents. Furthermore, there seem to be certain dangers inherent in such a plan which its advocates apparently do not understand. The basic problem is "Who are the laity?" American Protestants have had several generations of practice in being effective trustees of higher educational institutions, but Catholics are just beginning to acquire the skills necessary to play this role. It may very well be that there are just not enough competent, resourceful, imaginative laymen to go around, especially if a large number of institutions begin a scramble to collect the available lay talent. As a matter of fact, if some of the business and professional men who presently decorate the advisory boards of trustees became the legal owners of the universities, there is a very strong possibility that the last stage of the school would be worse than the first; the religious who are presently the trustees of universities, however unskilled some of them might be, probably know more about higher education and what it takes to make an institution good than do the well-to-do Catholic laymen who are most likely to be appointed to the emerging boards of trustees. Some presidents of rapid improvement institutions would never have been successful in their reforming innovations if they had had to contend with the kinds of lay trustees who might have been peering over their shoulders had the school been "turned over to the laity."

There are at least three other ways in which the appointment of reasonably competent presidents could be assured without so drastic a structural reform. The first functional alternative is quite simple: the religious order should make certain that the

[4]Most of the new appointments we encountered in the course of our 1965-66 research indicates a notable improvement in the type of men and women selected for administrative responsibilities. But still there were a number of appointments that seemed to be characterized more by their "safety" than by any other consideration.

superiors who appoint higher educational administrators know what higher education is all about. Such a superior would pledge himself to respect the freedom of the school. It might be required of a provincial, for example, either that he had taught in a university faculty or that he turn the responsibility for recommending or selecting presidents over to an assistant who had broad university experience.

A second "functional" alternative would be to specify far more clearly the legal relationship between the school and the religious order. At the present time, the canonical nature of the relationship is such that the religious order has all the rights and the privileges and the school has few, if any. But the canon law could be modified so that a school would actually be a separate financial corporation, with its financial operations not legally responsible to the religious order but responsible to its own board of trustees.

Similarly, the canonical provisions could permit the administration of the school independence in decision making and guarantee that its decisions would not be overruled by the provincial or the religious superior. Thus, the school would be free to hire and keep its faculty without being obliged to accept any member of the religious community the provincial should assign. Nor would the school be obliged to accept the loss of any member of the religious community whom the provincial should wish to withdraw from the faculty. Similarly, the top administrators, the financial officers, the student personnel directors should be people chosen for these jobs by the president, independent of any decision the provincial or superior might make.

In practice, in some institutions these rights and freedoms are already safeguarded. But there is nothing to prevent them from being terminated at any time, and there is nothing to force the provincials in other religious orders to grant such rights and privileges. Higher educational institutions could recommend reforms in canon law and in their own constitutions that would make a much clearer specification of the relationship of the university and the religious community possible—a recognition that without certain broad areas of independence, it is very difficult for the higher educational institution to improve academically and to become a full-fledged member of the American educational enterprise.

A third alternative would be to make the existing legal boards of trustees independent governing bodies. Thus the provincial could appoint to the board of trustees some of the most highly qualified members of his community and then change the legal nature of this board of trustees so that it would be self-perpetuating by electing its own members (either restricted to the religious community or including a certain proportion of laity) for specified terms of office. In this way, the school would still be owned by the religious order, but the provincial would not have the burden or the responsibility of supervising its operation and selecting its officers.

None of these alternatives, nor any combination of them, would automatically guarantee academic growth. But in the present highly fluid transitional situation, careful experimentation with these alternatives is definitely in order. In our discussions with Catholic administrators, some men argued that ecclesiastical law would not permit such experimentation. They may be right, but there is nothing sacred or immutable about ecclesiastical law, especially not in the present period in Roman Catholic history. If ecclesiastical law needs to be changed in order to allow Catholic higher educational institutions to achieve their goals, it seems perfectly clear that ecclesiastical laws ought to be changed. They might even be relatively easy to change.

CONCLUSIONS

In this report, we found that Catholic higher educational institutions improved for approximately the same reason that most small- or medium-size educational institutions improve—good leadership. We found that some institutions were improving rapidly and were becoming quite presentable American colleges and universities, and that others were not getting the leadership they needed or deserved, largely because those in positions of responsibility for selecting leaders did not know what sort of leader was needed or were afraid to appoint the kinds of leader needed. There are, obviously, not enough good college presidents to go around. But if anything was clear to us at the end of this study, it was that there are far more competent people available in the Catholic higher educational enterprise than have actually been appointed to key administrative positions. Until this pool of talent is utilized, Catholic colleges are not going to be nearly as good as they could be.

But the Catholic schools are not so terribly bad. They may not be in the top twenty of the American higher educational institutions, but at least some of them are moving rather vigorously in that direction. Most of the problems Catholic schools face are not unique in themselves, but are problems that they share with the vast majority of non-Catholic colleges and universities. The complaints of faculty, students, and administrators in the thirty Catholic colleges were reflections of the complaints we heard at the six non-Catholic schools. The real tragedy of Catholic higher education is not that it is so very bad but that it could so easily be so much better. The dramatic progress of the rapid improvement schools demonstrates that there is vast potential for striking improvement if only there were more leaders who would seize the opportunities that exist. Not only is it possible for more Catholic colleges to make striking progress and to become fully respectable members of American academia, it is possible, as St. Mary's College and a few other schools clearly demonstrate, for Catholic academia to make its own unique contribution to American higher education.

Appendix

The Objective Correlates
of Academic Improvement

Since it clearly was not possible to visit all Catholic colleges and universities in the country, some procedure had to be found to select those schools to be visited. Initially, it was decided to limit the candidates to those Catholic institutions that fell into the National Opinion Research Center's 1961 and 1964 representative samples of American colleges and universities, in order to take advantage of special data available on these colleges. Thirty-nine Catholic institutions were included in these samples, of which twenty-four were men's or coeducational colleges and the remainder were women's colleges.

Because this number was too large to allow adequate field coverage of all institutions, we had to limit the sample still further. In doing this, we wanted to be sure that the entire range of colleges was covered—the greatly improved colleges, those holding their own, and those not keeping up with the rest. In order to insure that all three types of colleges would be visited, an index of improvement was developed, based on objective characteristics of the colleges—changes in the quality of the library, the faculty, and the amount of funds available. Such an index also provided a means of validating, at least partially, the subjective impressions of the field staff. A set of schools was selected in such a way as to cover the whole range of the objective improvement scale, but the field research team was given no information about the position of any school on the objective improvement scale until all field visits had been completed.

Since no objective measure of the academic quality of colleges is available for two points in time, it was not possible to develop a direct measure of institutional improvement. It was necessary to

This Appendix was written by Donald J. Treiman.

attempt to develop an Index of Institutional Improvement from a set of organizational characteristics of colleges for which measurements at two points in time were available—viz., the tuition cost, the per-student library holdings, and the proportion of the faculty who are laymen. By comparing these characteristics at two points in time, one can observe the pattern of change for each school. But, while it is likely that the improvement of a college has something to do with increase in some of these values, precisely which organizational attributes of colleges are crucial for their academic improvement is still an open question. Thus, before using variables of this sort, it is necessary to validate their relationship to academic improvement.

To do this, we have tried to predict the academic quality of a college from a number of its organizational attributes. For want of a better indicator, we used the proportion of a college's seniors planning to go on to graduate or professional school as an indicator of the academic quality of the school. While it is recognized that there are many other possible definitions of academic quality, some of which may accord better with the goals Catholic institutions set for themselves, this is the only indicator available for all schools in our samples. Moreover, the measure is quite plausible on its face—a school's academic orientation should be reflected in the proportion of its graduates seeking intellectual careers that necessitate post-graduate education. It should be noted, however, that this measure is not a very good one for women's colleges, which typically have rather different goals for their students. Since the primary emphasis of this project was on men's and coeducational schools, women's colleges were eliminated from the analysis. As the first step in the analysis, a set of organizational characteristics of colleges—tuition cost, proportion of lay faculty, and per-student library holdings—were used to predict the proportion of seniors planning to attend graduate school. Some justification of these items seems in order.

Tuition cost was included both because it provides the single most important source of revenue for Catholic colleges and because it may be taken as an indicator of a college's position in the academic marketplace. Excellence must be purchased; revenue is necessary if a college is to pay its salaries, build its library, provide laboratory equipment, and so on. Clearly, the more revenue a college has, the better able it will be to provide the material underpinnings of academic excellence. Moreover, the size of tuition may reflect the desirability of a college from the standpoint of student. If a college is perceived as providing an excellent education, it can charge high tuition and still attract students. It may be that because they are perennially pressed for funds, all private colleges in America, Catholic and non-Catholic alike, charge "all that the traffic can bear." If this is so, tuition is a good indicator of how excellent a college is perceived to be.

As it turned out, tuition costs proved the best predictor of graduate school attendance, and the regression equation on which the choice of schools was based consisted essentially of a regression of 1964 tuition on 1956 tuition. The ranking of schools made by interviewers for which the high rank-order correlation was achieved (as described in the text) was based on this initial regression. The validity of the procedure used will be described in further detail in the following paragraphs.

It is likely that the academic quality of a Catholic institution is enhanced by having a large proportion of laymen among its faculty. When a college appoints a laymen, it is free to choose the best man it can get, and to promote him or dismiss him strictly on his academic merits. However, when the faculty is composed largely of members of the religious order that controls the college, this freedom is severely restricted. A man's place in the order comes to have relevance and may take precedence over his academic qualifications in determining his academic position. Moreover, where religious form a relatively large portion of the faculty, the faculty is likely to be dominated by the religious order. Under these circumstances it may be hard to attract first-rate lay faculty for the remaining positions.

Because the library is the principal research facility of the scholar, the emphasis a college or university places on the quality of its library is a good indicator of its commitment to academic excellence. Although the size of a university or college library is a somewhat crude measure of its excellence, it is obvious that the larger the number of volumes, the greater the variety of holdings. Because large schools must necessarily have large libraries in order to provide even minimal service for their students, the best indicator of library quality is the number of volumes per student.

In order to predict graduate school attendance from the organizational characteristics just reviewed, we regressed the proportion of students planning graduate school (P) in each of the twenty-four male and coeducational colleges on tuition charge (T), proportion of the faculty who are laymen (L), and number of library volumes per student (V). Since our information on graduate school intentions of seniors came from both NORC's 1961 and 1964 samples of colleges, it was necessary first to adjust the 1964 figures to the 1961 metric. An adjustment equation was arrived at by regressing the 1961 proportions planning graduate school on the 1964 proportions, for the fifty-five colleges and universities common to both samples. Data on tuition charge and library size were taken from the 1956 edition of *American Universities and Colleges*. Data on the proportion of faculty who are laymen are from *Official Guide to Catholic Educational Institutions*, 1959 edition. Data on student body size used to construct the variable, "library volumes per student," are from the 1957 edition of the U.S. Office of Education publication, *Opening (Fall) Enrollment in Higher Education*. The figures for total enrolment were used.

The least squares solution of our regression predicting graduate school attendance rates is given, in standard form, by

$$P = .559(T) + .209(L) + .146(V).$$

The amount charged for tuition is clearly the strongest predictor of graduate school attendance rates, but the proportion of faculty who are laymen and the number of library volumes per student add to the predictive accuracy of the equation. Together, the three variables account for about 45 per cent of the variation over schools in the proportion of graduates continuing their education ($R = .66$).

Although the proportion of students from a given college going directly on to graduate school is not, as we indicated above, a completely valid measure of institutional quality, the fact that the three organizational variables—tuition charge, laity of faculty, and library size—predict graduate school attendance fairly well lends some confidence to their utility as surrogate measures of academic quality. Hence, it seems reasonable to suppose that change in these variables is associated with change in institutional quality. For this reason, we decided to use these three organizational variables to construct an Index of Institutional Improvement by which our sample of schools could be hierarchially ordered.

To construct our index, we chose to compare the three characteristics of colleges at two points in time, as close as we could get to 1956 and 1964.[1] Rather than using the simple differences between the 1956 and 1964 values on these variables, we took account of secular trends by scoring each school in terms of its departure from the average increase. This was accomplished by regressing the 1964 score on the 1956 score and taking the residual from the regression. This procedure amounts to considering proportional increases, rather than absolute increases, and thus removes a bias in favor of schools that had high values on those variables in 1956.

Our next task was to put the scores for the three variables together into an index. Here two possibilities existed: (1) to weight the variables according to their contribution to the prediction of graduate school attendance; or (2) to take a simple average of the three values. The justification for the first alternative rests on the assumption that the same variables that best predict graduate school attendance on a cross-sectional basis will be most highly associated with academic improvement over time. Since there are no good grounds for accepting this assumption, we felt that a simple average of the residuals from each of the longitudinal regressions would provide the most appropriate Index of Institutional Improvement. However, since the three variables are measured in different metrics, it was first necessary to convert them to standard form by dividing each residual by its standard deviation. Then the index scores can be interpreted as average standard deviations from the mean level of improvement.

As was indicated above, the purpose of developing such an index based on objective characteristics of colleges was to provide

[1]The sources listed above provided data for the first period, "1956." The 1964, 1963, and 1965 editions, respectively, of these three publications provided data for the second period, "1964."

some validation of the subjective rankings of improvement made by the field staff. Because the field staff had a special interest in some of the twenty-four colleges, these were automatically included in the list of schools to be visited. To select the others, the field staff was given its choice from the subset of schools falling within the same third of the rank order. In this way, fourteen of the original twenty-four colleges were chosen for field visits.

So the question remains: How good is the subjective ranking of institutional improvement made by the field staff? In order to determine this, we computed the product-moment correlation between the subjective rankings and the objective scale scores, for the fourteen colleges that were ranked; $r = .62$, indicating that nearly 40 per cent of the variance in the subjective rankings is accounted for by the average deviation from the secular trends in tuition rate, laity of the faculty, and per capita library size. Considering that these variables are but crude surrogates for measures of institutional quality, and that change in these characteristics is conditioned by many factors other than degree of emphasis on improvement, we may consider the size of the correlation to be impressively high. At least it allows some confidence that the subjective impressions reported in the body of this monograph are not completely amiss.

References

AHERN, P. H. *The Catholic University of America, 1887–1896.* Washington, D.C.: Catholic University of America Press, 1948.

ASTIN, A. W. *Who goes where to college?* Chicago: Science Research Associates, 1965.

BARRY, C. J. *The Catholic University of America, 1903–1909.* Washington, D.C.: Catholic University of America Press, 1950.

———. *Worship and work: Saint John's Abbey and University, 1856–1956.* Collegeville, Minn.: St. John's Abbey, 1956.

DONOVAN, J. *Academic man in the Catholic college.* New York: Sheed and Ward, 1964.

ELLIS, J. T. American Catholics and the intellectual life. *Thought,* 1955, **30** (Autumn), 351–88.

GLEASON, P. The crisis in Catholic universities: A historical prespective. *Catholic Mind,* 1966, **64** (September), 43–55.

GREELEY, A. M. *Religion and career: A study of college graduates.* New York: Sheed and Ward, 1963.

GREELEY, A. M., and ROSSI, P. H. *The education of Catholic Americans.* Chicago: Aldine Publishing Company, 1966.

HAMILTON, R. N. *The story of Marquette University.* Milwaukee: Marquette University Press, 1953.

HASSENGER, R. (Ed.) *The shape of Catholic higher education.* New York: John Wiley, 1967.

HOGAN, P. E. *The Catholic University of America, 1896–1903.* Washington, D.C.: Catholic University of America Press, 1949.

IRWIN, M. (Ed.) *American universities and colleges* (7th ed.). Washington, D.C. American Council on Education, 1956.

JACOB, P. E. *Changing values in college: An exploratory study of the impact of college teaching.* New York: Harper, 1957.

MCCLELLAND, D. C. *The achieving society.* Princeton, N.J.: Van Nostrand, 1961.

MCMULLIN, E. Philosophy of the United States Catholic college, a survey. University of Notre Dame, 1966. (Mimeo.)

NATIONAL CATHOLIC WELFARE CONFERENCE. *The official guide to Catholic educational institutions in the United States.* New York: Catholic Institutional Directory Company, 1959.

221

POORMAN, R. O. An analysis of the relationship between the concept of shared decision-making and the vow of obedience in religious institutes in Catholic higher education. Unpublished Ph.D. dissertation, University of Notre Dame, 1964.

POWER, E. J. *A history of Catholic higher education in the United States.* Milwaukee: Bruce, 1958.

UNITED STATES OFFICE OF EDUCATION. *Opening (fall) enrollment in higher education, 1957.* Washington, D.C.: Government Printing Office, 1957.

WARKOV, S., and GREELEY, A. M. Parochial school origins and educational achievement. *Amer. sociol. Rev.,* 1966, **31**, 406–414.

WILLIAMSON, E. G., and COWAN, J. L. *The American student's freedom of expression.* Minneapolis: University of Minnesota Press, 1966.

Index

AAUP, 13, 15, 65, 81, 82, 83, 93–94, 95, 107, 109, 110–111, 114, 116, 120, 122, 147, 190
AAUP ratings; *see* Faculty
Academic freedom; *see* Administrators; Faculty; Index of Forbidden Books; Students
Academic improvement: and academic freedom of faculty and students, 6, 7, 104, 207; and alumni and parents, 100; and competence of administrators, vi, 9, 10, 18, 20, 99, 102, 103, 104, 213–14; and development offices, 100; and environment of institution, 102–103; and faculty participation in academic affairs, 6, 101–102, 104, 207; and financial resources, 5, 7, 9, 100, 103–104, 207; and freedom of administrators, 10, 207; and graduate programs, 101, 102, 207; and lay administrators, 102; and liberality of student regulation, 102, 207; and location, 6, 7, 9, 99, 100–101, 103, 207; and loyalty of students to school, 103; measures of, 1–2, 215–20; and paternalism of administrators, 6, 7; and presidents, 7, 9, 57, 61, 71, 75, 77, 87, 97, 99, 102, 103, 104, 171, 207, 208–210, 213–14; and relation to religious community, 6–10; and size, 6, 104; and social and economic class of students, 5, 100, 207; and values of religious community, 6–7
Administrators, vi, 5, 8, 9, 10, 11, 20, 48, 57–64 *passim,* 74–80 *passim,* 89–92 *passim,* 97, 108, 109, 111–12n.; and academic improvement, vi, 6, 7, 9, 10, 18, 20, 99, 102, 103, 104, 174, 213–14; competence of, vi, 9, 10, 18, 20, 62–63, 76, 86, 87, 99, 102, 103, 104, 119, 141, 143–44, 146–49, 155, 157, 159, 171, 174–75, 199, 209, 213–14; confidence in faculty of, 80, 82,

84, 126, 140; confidence in presidents of, 63, 71, 74, 75, 77; enjoyment of jobs, 147; freedom of, 9, 10, 144, 172, 174, 176, 203, 207, 212; lay, 78, 102, 203, 207; morale of, 76, 208; paternalism of, 6, 7, 142–44; religious, 27, 67, 113; training of, 27, 139, 144, 147, 168–71; *see also* Presidents
Ahern, P.H., 22
Alumni, 5, 100, 151–52, 208
Astin, A., 48, 49

Barry, C.J., 22
Beckwith, J., ix
Bradburn, N.M., ix, 11, 12, 99

CUES; *see* Pace College and University Environment Scales
Carnegie Corporation, x
Carroll, J., 24
Catholic colleges and universities: admissions standards of, 63, 78–79, 92, 118, 159, 160; alumni of, 5, 100, 151–52, 208; athletics programs of, 56, 73, 88; coeducational enrolment of, 56, 73, 95–96, 182; communication in, 63, 67, 71, 96, 126, 155–59; cooperation of, with chancery offices, 163–64; cooperation of, with other Catholic colleges and universities, 22n., 30, 164–67, 169; curricula of, 27, 28, 97, 118, 194; curricula of, in philosophy, 135–38, 140, 160, 173, 178–79; curricula of, in physical sciences, 138–39; curricula of, in social sciences, 139–40, 165; curricula of, in theology, 68, 134–35, 138, 140, 160, 173, 178–79, 194, 196, 202; development and planning offices of, 63, 76, 92, 100, 151, 161–62; enrolment of, 29–30, 55, 56, 73, 88, 107, 161; environment and atmosphere of, 48–51, 52, 102–103, 113, 114, 152, 183, 193–94, 196, 197, 202, 203; expansion of,